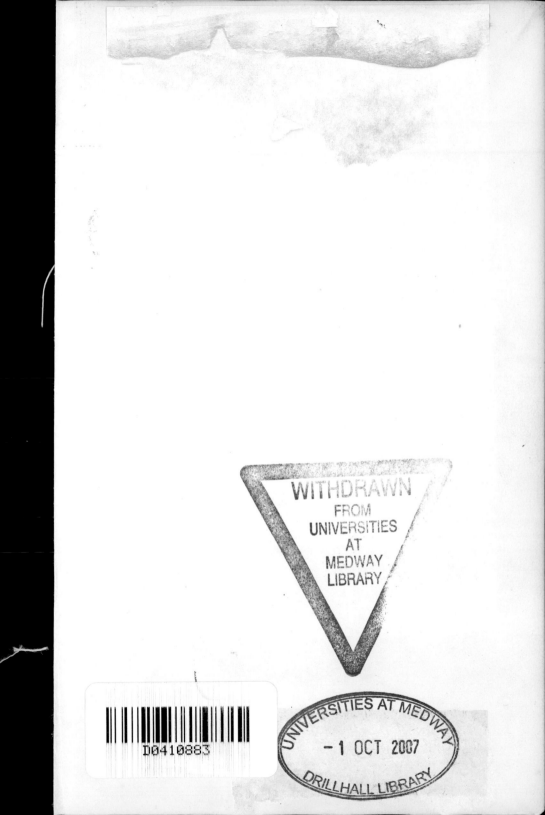

KENT

KENT

by

RICHARD CHURCH

Bernage came to see me to-day; he is just landed from Portugal, and come to raise recruits: he looks very well, and seems pleased with his station and manner of life: he never saw London nor England before; he is ravished with Kent, which was his first prospect when he landed.—JONATHAN SWIFT, *Journal to Stella*
25 August 1711

Illustrated and with a Map

London
Robert Hale & Company
63 Old Brompton Road, S.W.7

First published in The County Books Series 1948
Reprinted 1949, 1950, 1953, 1957, 1961, 1963 and 1966
This edition May 1972

ISBN 0 7091 2550 X

PRINTED IN GREAT BRITAIN BY
LOWE AND BRYDONE (PRINTERS) LTD., LONDON, N.W.10

CONTENTS

ILLUSTRATIONS

ILLUSTRATIONS

ACKNOWLEDGMENTS

The illustrations above, numbered 6, 19, 22, 26, 28, 40, 41, 42, 44, 45, 46, 47 are reproduced from photographs by Mr T. Edmondson of Folkestone; 14, 27, 32, 33, 37 and frontispiece by "The Times"; 4, 10, 17, 18, 29 by "Country Life"; 38, 48 by Aerofilms of London; 3 by Fox Photos Ltd of London; 49 by Mr Reece Winstone, A.R.P.S., of Bristol; 39 by Photopress of London; 34 by Hamlin's Photo-News Service Ltd of Folkestone; 35 by Hudson Photo Service of Dover; 31 by R. H. Goodsall. The remaining 18 are reproduced from photographs supplied by Sport & General Ltd of London.

EQUALLY TO ALL KENTISH MEN, AND
ALL MEN OF KENT

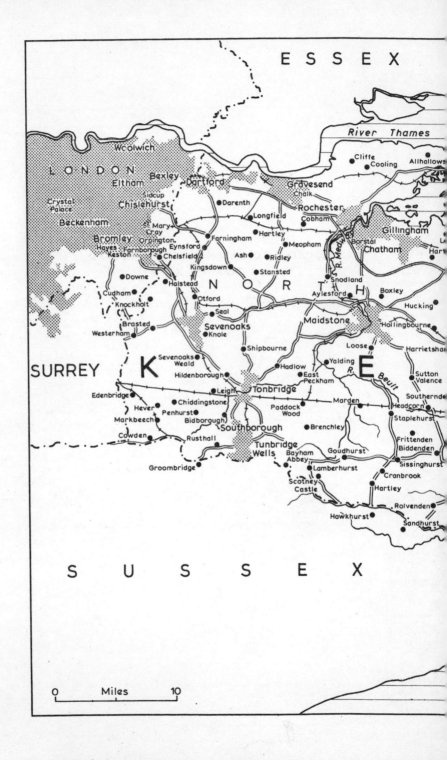

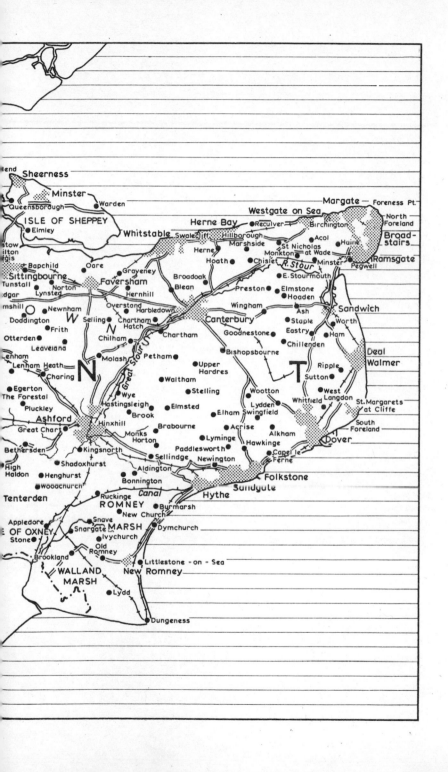

CHAPTER I

BACKGROUND AND UNDERGROUND

THE literature about Kent stretches from Greenwich to Maidstone, book by book. And then the original documents, pamphlets, and title deeds carry on from Maidstone to Canterbury. So there is no object likely to be served by my writing another guide book, or elaborate piece of topography. Indeed, I have no excuse at all for writing this book. All the books about Kent have been written. If I were not infatuated, desperately in love with Kent, I should more sensibly realize this, and be content to stand afar off, worshipping. But what a poor sort of man I should be; what a faint-heart. No; having been subjugated by Kent, that fair lady of the English counties, I will let that desperate condition work upon me explicitly. I will say my say about her, though she may not notice or approve, nor I be cured.

I have no credentials to say that say. I am neither a Kentish Man nor a Man of Kent, like Christopher Marlowe, Herbert Baker, Edmund Blunden, or Frank Kendon. I am a Cockney. But so was Geoffrey Chaucer, and he wrote of Kent amply and with great affection. He was one of her first articulate lovers. So why should not another Cockney voice his adoration, later in her history, at a moment when she has suffered somewhat, and had her beauty marred by front-line exposure to the ravages of the barbarian, who threatened to rape her, but did not succeed?

When I say that I am neither a Kentish Man nor a Man of Kent, readers may be puzzled by a suggestion of pedantry in the distinction. It will not be easy to disabuse them, for there has been so much argument about the difference between the two kinds of native, and still the matter is not definitely settled. Some pseudo-historians of the county insist that the distinction goes back to the times of the Teutonic waves of invasion, in the early Christian centuries after the Romans had shrunk from our shores to concentrate protection around Rome against that dreadful tide from the north-east. Their

B   I

theory is that the Kentish Men are descended from the Saxon invaders, and the Men of Kent from the Jutes who came later from the Chersonese Peninsula and drove the Saxons to the western part of the county, settling themselves east of the Medway and in the Isle of Wight and the New Forest. The venerable Bede, our first great English savant, put that theory on record in the eighth century, and it still persists because of its likelihood. There is a faint element of difference between the peoples of the two halves of the county. Most noticeable, I think, is the strain of dark wildness, of fantasy perhaps, in the west and south, where a streak of Celtic British blood persists. But I shall say more about these matters later.

I doubt if there is much sound ethnological basis for all this speculation. Frankly, we do not know what mixings and stirrings took place in those centuries of confusion between the departure of the Romans and the coming of William of Normandy, our first great bureaucrat. Sir Herbert Baker, the architect and friend of Cecil Rhodes, was born within the area of the Kentish Men, in the fifteenth-century house called Owletts, at Cobham, on the uplands which rise from the Thames and the Medway estuary, about five miles from Rochester, and standing on the Watling Street built by the Romans. He has recorded in his autobiography that "it is commonly assumed that the Medway divides the Men of Kent in the east from the Kentish Men in the west. But I prefer another tradition, which holds that an old kingdom of the Men of Kent included what is now all the county, and that the Kentish Men were those who owed allegiance in the border districts south of the Thames." That is a good example of how individualistic one may be about this matter.

Those border districts of which Sir Herbert writes are a lively theme. They represent country of surpassing loveliness, upon which man, in the manner of our forefathers, has woven a patchwork quilt of border fields, copses, lines of beech, brooks, and mossy banks once haunted by the red squirrel and now haunted by the grey. It is a good pastime to try to trace some of those borders, in such a district, let us say, as that running south from Titsey (a lovely name, meaning *fairy waters*, like the equivalent village and lake in the Black Forest

of Baden—Titisee), down through Limpsfield, Limpsfield
Chart, Crockham Hill, Kent Hatch (at one time, in the
Nineties, a famous literary settlement), Chartwell where Mr
Churchill lives, Mariners, Froghole and so over Toys Hill to
the valley that drops from Westerham, just in the Kent
border, down to Sevenoaks. I hope, in the course of writing
this book, or rather of *living* it, to take that path.

Sir Herbert also refers to "the old Kingdom of the Men of
Kent," and that too carries a long story—this time through
the centuries rather than through field and woodland. But
before looking at the story which man has put upon the county,
it will be more orderly to look at the stage itself, and to see,
in a rough and ready way, what its dimensions and shape are,
and how it is supported.

The geography of Kent is a complicated one, owing to its
variety of geological outcroppings. Its charm and many graces
are due to this. The county is sixty-four miles long from the
North Foreland to London, and at its widest is thirty-eight
miles from the Isle of Sheppey to Dungeness in the south. The
area is nearly a million acres, or just over fifteen hundred
square miles. In size, Kent is the ninth English county. Those
are the dimensions of the stage.

It is not so easy to describe its character. To begin with,
that character has altered, and goes on altering, considerably
even within the short period of time that carries records of the
presence of man. One outstanding event in this drama of the
rocks is that between the Paleolithic and the Neolithic periods
of prehistory, the British Isles were severed by the sea from
the Continent. A fanciful person might imagine that, long
after this change took place, there lingered on right into
historical times a sort of ghost-scene of the earlier Europe
when the Thames was a tributary of the Rhine—a geographical influence still potent to affect the manners and
emotions of human settlements this side of the chasm. Kent is
more European than any other part of England. Matter-of-
fact people will say that this is due to its obvious proximity to
France, and that it is the front door of England. That is so;
but there may be something more—a looming over from the
geological past, so that the traffic, intercourse, modes of life
that went on hundreds of thousands of years ago when there

was no dividing sea *still go on* ! How absurd ! Yes, but the dog, before he goes to sleep, still treads down an illusory patch of grass (faded long æons ago) on the kitchen rug. And man has such survivals too. Some of them may be the underpinnings of our medieval history, helping to make Kent and Normandy one social entity.

As though to refund a little of what it snatched away so long ago, the sea has since paid back, in dubious coinage of dreary and sterile sands, stretches on the south-western shore, bordering on Sussex, and round the Thames Estuary. When Julius Cæsar landed first in Britain, the sea ran through what is now the valley of the Stour, and Thanet was an island. Odd barterings between sea and shore go on still all round the coast. In the devious channels on the Kentish bank of the Thames Estuary the strange give-and-take is never at rest. It must be a pilot's headache. It needs a pen like that of H. M. Tomlinson, so skilled in maritime affairs, to write the history of this mermaids' marketing. I wonder how the natives of Sheerness, Chatham, Rochester, and Gravesend, dwelling amid such instability, manage to keep any moral sense at all.

One structural principle in the shape of the county is that all the rivers run roughly north or south. This is due to the fact that, away still further in geological time, a great whale-back of chalk ran west-east across the county. As it weathered down, like a decaying molar, its top went first, and a ridge formed that gradually increased until it became a long valley with surviving chalk heights to flank it north and south. They are still there, known respectively as the North and South Downs. But before that took place, the rivers were already well defined within their respective beds, cut through the original heights which formed their watershed. And there they are still, in their original valleys. The most pronounced examples are those of the Darenth and the Medway, which afford breaks-through from the Thames valley to the hinter-land of the Weald, which the long inland valley is now called.

This slow sculpturing by time has thus left the county divided into what may roughly be called four areas, or charac-ters : the Thames flats and inlets, the chalk North Downs, the Weald, and Romney Marsh. Now these areas are so dis-tinctive, so indissoluble each into the other, that I may be justified in·calling them *characters*. Round about Appledore, for instance, at the top of Romney Marsh, you will rise suddenly out of the desolate flats, and within a few hundred yards will come to a totally different landscape and people. The Men of the Marsh keep to themselves. They have their own laws and know little of what goes on among the foreigners up in the Wealden hills (that low ridge of enchanting beauty between the North and South Downs).

The people of the Weald, again, are different in habit and character from those who inhabit the chalk downs. The nature of the land on which they have been nurtured for centuries has gradually shaped in their subconscious minds an inheritance of instincts, superstitions, necessities, and pleasures; and each environment has acted as a watershed of the spirit for these groups of folk, drawing them off more and more into their district differences.

But even so, these four geographical aspects of the county cohere. They form as it were the superstructural variations of the great geologic mass beneath. This is unique in formation, a paradise for the student of the rocks. The great strata come sweeping like formalized waves (as in a Chinese painter's seascape) across from the larger mass of European land. Edge-on to the surface, they break off and thus reveal the earth-history in section, through the Secondary, Tertiary, and Post-Tertiary Systems. First come the silts from the sea, which are now Romney Marsh. Then the next upfold consists of the Wealden Beds, mainly a mixture of clayey gravels known as the Hastings Bed, a subsoil that stretches right up to the heights of Goudhurst and Cranbrook, ending suddenly as the mid-county hills drop down into the Weald proper. That soil is like the Garden of Eden. It grows fruit so abundantly that the land is worth its weight in gold (and well the farmers in that district know it!). It has some funny tricks. Here and there it will have a streak of venomous white clay that is more like gutta-percha than honest soil. Woe betide the unfortunate gardener who, during a bit of landscape-designing, or in the digging of a sump or well, turns up some of this stuff. I once did it to my cost, and had a sore patch in my garden for three years afterward.

But that Hastings Bed soil in general is, as I say, a

gardener's joy. It is self-drained and warm. It is freely aerated, and it contains the right salts of iron for plumping out stone fruit and making apples and pears ripen to the full. I have ripened Turkey figs in the open air on this soil; and a four-year-old grape vine on a south wall gave me a hundred and seven bunches of black grapes, sweet as muscats.

One of the causes of the varied beauty of the land on this Hastings Bed is the outcropping of ironstone rocks, such as the famous Toad Rock on Tunbridge Wells Common. Iron was formerly worked throughout this stretch of country. The railings round St Paul's Cathedral were made at Lamberhurst, on the border of the county where it passes into Sussex. This medieval industry, which gradually died as the oaks used for fuel in the smelting were used up, survived almost·until the nineteenth century. The foundry at Lamberhurst ceased work about 1765.

Bunching up from below this bed is the Wealden Clay. I don't say much about that. It has a cold look. To come down from the heights of Goudhurst or Brenchley on a winter morning to the level of the Weald, facing north, is like going down into a well. The air takes one by the throat. Yet once you get down among these meadows and meandering streams (mainly tributaries of the Darenth and Medway) you find much to delight the heart. It is a land of sleep; trees by waterways, sluices and forgotten stretches where pike lurk; huge hop-gardens where the annual bacchanalia takes place every September, when the hordes of hop-pickers come down from London to live in the open and to litter the countryside with an incredible amount of filth which the rich farmers miraculously tidy up outside a week of the end of the season.

The next wave of solidity as it breaks to the surface is known as the Lower Greensand, which takes the form of a hilly ridge running from Westerham and Sevenoaks (a part of the county much beloved by me) right across to Hythe, at which place it can be seen sticking up as a rampart along the old military canal. This range of hills, six hundred to seven hundred feet in height, contains beds of limestone, quarried as "Kentish Rag," principally in the Maidstone district. It is an attractive building stone, for it wears well, and has a rich range of autumnal umber colours that seem to change with the weather, though its basic colour is a blue-grey that we recognize in so much of our medieval gothic masonry. How the name rag-stone arose I do not know, though it probably is a corruption of ragged stone, a term for rock quarried in slabs. Many of the oast-houses along this ridge of hills are built from it, so that they have an air of much greater antiquity than in fact they possess.

One other stone found on this ridge is that quarried at and known as Bethersden marble. It is a limestone which can be polished, as can be seen from its use in the church towers at Headcorn, Smarden, Biddenden, and Tenterden, and on the altar stairs at Canterbury Cathedral. It is a handsome stone, superb for rock garden work.

From below this stratum there emerges a thin sandwich streak known as the Gault Clay, a stiff blue clay a hundred feet thick. It makes good bricks, and it contains many fossils. Round about Folkestone is the place where they are most abundant, more than in any other part of Britain. A recital of some of their names sounds like a catalogue out of the Old Testament : ammonites, hamites, and other allied cephalopods, with nautilus and belemnites; bivalve and univalve shells of wide variety; crustaceans of several kinds; small corals and foraminifera; teeth and bones of fish and reptiles; and a few plant remains. Many of these awe-inspiring relics of the childhood of Mother Earth still possess their original pearly iridescence, and can be separated from the soft clayey matrix with delicate markings and ornamentations intact. But they usually decay rapidly when exposed to the action of the air and the iron salts which accompany their excavation.

The Gault Clay is separated from the chalk of the Downs by a paper-thin layer of Upper Greensand, never more than twenty feet thick. But without it, I suppose, we might in Kent be the poorer for a few botanical specimens, and their accompanying butterflies and bugs and beetles.

And now the chalk ! How does one begin to talk about this unique formation? It has so pronounced a character, and affects man and his works so intimately, that it becomes a world unto itself. Chalk underlies all the geological formations in Britain along the eastern and southern sides. The one-time semi-alpine range that ran along the south

forming the backbone of Hampshire and the Home Counties
on the southern side of London, ran also across the Channel
into France. The edges or crater walls of what remains of that
range now form the Upper Chalk of the North Downs, with
a thickness of some thousand feet. This chalk is almost pure,
a soft, soapy pre-limestone, richly aerated and studded with
flints. How familiar it is, and how perpetually strange; as a
remnant of deep-sea life comparable to the coral formations
of the Pacific. As it gets deeper it becomes less pure, and
harder. Fossils in these lower beds of Middle and Lower
Chalk are of so vast an age that they represent a fauna that
was extinct before that life represented by the surface fossils
appeared. And all are very different from existing sea-life.
What is first remarkable about the chalk country is its
simplicity, its monotony of character. This, its most identifi-
able feature, is preserved wherever there is an outcrop of
Upper Chalk.

Of the nature of that simplicity there is so much to be said
that I propose not to say it here, in my preliminary survey.
I may better be able to deal with it when I start my wanderings along the North Downs, and once more make close contact with that landscape which is perhaps the most light and
lyrical of any in the world. When I think of chalk I think of
fritillaries in their thousands, of harebells and scabious
shaking above sweet-scented thyme, of dry-backed slopes
blazing under the sun, of rabbit droppings outside arid
burrows below juniper bushes. And I think of south-west
winds blowing against those slopes and whistling in the
grasses and flowerets dwarfed by centuries of sheep-cropping.
But such thoughts will not now get us further with our contemplation of the foundations of the house, the geological
base upon which Kent stands. Sufficient now to remark that
the signature of Kent, the white cliffs of Dover and Folkestone,
is in chalk. Chalk stands at the entrance to the county and to
the Kingdom. It crumbles in the hand, yet there it has stood
throughout history, keeping the sea at bay, and holding off
the enemies of the people of England, so long as that people
has been united within itself.

Behind that chalk face, in the downs behind Dover and
Deal, some ill-favoured experts discovered a seam of coal

about fifty years ago. Thank Heaven it is two thousand feet deep, and not too economical to work. May the seam run out before industrialists begin to settle round it like flies round a festering wound.

The chalk ridge runs right up to the outskirts of London, at Croydon, Addington, and West Wickham; and at the other extreme it forms the whole of the Isle of Thanet, which used to be separated from the mainland by the broad channel that is now the estuary of the River Stour, outflowing to Pegwell Bay and the ancient towns of Sandwich and Richborough.

That, roughly, is the substructure of our county, a series of sloping geologic scrolls setting back into the interior of the island, so that Kent stands firmly on a mighty bastion above the sea, in a posture of self-withdrawing from the mainland. Yet it is a child withdrawing from its parent, Normandy. The character of Kent has been formed by more than proximity to the mighty personality of France. Kent is the daughter who lives next-door. Kent has married into England. People who know Normandy will recognize the relationship. Normandy has the same sort of scenery as Kent; rolling hills with intimate and lavishly fertile valleys. But for the absurd regulations (they hardly have the dignity of laws) imposed by industrial interests and the prejudices of puritanism, Kent would have her vineyards too, or at least would drink the wine of France as a natural right; and her cheeses would be as subtle as those of Pont l'Eveque, or Port Salut, or Brie. Instead, she has to eat the harsh, immature substance known as colonial Cheddar, or those nasty cubes of byproducts from the plastics industry, wrapped in leadfoil and given a trade name in which the bastard word "kremey" predominates.

However, she has her substitute for the vineyards. Her hop gardens are a sacred cult. Nobody who has not lived amongst them may know how deeply they enter into the life of the people of Kent. The whole domestic economy centres round them. At three periods of the season, extending each over several weeks, the women have to leave their home duties for odd moments, so that they may spend their working days in the gardens—first, with the stringing of the poles, second, with the twirling of the young vines when they begin to run, and third, with the hop-picking at the crown of the year. And the equivalent of the treading of the grapes is the drying of the hops in the famous round kilns (which strangers often mistakenly call oasts). The oast is the whole building, consisting of the receiving barn, the drying floor, and the kilns. But this drying is a matter which must have more close attention later, when we are down in the Weald one mild September night, and the strange, haunting bitter-sweet smell of the hops is abroad over the county. It is a religious festival, older than the rituals that Augustine brought to Canterbury in A.D. 597. It links Kent with that classic world round the shores of the Mediterranean from which all our consciousness of civilization has sprung—the world of Homer, and those who came after him; softening, rarefying the crude heroism, giving it a moral force, and lifting its superstitions to a higher level of philosophy and social procedure. Just as Walter Pater saw the uncrowned Apollo wandering, an outcast, in the fields of medieval Europe, outside the monasteries, so I can see, when I have snuffed sufficiently of the odour of the drying hops, the poet Theocritus, and the more than poet Virgil, flitting like shadows through the green geometry of the Kentish hop-gardens, whispering their songs of the wisdom of the vine, putting their spell upon the natives, to make the process sacred at this time of the year.

All this, maybe, is as much to do with climate as with geographical position. For the climate of Kent is distinctive too. I like to think that Kent is warm because it escaped (but only by the width of the Thames estuary) the great ice-sheet that crept over northern Europe after the close of Pliocene times. That simple fact holds perhaps many chapters of the early history of the human race. It means, for one thing, that there may have been human settlements in Kent, the edge of all possibility of life. There for ages the poor creatures, doomed to so vast a future, may have lingered, watching and unconsciously waiting at the rim of that ice-cap, that Nothingness, for the great recession to begin, the first trend toward the new story of mankind.

Would not this mean that the hearths of Kentish people, the very nature of their *lares*, are of an older standing, and are linked without fissure to those survivals of prehistoric ways and emotions and race-memories, those relics of a story that was wiped out by the last glacial sponge moving down from the North Pole over the upper halves of Europe and Asia? This would mean that the rest of England started afresh, from sterilized ground under the ice. And therefore it must have started from Kent, where the seed lurked waiting.

This is poetic contemplation; but, thinking along the lines it suggests, one is not surprised to find that when Julius Cæsar visited Britain, he noted in his commentary that the men of Kent were as civilized as those of Gaul; nor that, a thousand years later, William of Poitiers (the Conqueror's historian) said : "Kent is situated nearer to France, wherefore it is inhabited by less ferocious men than the rest of England." Again and again, in studying the history of the county, one is impressed by the closeness of this association with the main stream of European civilization. Under the Roman domination Kent quickly became assimilated, and was hardly ever an armed camp held down by force. It became the home of the administration, and was enriched with the comings and goings of the cultural traffic from Rome and Gaul. Its huge pottery industry (pottery of large dimensions was used for all sorts of odd purposes by the Romans) sent supplies all over Europe. Then in the Middle Ages the ecclesiastical ties were close. Many Abbots of Bec in Normandy became Archbishops of Canterbury, notably Lanfranc, the great administrator who came with William the Conqueror, and began the building of Canterbury Cathedral. So many historical matters are significant of that tie, as for instance when King Stephen wanted to found a Cluniac abbey at Faversham in 1147, to be colonized from the great Abbey of Bermondsey, he had to obtain permission from the Abbot of Cluny, and the Prior of La Charité sur Loire, they being the Superiors of Bermondsey.

But I am trespassing into my second chapter, which is to give a faint outline of the history of the county. I ought to be dealing here with its natural features, its "rocks and stones and trees," its flora and fauna. I ought to be giving statistics of these matters, but I won't, for I have no wish to prove anything, or to deceive anybody. Statistics are for merchants, politicians, and Civil Servants to juggle with, to further some plan that usually ends in a new restriction upon liberty, and a concentration of power.

But even so it is delightful to brood over figures and collections of names. A seedsman's catalogue is after all a statistical table! And so is a record of the flower-life of Kent. There is no end to such a record, and I cannot attempt it here. Maybe, as I progress on my latterday pilgrimage I shall learn much about the flowers and have more to say about them. Kent is said to be the richest county in all England in its wild flowers, especially along the Medway valley. So it is in fungi, this being due to the large extent of coppice wood laid down for the growing of hop-poles, to the numerous pine woods, and to the number of old trees surviving in the many parklands. The Victorian Judge Stirling, who lived at Goudhurst, did much in the exploration of the flowers and fungi in the county.

As for the insect life, Kent was formerly the richest in England for species and numbers, but over-cultivation and the absence of commons have reduced it. Still, however, it has a wealth of *Orthoptera* (earwigs, grasshoppers, crickets, cockroaches). It has sixteen kinds of ants, and is wealthiest of all the counties in *Coleoptera* (beetles). It is naturally famous for its immigrant butterflies; "they have so little way to fly." And of the more sophisticated monsters, the great white snail, the edible or Roman snail, is found throughout. I believe it is now known to have been native before the arrival of the Romans. If that is so, it is odd that so many are found near Roman settlements. I remember collecting huge specimens around the site of the Roman villa at Titsey, in the great wood above the present manor house, home of the Leveson-Gowers. That was a time-haunted wood, with avenues studded by huge bushes of the deadly-nightshade, whose coal-black berries shone in the green dusk like jewels dropped by folk long departed. In one of those glades I once saw a fox loping across. Suddenly his eye caught a gleam of light reflected in one of those sinister berries. He stopped, raised a foot, sniffed, approached and stared close at the berry. Then, his curiosity satisfied, he went on his way, melting into the gloom beneath the trees. A small incident, that happened on one of the grim days during the First World War in 1917. Yet it has shone in my mind ever since, as though it were of capital importance. That is how I am made, and how I shall write this book.

Enough has already been said about Kent being "the garden of England." But the truism is true enough. The cultivation and improvement of Kent's magic soil began many centuries ago. The barley grown between Chatham and Canterbury, along the northern slopes of the Downs dropping to the flats of Sheppey (many of which flats have emerged since Roman days), is thought by brewers to be the best obtainable. Wheat has always been a maincrop in Kent, and one notable feature of its cultivation has been the use of the "turn-wrist" plough, which has big wheels and is drawn by four to six horses. But much of that cultivation relapsed into pasture during the bad farming days of the nineteenth century, when Free Trade for one was found to be impossible without Free Trade for all. In 1867 over a hundred thousand acres were under wheat, but by 1907 this had dropped to forty thousand. Since the war, however, the leeway has been more than made up. I noticed one thing about this revival of wheat-growing. Fields that had lain for fifty or more years and then were ploughed for wheat in 1940 lacked the gripping power to prevent the heavy corn from blowing down during the August winds which come so heavily from the Channel over Kent. The next year the farmers rolled thoroughly after planting, and put their sheep to take down the first blades, so that the roots should spread accordingly, and in 1941 there was much less of this disastrous wind-play, which necessitated so much more labour and loss of corn.

But it is her fruit that has made Kent the Garden of England. Scientific methods began three hundred years ago, at Teynham in north-east Kent. Not far off from there is still to be found the biggest and richest cherry orchard in the county, near Sittingbourne. The second in size and quality is near Goudhurst, and I am sitting in it at this moment as I write in my workroom, which overlooks the whole of it eastward, on a warm southern slope well above the frost-line. But the really ancient fruit gardens and orchards are in the northern falls of the county, where the Thames alluvial soil breaks over the subsoil of the Lower Tertiaries and chalk. In 1576 the historian Lambard described the stretch of country from Rainham (near Chatham) to Blean Wood (near Canterbury) as "the cherry-garden and apple-orchard of Kent." And so it is still; but now the cultivation has stretched to the southern side of the North Downs, along the Wealden heights, where there is still no pollution of industrialism.

CHAPTER II

HUMAN GROUND

NOBODY will be willing to dispute that of all the English counties, Kent has the longest and most complex history. It has been the highway to the Mediterranean since the days of the Phœnicians, and probably long before that, for Paleolithic relics are profuse in the county. I should set the beginning of its story, at least in the latest unbroken phases, from those grim centuries, or perhaps millennia, of the last Glacial Age when, the rest of the country being under ice, shivering *Homo sapiens* left a few observation posts here and there along the great Chalk Barrier (as it was at that time) and in the forests rising behind it. How many years ago that was is a geological rather than an archeological problem. Man was too insignificant to matter very much, though possibly, outcropping at odd periods of time, one hairy, skin-clad individual here and there warmed his intelligence at the future, and speculated on what might be the outcome of those dim urgings that seemed, faintly, to be giving him and his fellow bipeds an ascendancy over the rest of the animal world, and over those relics of the giant, gorilla-like race whom he was gradually exterminating.

All that, however, took place long ages before the days to which the modern schoolchild is introduced, with a picture of naked savages dyed with nettle-juice, brandishing their spears pathetically in an effort to frighten off the approaching triremes of Julius Cæsar. That is an incorrect picture. The Celtic tribes who tried in vain to obstruct Cæsar's approach were already Romanized, like their neighbours the Gauls across the Channel. The woad-staining of which we read was purely a war ceremonial, like the regimental gear of modern armies. As far back as 200 B.C. these Celts were trading in soft metals and grain with the Greeks and Phœnicians, and for this purpose had instituted a coinage in gold pieces modelled upon the Greek coins of the age of Pythias. They also exported hunting dogs, skins, and even slaves and currency. Now these

15

last two commodities suggest a high degree of civil sophistication. Hearing of that activity, one expects to hear also of politics and rival parties. No doubt there were such rival parties, for the great question throughout those centuries before Julius Cæsar and Claudius settled it for them must have been whether or not to form some sort of close federation with the peoples of the mainland. I picture on one side the hierarchic Druidical party, conservative and religious, dreading their loss of spiritual power (and therefore of temporal) if new ideas were to be allowed to contaminate the insular beliefs of the oak grove, the mistletoe, and the cromlechs and altars to the Sun.

For the modernist and progressive party I picture the craftsmen and traders, whose outlook was more practical. They would look at the problem from the point of view of exports, contact with new processes, and raw materials, and not least with new ideas and designs, amongst which would be included certain aspirations to a greater personal freedom from the reactionary domination of the priests.

I suggest, as a corrective to the over-simplified idea which most people possess of the primitiveness of the Britons at the time of the Roman invasion, that we should imagine that Cæsar chose to time his expedition during a general election in Britain, whose issue was to be whether or not a large-scale trading agreement with the Romans should be concluded (with certain unspoken reservations about remunerative double-crossings with other Mediterranean powers such as the people of Tyre).

Such a counter-fancy will bring us some way nearer, probably, to what were the actual circumstances and conditions surrounding the comings and goings in those decades round about the dawn of Christianity that followed the full moonlight of the Greek genius. Archeologists have found in Kent : a sickle, pins, rings, skinning knives at Marden; funeral hoards at All Hallows, Minster, Leeds, Saltwood, Sittingbourne; various evidence that Bronze Age Kent was already developed more toward agricultural civilization than toward warlike barbarism. These people imported brass, pottery, glass, and ivory, and their plastic art in subtlety of design was not much below that which is familiar to us from the orna-

16

ments in the Book of Kells and the rhyme-schemes in the poetry of Dafydd ap Gwylim. In short, the Britons were a comparatively sophisticated branch of the Celtic family. From the swiftness with which they succumbed to the onslaught of the massive Roman impact, with its technique of the phalanx in mind as well as action, one might even surmise that the Britons were already somewhat softened by ease and prosperity when they were thus invaded. The people of Kent, at any rate, gracefully accommodated themselves to the new conditions, and continued their commerce and manufacture on an increased scale. Under Rome they became one of the greatest sources of pottery in the Empire, the district between Faversham and Rochester developing into one vast potters' field.

Alongside that industry there flourished the administrative life which was always so pronounced under Roman rule. The Roman Civil Service was comparable to that of the British to-day; tolerant, broad, slow, and depressingly impersonal. Officials of all grades made their homes in Kent, thus edging as near home as they could. Durovernum (now Canterbury) was a city covering about fifty acres, and was thus the same size as medieval Canterbury. Unfortunately the clumsy public works undertaken in the archiepiscopal city in 1867–8 (what a butter-fingered age that was!) destroyed most of the Roman remains. Durobrivæ (now Rochester), with its Roman bridge over the Medway, was a focal point of the large Romano-British population in North Kent. Its walls enclosed about twenty-four acres.

Most revealing of the sense of safety and settled conditions that rapidly obtained after the conquest was the fact that few military posts have been located in the excavations throughout the county. After the initial fighting against Cæsar, and against Claudius a century later, all such disturbances were carried much further north. It is probable that the only military post finally established south of the Humber and east of the Severn was at Regulbium, now known as Reculver, near Herne Bay. This place was also a Roman naval port, with Rutupæ (Richborough), Dubræ (Dover), and Portus Lemannis (Lympne), these bases being linked with each other by Roman roads, the most famous of which was the northern-

"It took place on that tower of the Crystal Palace"

most one running east to west along the Thames estuary (whose Kentish shore was then much nearer to the hills) from Canterbury to Rochester, and ultimately onward, under the name of Watling Street, to bisect England.

What must have been impressive in those four centuries of the Roman occupation was the grandeur of the human imposition upon the landscape. The Roman villas were so many and so vast in size. Even the lower civil servants' homes were spacious. The boxlike room seems to have returned with the Teutonic barbarism, and our subsequent settlement into a suburban contentment with all lack of elbow-room and the dignity it affords. The Roman villa at Boxted, for example, was two hundred and seventeen feet long by fifty feet wide. Its corridor was nine feet wide ! And to this one has to add the knowledge that the Romans built their walls some eighteen or more inches thick, and warmed their homes with a system of hypocausts (hot-air flues beneath the floors conveyed by a support of aerated bricks). How modern that sounds; like the advertisements for post-war insulation and heating processes.

Add to those noble dimensions the simplicity of design, the wise choice of site, the suitability of decoration, and you can imagine what the aspect of some of these famous sunfacing ridges of hills must have been. And there that life, with its amplitude, its hygiene, its Virgilian serenity, went on for four centuries. To have lived in the middle of that period must have convinced the accepting and educated Briton, who had travelled to Gaul and possibly on an academic expedition to Rome, that the world was settled for ever (as we believed in our nineteenth century). Imagine what correspondence went on, to and from the capital of the Empire, amongst these genial people, by now intermarried, Briton with Roman, and nurtured upon traditions that success seemed so thoroughly to justify. What exchange of rarities, objects of art, exotic plants for their gardens here or in Italy, what wines and garments, what gems of literature ! Kent must have flowered in those days—until the storm came out of the north-east, the Gothic storm of which we have just had another grim experience.

Unfortunately, our picture of this golden age of Roman

prosperity in Kent has to remain largely conjectural. Beyond an ample residue of funeral remains from the many cemeteries in the county, little else survives. No such palace floors as that at Bignor in Sussex have been found in Kent, and few relics of temples. The reason for this may be that the princes and hedonists preferred to live in more magnificent seclusion on larger estates, away from the administrative and workaday centre, which Kent speedily became. And again, since through English history Kent has continued in that role, as well as being the corridor to Europe, the "snows of yesteryear" have consistently been trodden underfoot and covered by new layers. From an archeological point of view, Kent's activity and progressiveness have been its undoing.

For example, just as philosophically as she adapted herself to the régime of Rome, she next absorbed the conqueror who followed. Note that difference. Roman culture could not be absorbed, it had to dominate. But the Teutonic invaders brought little culture. They were a wildly emotional people, intimidated by the cold wastes, the solitary forests where they had been generated. That intimidation made them a prey to nervous quickness. They trusted nothing, not even their own gods. Their Valhalla was as draughty as the world which they only half-inhabited, in fear and suspicion, over small, widely isolated communities, whose only politic was the small-centred equality, as of a jealous family, in which their settlements functioned. Such a system, if at that time it could be called a system, was not sufficiently developed to be able to stand impervious to external influence, especially if that influence should be the doubly wrought and authoritative environment which Romanized Britain was to offer.

So when the Anglo-Saxons and Jutes came in A.D. 443, some thirty years after the departure of the last Roman legions, they found Kent a coherent kingdom, under a Latinized British sovereign, Vortigern. This king had not only to face the wild sea-people coming from Schleswig-Holstein and round the mouth of the Elbe as far as Denmark. He had also to look over his shoulder at a threat from within the island. For the unsubdued Picts and Scots who had always remained withdrawn beyond the tides of Rome now came surging down from the north, a fire of irresponsible rapine as much beyond the Kentish King's rationalized comprehension as were the colder slaughterers from the sea.

He adopted the Roman technique, but forgot that he had not the Roman power to make that technique safe. He bribed one assailant to attack the other. The Saxons took the bribe, and drove back the Scots. The Jutes in particular, under their chiefs Hengist and Horsa, took a part in this double-edged game; but during the ten years spent in subduing the Scots, Hengist was steadily gathering more of his folk from Jutland and settling them in the island of Thanet. He married his daughter Rowena to Vortigern; by this and other means his power gradually percolated over the kingdom, until the time was ripe in 452 to fake a dispute about some small tax or other, when he seized the fortresses of Richborough and Reculver, sacked Canterbury, and marched on London. His way barred at Rochester, he turned south, and at Aylesford, by the Medway, defeated the Britons in a bloody battle in which his colleague, Horsa, was conveniently killed.

By this method, so archetypical of that which we have seen recently practised all over Europe by later seekers after Valhalla, Hengist possessed himself of a kingdom in Britain, and set about to substantiate and enlarge it. The Britons did not submit easily, and sporadic fighting, with occasional violent battles, went on until, in 473, Hengist firmly secured the throne. During these years the Saxons, shrewdly avoiding the claim staked out by the Jutes, were coming in round the coasts of Sussex, gradually extending westward after subduing the British mining fraternity of the Sussex Weald. This invasion provided an outflanking movement west and north of London, but it took a hundred years to accomplish this, during which time Kent existed in a sort of isolation, being consumed from within and from without. By the time Ethelbert, Hengist's great-grandson, ascended the throne of Kent in 564, a shadow life had been resumed in the little kingdom, over the skeleton of what had been the Roman fabric. For the next three hundred years settlements over the ruined cities, such as Rochester and Canterbury, gradually grew in size and function. Commerce with the Continent was resumed, and some sort of polity toward the greatly changed Roman Empire, in its Gothicized form as administered from Rome, enabled the seeds of civilization once more to germinate.

Ethelbert married a Christian princess, Bertha, daughter of the King of Paris, who brought with her a chaplain, the Bishop of Senlis. This priest established a church at Canterbury, on a site where a Roman Christian temple had previously stood. The gap between the Roman and the Gothic acknowledgment of this new Light of the World, kindled in Greece and Palestine, was a chasm of darkness. We can only conjecture again, as to its nature, by comparing it to the life of the small Germanic dukedoms in northern Europe during the succeeding centuries, dark spots fitfully glowing as the white heat of the Christian flame was directed at them from the south. Their language was crude, their folk-song guttural and monotonous. Even three centuries later, when the various dialects of at least the south and western Gothic settlements in Britain had been somewhat intermingled and softened by the influence of the monasteries, which were peopled from all parts, the literature of these Anglo-Saxons reflected a primitive life, as for example in the poem *Beowulf,* a typical heroic saga written in the dialect of Mercia, but copied out, and no doubt localized in declensions and vocabulary, in the Kentish monasteries. It is really a dull poem, hardly worth the trouble of mastering the complicated grammar; but if one does take the trouble to turn the key in that rusty lock, the reward will be a contemporary picture of life in the Anglo-Saxon world, which was the life of Kent for some five hundred years until the coming of the Normans.

It was a world that had its own quality; one not altogether sinister. Those small communities, almost family organizations, had about their social form a lightness and freedom which both the Roman and the feudal systems lacked. The circular strips of common land surrounding the settlements seem to symbolize a certain mental and emotional outlook on life which might be called the Gothic genius. But that method of cultivation did not take hold in Kent, as it did in the other kingdoms of pre-Norman England. The Germanic settlers here adopted rather the Roman measurements of land, which went in squares because the Roman plough did not turn the sod, as did the Teuton's, and ground had therefore to be cross-ploughed. For this reason Kent appears to have passed direct from the tribal and independent village system to that of commercial husbandry, without going through the intermediate stage of manorial husbandry common to the rest of England. Here again was another likeness to Normandy. The law of what is called gavelkind, established upon this practice, was a direct survival of Roman law, and it involved the direct family shareout of land, as opposed to inheritance by primogeniture. This has played a large part in the traditional character of the native of Kent, giving him an independence, and a bias toward economic an-archy (note that hyphen!) which has affected the course of the history of Kent during the centuries that followed, giving it a dramatic emphasis, and the habit of throwing forward champions of the people against any despots that tried to curtail liberty in this country.

With the revival of Christianity, after the lapse of nearly three centuries, the central Church took steps to augment the promise. Pope Gregory sent Augustine (who must not be confounded with *the* St Augustine, the North African mystic whose *Confessions* are still a cornerstone of the Latin Church). The second Augustine, born some three hundred years after the early father, was a man of administrative genius at headquarters in Rome, and he was sent, with some degree of worldly as well as other-worldly sagacity, to develop what was so obviously a favourable situation. He succeeded, for after landing at Richborough (though this is sometimes disputed—other scholars think it might have been Stonar) in 597, he converted King Ethelbert and thousands of his subjects. Another ancient Roman church, of St. Pancras, was rededicated in Canterbury, and later the King gave Augustine the site outside the city, where now stands the Cathedral. This was followed by the establishment of the first monastery, dedicated to SS. Peter and Paul, later known as St Augustine's Abbey.

Thus the continuity of European civilization was renewed in Kent, with the addition of that all-changing difference, that not quite new element, by which the individual, the "meek and the poor in spirit" (a conception which the Romans had overlaid in their borrowings from the Greek view of life) was by the doctrine of Christianity to be set with even more emphasis as a cornerstone of human society.

From that time, no matter how oppressive the story of man and his doings in Kent, his wicked lip-service to a faith that he betrayed in practice, his open pagan revolts against it, that story nevertheless has about it a lightness, an aeration, of spiritual idea. It becomes the story of England as we know it within our own experience; a knowledge that has been suddenly denied and interrupted by the outbreak of ancient superstition in Italy and Germany, and a temporary denial of all that has been so painfully and gradually built up during the last two thousand years.

That new idea, with its message of hope to the gentle of heart, spread over the impoverished and blood-drenched little Kingdom of Kent just as the wild flowers spread over the ruins of our modern cities in the recent war. While the island of Britain was still anarchic, however, fighting was bound to go on amongst the petty kinglets to decide which of them should be supreme and found a dynasty. For a time it looked as though this first Christian King of Kent would succeed, for he spread his rule as far north as the Humber, and married his daughter to the king of the lands beyond that. But nothing remained stable. Backwards and forwards, one after another in fatal quickness these seekers after power fought over the surface of the land, erasing from it again and again the first signs of a settled life, and a continuous record of man's creative effort.

In the course of this confusion, the Kingdom of Kent went under beneath a flood from Wessex, in 823, when it seemed at last that King Egbert would succeed in unifying the government of the whole island.

But no sooner was this promise emerging with some distinction than another wave of savages from abroad threw the embryo constitution into the melting-pot again. In 832 the Vikings landed at Sheppey, and proceeded to pillage the wealth which was beginning to accumulate round the first Christian communities. Canterbury and London were sacked, and nothing could be done to appease the savagery of these invaders until in 871 a man of genius made himself master of the whole of England, and set about to recivilize the ravaged land. The story of King Alfred need not be retold here. But that story is one of horror and destruction for Kent. Once again it was the landing-stage for the invader, and battle after battle was fought over its fields and towns. Gradually, through a sea of blood, the Danes spread their authority, until in 1013 Sweyn, their leader, made himself King of England, and Ethelred the Unready fled to Normandy.

Even so the destructive warfare went on, for the rival royal families divided the country into factions clashing in civil strife, more violent than ever. Canute defeated and slew Edmund Ironside at Ashdon, in Essex (the little village where Henry VIII is said to have married Anne Boleyn in the parish church), and once again united the country under his rule.

But at this time a lord in Kent was increasing his power. Godwin, Earl of Kent and Sussex, may be called the first king-maker in our history. He played this game of living chess with the greatest *expertise,* and finally succeeded in putting Edward the Confessor on the English throne in 1042, and in marrying his daughter to the King. From that time the intrigues took on a larger and European significance, and Kent merged its dynastic interferences into those maintained by the kingdom as a whole. Henceforth its history was to be a local one. Kent was already Normanized, partly by its now considerable trade interests, and partly by its religious ties. It was the centre of Christianity in England, and by now the faith had become sadly tied up with temporal power and its lusts. The Archbishop of Canterbury, Godwin's stumbling-block, was really an ambassador of William of Normandy, and so too was King Edward himself.

The Saxon rule, if such an internecine turmoil can be called a rule, was over. A larger, more politically and economically organized order was to take the place of all those frustrated beginnings toward a settled society and culture. That Saxon period had its beauty, however, as can be seen from an examination of its few surviving bits of handicraft : jewellery, weapons, pottery, etc. There is grace, lyric freedom, which makes this work compare with that of the Normans as the lovely filigree made by the people of Ur compares with the monumental solidity of Egyptian art.

. In fact, the coming together of the Saxons and Normans on English soil was only the merging of two branches of the same Frankish westward flow. Their consolidation therefore had about it a foreordained homogeneity that promised the strength to come, the secret of our marked English characteristics which have put so pronounced an impression upon the story of Europe. I said earlier that Kent and Normandy had geographical features in common. Green, the historian, confirms this. "A walk through Normandy teaches one more of the age of our history than all the books in the world. The whole story of the Conquest stands written in the stately vault of the minster at Caen which still covers the tomb of the Conqueror. The name of each hamlet by the roadside has its memories for English ears; a fragment of castle wall marks the home of the Bruce, a tiny village preserves the name of the Percy. The very look of the country and its people seem familiar to us; the peasant in his cap and blouse recalls the build and features of the small English farmer; the fields about Caen, with their dense hedgerows, their elms, their apple-orchards, are the very picture of an English countryside. On the windy heights around rise the square grey keeps which Normandy handed on to the cliffs of Richmond or the banks of Thames, while huge cathedrals lift themselves over the red-tiled roofs of little market-towns, the models of the stately fabrics which superseded the lowlier churches of Alfred or Dunstan."

Thus it was inevitable that Kent, with its now long-sustained history of traffic in European affairs and wealth of material things, should combine, like to like, with the culture and commercial nucleus of Normandy. From the fusion of the two peoples, true scholarship and intellectual ascendancy were to emerge. William, half pirate and half religious statesman, proved to be a man who saw the strategic value of uniting that culture and that material wealth under his rule, and he protected both these sources of power by setting out to curb the barbaric self-interests of all the land- and slave-grabbers who at that time, as through all time, had proved to be the greatest enemies of comfort and learning. Those small barons have their equivalent in all forms of society. To-day we see them as industrial reactionaries and municipal racketeers, bent only on feathering their own nests at the expense of the community, and ready to spoil any project towards the greater ease of life should it interfere with their own seekings after power and wealth.

As an aid to the estimation of the character and stature of William, who was to affect the fortunes of Kent so markedly, it is interesting to quote from a contemporary who watched him at work. "In choosing abbots and bishops, he considered not so much men's riches or power as their holiness and wisdom. He called together bishops and abbots and other wise counsellors in any vacancy, and by their advice inquired very carefully who was the best and wisest man, as well in divine things as in worldly, to rule the church of God." That, surely, is an intimation of new grades of thought and social conduct introduced into English life at that time. I mention it here because it floodlights the history of Kent, which hitherto had been in semi-darkness behind a curtain of blood and fire. From now on such men as the two great Italian gentlemen, Lanfranc of Pavia, and Anselm of Aosta, were to rule at Canterbury, successive Archbishops who brought with them new conceptions of moral and mental discipline. Lanfranc was a master of both Roman and Canon law, through which he proceeded to reorganize the life of the country through the administration of the King. Anselm was a spiritual illuminant whose saintliness was an antidote to that side of the King which he had inherited from his Nordic forebears, the side that made him at times break out with cruel reprisals of destruction, torture, and death against any who opposed him or frustrated his valuable designs.

Now this book is not a history of Kent. It is a record of my own contacts with and delights in the county. Little purpose therefore would be served were I to continue with details of dates and events through the succeeding centuries during which England gradually took its place in the comity of Europe. I have shown how the primary ingredients of character of the natives of the county were introduced into it. From now on it has been a question merely of stirring the pot. And very vigorously it has been stirred, for at no time has Kent been allowed to stagnate. Everything that has happened to the English people, has happened to the people of Kent first; so far, at least, as that happening has occurred from the Continent. Kentish folk have been the watchers at the door, and therefore their consciousness has always been a quick, nervous one. They have been prompt in political and martial action. The first signs of an organized demand for democratic rights by the people came from Kent, which by the fourteenth century was the richest county in the Kingdom. A contemporary rhyme summed up the economic position of the county thus :

> A Knight of Cales,
> A Nobleman of Wales,
> And a Laird of the North Countree;
> A Yeoman of Kent
> With his yearly rent
> Will buy them out all three.

It was natural that the people who slaved to produce this wealth should grow restive, especially at periods when the screw was put on too tightly by some ruler who lacked the wisdom to disguise his rapacity. Richard II was such. He came to the throne thirty years after the Black Death, the scourge that swept Europe and carried away half the population. The resultant shortage of workfolk broke down the balance of the feudal manorial system, which had worked adequately since its imposition by William three hundred years earlier. Trevelyan says that "in a society accustomed to very slow changes in conditions of life, the market value of labour had been doubled at a stroke. The consequence was twofold. The labourer who was already free struck for higher wages, while the villein whose labour was not free struggled against the legal demands of the bailiff for customary services which were now worth more to both parties; gradually he was led on to demand his full freedom, the right to take his labour where he would, to plead in the King's Court even against his own lord, and to be free of irksome feudal dues. Lords and bailiffs were in a terrible dilemma. Half the domain land, half the rent-paying farms were lying untilled, turf and bushes overgrowing the strips, the ploughmen dead, the thatch falling from their deserted hovels. And the survivors were rising in open mutiny against law and custom, and sometimes also against what was economically possible. The world seemed to be coming to an end."

Now this came on top of another great change which was already disturbing the social balance of the country, and especially those parts of East Anglia and Kent which were the most developed industrially and commercially. The wool trade had begun to prove so remunerative that Edward III had devised a scheme of manufacturing the wool at home instead of exporting it all to Flanders and elsewhere. He brought over Flemish weavers to instruct the English workers, and these master craftsmen settled in England, to become the nucleus of that powerful middle class which was quickly to take a hand in the control of the country's destiny. Their noble houses can be seen in Kentish towns to-day, masterpieces of domestic architecture. On the outskirts of Cranbrook, for example, in a tiny hamlet called Wilsey Green, there are three of these fine mansions, standing tightly with their great king-beams across their vaulted halls. Tenterden, Goudhurst are two other of the many villages where relics of the fruits of the greatest medieval industry throughout Europe still survive. In Goudhurst there is a long row of cottages beside the church. They were once a weaving establishment, and on the beam ends of one of them are still to be seen the little figures denoting the trade.

A most interesting little study of this wool trade of the Middle Ages is to be found in Eileen Power's record of the history of the famous Flemish house at Coggeshall, near Colchester. What she says there can be applied approximately to most of the similar houses scattered up and down the Kentish towns and villages.

Now alongside this economic and political fermentation, there was growing up a religious one, which had been set in motion by a man of great genius, John Wycliffe, who in his foundation of the society of the Lollards began a scholarly and truly spiritual revolt against the gross degeneration of the Roman Church, which by this time was already obstructionist and firmly on the side of property, as it has been ever since. The Church was to crush for a century this effort to cleanse Europe once again of the habits of self-interest and materialism. Wycliffe's teaching (and his translation of the Bible) spread to central Europe, where the Moravians (the Hussites) sustained it with Teutonic gravity. But not until the brutal and coarse Martin Luther came a century later did the movement really shake the complacency of the established priesthood.

Now in Kent these two European problems took on a dramatic focus. A priest in Kent, a Yorkshireman named John Ball (about whom William Morris has written a book which is a wonderful evocation of the England of that time), went about preaching on the text

> When Adam delved and Eve span,
> Who was then the gentleman?

. His eloquence so stirred up the smouldering brands that at last, in 1381, Ball was imprisoned in Maidstone, with the result that another Maidstone man, Wat Tyler, following an incident in which a tax-collector was killed by one of his victims, marched to London with a following of Kentish folk and summarily murdered the Archbishop of Canterbury and the Lord Treasurer, the figureheads of the forces of oppression. The impressionable but weak King met the insurgents at Smithfield and promised them a general pardon and a charter of liberties. But the real governors of the country, the jacks-in-office, the red-tape men, gradually watered down the promise, and finally even greater repressions followed.

Seventy years later another rebellion came from Kent, under the leadership of Jack Cade, following the failure of a petition to the King called "Complaint of the Commons of Kent" in which his attention was called to the peculation and tyranny practised by his tax-collectors. Cade, an Ashford man, led twenty thousand men as far as Sevenoaks, where he met Henry VI's forces and beat them. Cade made his head-quarters at the Hart Inn, which I like to imagine was on the site of the White Hart where Mr Pickwick met and engaged Sam Weller. The rebels marched to London and executed Lord Say and Sele, whom we remember because of his flattering verse about the Kentish people, which he composed in the vain hope that it might save his head. Here it is :

> Kent in the Commentaries Cæsar writ,
> Is termed the civilest place of all this isle;
> Sweet is the country, because full of riches,
> The people liberal, valiant, active, wealthy.

However, this rebellion, like its predecessor, petered out. Cade died ignominiously, after frittering away his success. The people at that time had no experience of authority or organization. They were like children suffering at school under brutal masters. What could they do about it? Only time could say, and time was not yet ripe.

The other outstanding disturbance which originated in Kent was that led by Sir Thomas Wyat, of Allington Castle and Boxford Abbey, near Maidstone (both places now only ruins). This gentleman of the county was the son of a more famous father, for Sir Thomas the elder was a diplomat in the reign of Henry VIII, whose service abroad brought him closely into touch with Italian and French writers. He returned to England an accomplished poet, and had the distinction of being the first to write sonnets in the English language, a form that was to blossom in the Elizabethan Age through the genius principally of Edmund Spenser and Shakspeare. To have done this is, to my mind, a memorable achievement, for this slight monument to Wyat's work will survive long after the labours of kings and statesmen are forgotten.

The younger Wyat led the men of Kent against Queen Mary, who proposed to marry Philip of Spain and to reimpose the rule of the Roman Church in England. This the democratic and Protestant county resented as a threat to their liberty, though heaven knows it was little enough at that time. Nothing came of this effort, for the citizens of London, oddly enough, sided with the Queen, and slammed the doors of Ludgate in Wyat's face. He was executed on Tower Hill, his abortive rebellion also costing the lovely and gentle Lady Jane Grey her life, and almost implicating the future Queen Elizabeth.

But all this politics is general knowledge. Kings and governments are interesting, no doubt, and they play an important part in the lives of private individuals, principally by moulding the environment (or destroying it!) in which those individuals have to live their lives. I am, however, impatient to get to those people, here and there, in particular places, and to give up this *deus ex machina* trick of looking at them and their county of Kent as a whole. The world is too much given to abstractions to-day; maybe it always has been, through one official machine or another : the Church, the State, the Trade Union, the Statistical Department, the Big Business. How dreary, hateful, and dangerous it all is. Give a man a date and a number, and his soul is in peril. He is about to be destroyed by a dossier inscribed with his name. How shall he escape? How may I help him to escape?

I know how : by joining company with him, by coming into contact with him, flesh and blood, in the place that is his place, where his roots are. I will wander about until I find him there, and can approach him no longer through the diminishing lenses of the fog of time and space, those agents of the historian and the geographer. Let me be neither of these professional people. Let me be nobody; a quiet anonymous wanderer about the lanes and fields and gardens of Kent, with the gift perhaps of invisibility, if I should need it; but usually with a substantiality that will make me welcome for my own sake amongst the villages and farms, where I shall find men and women, children and dogs, willing to talk, laugh, and bark; no learned stuff, no conscious stuff; mere time-of-day exchanges whose platitudes mean so much, like the smell of earth when the wind is in the south, like the inarticulate crying of plovers racing over a cornfield when the blades are small and sharp, just out of the ground. It is out of the nothingness of things that we learn all about them; the days when little happens, except the sun shining, or the rain drumming down, or a cock crowing with distant, chilly defiance before dawn; or a bat creaking about in the dusk at the end of a summer day and long physical labour. These are not history, for they have no thesis or argument. But they are life, and it is the life of Kent that I want to record. I do not want to record records.

No; but even so, it is one of the paradoxes of life that we cannot fully appreciate its simplicities until we have won a certain sophistication of mind that puts us slightly out of focus, as it were; removes us a little from the stream of continuity so that we may see how one day affects another day; how a Roman gesture made at Durovernum in the second century after Christ contributes a tiny influence toward the placing of a Saxon hearth in Canterbury five centuries later, which in its turn commands the angle of a certain timbered dwelling in

Tudor times, thereby affecting the dimensions of a multiple bazaar in the twentieth century. That may sound fanciful; but it symbolizes the understanding which a reading of history gives us. History is really the compost heap from which we feed the roots of love and enjoyment. When an archeologist handles a sherd, his fingertips re-create with infinite definition the whole way of life of Roman, Saxon, or Tudor Britain.

That is why I have dared to begin this serenade to Kent with some historical and geographical strummings. I have made enough of them, I hope, to set the background in time and space concretely, so that wherever I go, and whatever I may touch here and there in the county, that rich undertone will respond.

And why have I cut off the historical survey abruptly in the middle of the sixteenth century? Because from that time Kent did not act as a unit in the drama of England. The whole of its activities are still to be dealt with; but I believe it can most naturally and humanly be done by keeping those activities to their own localities, where they wait for me to discover them casually, and not in the detached, scientific way of the historian. We shall want to find out about the story of the Cinque Ports, for example; or the commerce that has been going on along the Weald for several thousand years. Well, let us wait until we get there. Maybe we shall meet with people, workmen or idlers, masters or nosey-parkers, who will want to talk. Many will be bores. But bores have their uses, even in Kent.

The restored Hall of Eltham Palace
The view from Otford Mount

CHAPTER III

THE HINGE OF THE FAN

LOOKING at Kent as a general shape, one might call it a fan. The hinge to that fan—and a jewelled hinge—is, or was, the Crystal Palace on Sydenham Hill.

That statement may be just a geographical fact to most readers. To me it is a highly emotional reality. I will explain why; and the reason why I explain it here is that now is the time, after our historical and other sketches of Kent, to set out on our personal explorations, our living and physical topography.

Now topography, like charity, might well begin at home. Home is the first thing we see, and recognize. It is our point of foundation, on which we build our estimate of the universe. And by home, I mean our first home, the home of our childhood; for that, no matter if it be an unhappy one, is likely to be the only permanent and unshakable factor in our lives. All that comes to us when we are grown up has an infection of the temporary about it. We may build ourselves noble country houses after making our fortunes and fame; but they are always slightly intangible; places where, in spite of all our efforts, we are only lodgers. No; I suppose that in the long run, only birth and death, the cradle and the grave, are the twin points of home, the surviving certainties.

My real home, then, was Dulwich. At the turn of the century it was a sleepy little village, inhabited by a few natives who seemed to have been forgotten by the great evolutionary movement of London, whose cancerous growths of suburban pink houses were flowing rapidly in every direction in the years before the 1914 war. For ten years previous to that unhappy one, the fields and farms outside the Victorian suburbs of London were a sight such as the world will probably never see again. First the main roads of the outlying villages—such as Lewisham, Sydenham, Norwood, Streatham, Wimbledon —were desecrated. Existing houses, many of them lovely things surviving from the seventeenth and eighteenth cen-

D   33

turies, lost their pride and became derelict or slummy. Many of them were built round with disgusting little jerry-built semi-detached boxes. Their fronts were torn down and flash shop-windows put in, leaving a faded upper story of Georgian windows, blind relics of a past that had both shape and history. Little tea-shops, bicycle shops, laundry depots, brought a new traffic to the ground floors, while above, in the bedrooms, lumber and filth collected.

Along the roadside, where once their gardens had reached with hedges of laurel and briar and thorn, temporary hoard-ings were put up, on which the advertising firms spread their hideous posters, layer upon layer of paste and paper that wind and weather worried into shabbiness. Behind those hoardings might still be seen relics of the old hedges, desecrated probably with muck thrown over or behind the boards; dead cats, old tins and bottles, umbrella skeletons, bits of bedsteads and bicycle frames. What an age that was; the Edwardian transition from the ugliness of the Victorian opulence to the squalor that awaited the avenging outbreak of war. Nobody has described it better than H. G. Wells in such books as *Kipps, Tono Bungay, The War in the Air, Love and Mr Lewisham.* He showed in those sociological tales how the new pert, philistinish-and-proud-of-it generation of lower middle-class were emphasizing themselves as they grew some-what better off in wages and mass-produced food, furniture and clothes. His Kipps, his Bert Smallways (who kept one of those hideous little bicycle shops near Bromley, forerunners of the garages and petrol pumps which are now the symbols of our times and culture) were spokesmen of those self-assert-ing people who were determined to have no more nonsense about superior manners and the graces of tradition and cul-ture. They wanted bikes, motor-bikes, dinky little two-seaters, pinky little tea-shops on the road, handy little bluebell woods where they could loll and sweat, leave their food litter and their love-signs, before tearing up the last of the flowers and rushing back along the outraged highroads to a back-street semi-privacy that still stank of the Victorian moral sediments, the dregs of something that in its day had been respectable and even noble.

When I first knew Dulwich it had not yet been invaded by

this sort of thing. It had a village integrity and form. It was dominated, winter and summer, by the old College and Picture Gallery (relics of Edward Alleyn's charity), and by the old country house known as Beech House, which stood sideways to the road beyond the village school (the Dulwich Hamlet School of football fame).

That school was my school, and still I can recollect sitting in class on a summer day, staring entranced out of the window at Beech House shimmering in the heat, pigeons shining white on its red-tiled roof, and the creepers and roses hanging round its windows, so that it merged into the great beech-tree and the elms and poplars surrounding it. Those were the days when willows and Shakespeare, sunsets and Milton, were all stirred together in my imagination, a sort of spiritual punch bowl that kept me in a state of perpetual drunkenness and bemuscment, so that I went my way to and fro over the surface of the world "stumbling on melons," too rich, too dream-laden.

What a beautiful place in which to grow through those years of dawning consciousness and intelligence! I recall walking up to the Crystal Palace, along College Road, through the Tollgate, past the Dulwich Wood where Robert Browning as a boy used also to wander, learning the nature-lore that was to inform so much of his baroque verse. That walk, a weekly pleasure, taken always with a brother dearly loved and in those days worshipped as an elder oracle of wisdom and artistic creativeness, often ended in a visit to the Palace, after a loitering stand by the walls of the Crystal Palace Parade, to enjoy the superb view over London, an aspect which set St Paul's hovering in mid-air, and the great buildings along the Thames-side equally insubstantial, part of the "sudden city of dream-spires."

In those days the Crystal Palace was already somewhat derelict, its crystal panes grown cataracted, with occasional spots where the glass was gone. But not many weeks would pass without the old giant waking up and welcoming some festival or other; a band contest, a Policemen's Fête, firework displays ("Brocks' Benefit") and of course the annual Handel Festival, with the performance of the *Messiah* in the great central hall.

My brother and I went to all these occasions, and usually enjoyed them, as well as the shows in the little theatre within the Palace. The plays, the various great occasions, the crowds and spectacles are all confused in my memory now, and as dead and extinct as the stone prehistoric animals that stood about the lake at the bottom of the grounds. But one thing survives, isolated and intact. It is the moment of my first look-out over Kent when I climbed the great tower at the eastern end (the waterchute end) of the Palace.

I still find myself tongue-tied when I try to describe what that meant to me. It has something of *Pilgrim's Progress* about it. I am Christian gazing at the prospect of the Celestial City. I remember, too, how when I first read Keats's sonnet on Chapman's Homer, and came to the lines about "stout Cortez staring at the Pacific, and all his men looking at each other with a wild surmise, silent upon a peak in Darien," I immediately recognized those men and their emotion. I was already one of them, and had shared their experience. It took place on that tower of the Crystal Palace, and my Darien was Kent, the land of promise and unknown adventure, where later, as I grew bigger and possessed a bicycle, I was to explore, every fine Saturday, with my brother; ferreting out, as only boys can do, every by-lane and odd copse and wayside station, every cottage where teas might be eaten and maps consulted. But when a man finds himself becoming senti-mental, he ought to lock himself up somewhere alone, until the indulgence is past. So I will not enlarge on those Saturday adventures, when the bicycle itself was part of the ecstasy, and the possession of a new kind of oil-lamp, or a speed-gear, something to brood over like a lover.

But I hope that what I have to say about Kent, in the follow-ing pages, will unconsciously recapture something of the rapture with which I looked, as a boy, over her fields and vast stretches of woodland, hill, and valley, all of it distance-hazed, too bright to look upon. Of course it is an impossible hope. What I saw then was Atlantis, perhaps, or Tir na nOg, the perpetual land of To-morrow, where Time and Life and Love lie all before you, and there is nothing stale, nothing familiar.

Never mind. What we can still see, in the eye of recollec-tion, is good enough to point the way, and to give this book some sort of shape. We will enter Kent by this back door, which is the same door that Ptolemy took when he came as geographer to Britain two thousand years ago. So let us turn our backs on London, and face the sun.

Immediately below us, to our left hand, lie Sydenham and Penge. They still have, from this height, something of their past seclusion and foliage. Once they were places of retreat for the successful merchants of the nineteenth century, who built large houses amid dropping terrace gardens where the nightingales sang, and the terraces looked over the south to the Weald and the warmth. You can imagine the croquet on these lawns, among the formal flower beds, the monkey-puzzles and the double-red may trees. You can picture the greenhouses with their palm courts, their chrysanthemums and orchids. You can hear the carriages spanking up from the station, or right out from Town, along those tree-arched roads with their steep hills and their stretches of ancient commonland now roped off with white posts and chains, and shaded with great chestnut trees.

Alas, the tumescence of the Great Wen has broken down that dignified suburban life. No longer can a foreign musician, as did Mendelssohn, stay in those great semi-country villas and write his "Spring Song" (Mendelssohn did this on Denmark Hill, closer still to London.) Population has pushed all that seclusion away. In 1821 Penge, the door to Kent, was a tiny hamlet of two hundred and twenty-eight people. Twenty years later it was still only two hundred and seventy. Then the great Industrial Change began to ferment. By 1851 the railway had come out and the population went up to 1,169. In 1861 the re-erection of the Crystal Palace (after the closing down of the Great Exhibition in Hyde Park) brought more inhabitants, and more building over the green fields. The population was then 5,000. By 1871 it had more than doubled, becoming 13,202, with resultant ugliness in municipal life that called down the wrath of John Ruskin in his book *Fors Clavigera*. (He too sat on Denmark Hill and watched events.) By 1921 the one-time hamlet was an indistinguishable suburb of 25,000 dwellers.

The boundary still stands, however, at the east end of Crystal Palace Parade, where once stood the Vicar's Oak, an ancient mark of the frontiers of the counties of Kent and Surrey. But the parish was more ancient still, for its very name suggests its age, Penge being a Celtic word denoting a wood-end (like Pencoed in Wales). The odd thing is that the hamlet was in the parish of Battersea for nine hundred years, from Saxon times. William of Normandy granted it, with Battersea, to the Abbey of Westminster as purchase price for the regalia of Edward the Confessor, who had lodged his valuables in the Abbey. Now Battersea seems to belong to another world, though it is only seven miles away in south-west London, a place of flat and foggy back streets, a working-class district of much poverty and meagre respectability, with whitewashed yards to the tiny houses, where the natives keep their hens and rabbits in tiers of hutches.

Right up to the nineteenth century Penge was mostly common land, on which the people of Battersea had grazing and wood-cutting rights. Patches of Royal Forest survived for many centuries, and we read that Sir Richard Grenville's famous little ship, the *Revenge*, was built from oak felled in the woods of Norwood, which is the parish at the western foot of the Crystal Palace. It lies, to our right hand, immediately below, dropping steeply down from Norwood village, which clusters round the end of the Parade. Down those slopes, as also down the nearer ones of Sydenham and Penge, opulent houses still stand, many of them fallen into shabby-genteel condition, and their gardens gone to melancholy, with fallen fences, briars across the paths, and all the rest of those characteristics of the deserted garden, and the voices now silent, and the lamps gone out, and an echo of the ballade "Où sont les neiges d'antan?"

There lie Penge, and Sydenham and Anerley, three surviving hamlets now lost under the tide of bricks and mortar. One can go down and explore, and find a few surviving things of interest, evidences of the personality of place. Margaret Finch, Queen of the Gypsies, lived in Penge, dying in 1740 at the age of 109. From her habit of sitting with her chin on her knees, smoking a pipe and contemplating the folly of mankind, she grew stiff, and the corpse could not be straightened out, so that she had to be buried in a large square coffin.

Thomas Campbell, the poet who wrote some vigorous

patriotic verses (notably "The Battle of the Baltic") lived in Sydenham, and so did Tom Hood, the lovable Cockney punster. There was also a local poet named John Gwyer, a potato salesman, who combined business with pleasure and wrote selling-slogans for his neighbours to put up over their shops in the High Street (he was thus before his time, for he would have been paid two thousand a year to-day for that sort of thing, and he could have given up selling potatoes, or doing anything else useful).

H. G. Wells, whom I have already cited as a historian of the horrible disease which swept industrial England at the beginning of the century, was born in Bromley, which lies immediately in front of us in the middle foreground, about seven or eight miles into the county, beyond the hill of Shortlands. This was once a lovely district, and I remember Bromley with its steep High Street and compactness. You should see it now! All the growth of brickwork that was smart in 1910 is now outmoded. Networks of meaningless and unfocused streets stretch out like the veins on a drunkard's nose. The Picture-house, the Multiple Store, the Sixpenny Bonanza stand with their gaudy façades blotching the High Street. But perhaps we shall not have to go to Bromley, so why anticipate depression?

Anerley, just beyond Penge, was for many years the home of our great contemporary poet and fantasist, our trafficker with the widdershins side of life, Walter de la Mare. That will immortalize the parish, and in a hundred years' time pilgrims will come from Brazil and Chicago and Chungking to see the villa where the poet lived in the days of his obscurity, when he was known only to a "little clan." Another poet, John Freeman, also lived here. This poet suffered from an amateur's garrulity in his verse, and most of it is already retreating into the mist out of which it emerged.

I wish we could take a peep from our Topless Tower of Sydenham at the flat end toward the eastern debouchement of the Thames through the great City. There lies Lewisham, leading eastward below Blackheath, past Shooter's Hill, and out by Eltham along the great Dover Road. Lewisham is lost in the London haze, and most of it is also obscured by the nearby slope of woody hillside dropping down to Dulwich behind us. And we must not look behind now we have once started on our great fanwise exploration. It is a pity, because Lewisham was a place of distinctive beauty, with a High Street rich in finely proportioned period houses, and old posting-houses, such as the Geórge, and architectural delights such as Colfe's Almshouses, and the little side-street known as Exchequer Place. At a noble old house called the Limes, built in the seventeenth century, John Wesley made his country retreat. All that road, however, is a sad example of the desecration of which I have spoken earlier in this chapter, with the dwellings of the past sinking into an old age of garish prostitution as garages, or multiple-store branches with painted fronts. A history of the district was published in 1908 by Leland Duncan, printed locally. Such a book is a fine example of work done reverently for a defined and local purpose.

Before I leave what are now called these inner suburbs, I must record the schoolfellow of forty years ago who used to cycle into Dulwich village every day, wet or fine, right over the great hill from Norwood, on the Surrey side. He was a little boy, remarkable for his courage and liveliness. But while he was still at the elementary school with me he found his vocation, which was religion. He had genius in this matter— a matter much more rare than we imagine in our world of conventions and faded rituals—and I possess still, in my mental treasury, the surviving riches that he gave me from his extraordinary vision of the realities of a substantial relationship with the idea of Godhead. Nothing was too odd to be assimilated to that strange inner vision which made this boy so outstanding. His face shone with it, and his gestures and mischiefs were part of its information. He would read a passage of Shakespeare (I recall the scene where Ferdinand and Miranda discover their tenderness toward each other on the golden sands, in *The Tempest*) and make it a symbol of his own new discovery of the passion and significance to be found in every detail of day-by-day existence—a schoolboy's existence. There was no doubting such illumination. The boy's whole body was singing with it.

This boy, Edgar Sydenham Richards by name, has a place in this book because he also was an infatuate of Kent, and was often my companion on long rides of exploration along the secret valleys of Addington and West Wickham, Keston and Downe. On one occasion we rode early one Sunday morning from our homes, he from Norwood and I from Dulwich, meeting at the top of the hill by the Palace, and making our way past West Wickham church over the top of the downs by the back lanes to Titsey and Westerham, in which old, sleepy townlet we left our bicycles at the inn, and went to Holy Communion at the church, returning to the inn for a great breakfast of two eggs and a gammon rasher for each.

But I am getting too far afield. We are still looking out from the Palace Tower, picking out the near approaches of the county as it spreads its vanes south-east out of London. Out of sight along our left-hand view, or rather below it, lies the more public way into Kent, parallel with the Thames, down the Old Kent Road and through Lewisham High Street. What a sordid experience that is to-day. But I have already said enough about such changes. It is hard, however, to recall that Lewisham gets its name from the Saxon Leof-suhaema, as it was named in a charter granted by King Aethelred in A.D. 968. It meant "my dear son's farm." What would the dear son think if he could see the High Street to-day, with the stream boxed in cement, and the multiple stores, all of them architectural monstrosities; and the dirt and squalor resulting from the war? All these London approaches into Kent suffered badly from the enemy bombardment.

These parishes have a sadness about them now; something faded, something ghostly. This spirit, lingering from a greater past, gives their trees and streets an almost hectic quality, an intensity of beauty that the open country does not possess. Think of Honor Oak, where Queen Elizabeth used to sit on her walks from Greenwich Palace, her favourite residence. And think of Blackheath, above the Palace, the scene of so many pageants and meetings. Greenwich itself is both small and big enough to write a book about. Its exquisite little park, crowned by the world-measuring Observatory, is similar in shape and view to that of Richmond on the other, western side of London. Its hill looks up Thames in the same way; but what a different Thames. This stretch of the river seen from Greenwich Park contains the wealth (and the grime) of the

Empire. Canaletto, in the eighteenth century, loved to paint his lucid pictures, so clear-cut and sharply defined, from this hilltop. There looms St Paul's again, more solidly set on the earth than when seen from the heights of Sydenham. And look at that floating crane being tugged down the river from one of the inner waters of the dockland labyrinth; Surrey Commercial, West India, Wapping perhaps. I need H. M. Tomlinson's knowledge and magic to describe those somewhat sinister folds. There they lie, a continuous aspect of masts, funnels, derricks, towers, and granaries. And from the whole of that vast scene there goes up continuously a faint humming sound. It is the sound of the homing bees of the Empire, nuzzling their way into the central comb, which grows and grows, dripping its gouts of honey in careless opulence, to which the dirt of time clings, and strange parasites from all quarters of the world. Out of this welter Greenwich Park rises clean and formal, still as Canaletto must have seen it, and still rather like one of Rex Whistler's wall decorations, with domes and noble façades, and newly brushed trees, and porcelain daffodils clustered at their roots, in the almost artificial grass.

Like Lewisham, Greenwich (really a part of Blackheath) goes back in its record to ancient times. A Roman, soon after the landing of Cæsar, built a villa there. There is documentary evidence of the park of Grenevic (the "green village") being given by King Alfred's daughter Elstrudis in A.D. 918 to the Abbey of Ghent : but by this time it was already an ancient place, for it had been civilized for centuries, during the whole of the Roman occupation. Watling Street, the most famous of the Roman roads, passed over Blackheath, a wild place with a formidable reputation for robbers. The Park was laid out and fenced on the northern slopes of the Heath about the middle of the seventeenth century. Evelyn, the scholar-diarist, whose house was leased for a time by Peter the Great of Russia, who came over to study our methods of naval shipbuilding, records in March 1664 : "This Spring I planted the home field and west field, about Sayes Court, with elms, being the same year that the elms were planted by His Majesty in Greenwich Park." Charles the Second employed that landscape gardener of genius, Le Notre (who laid out Versailles,

Fontainebleau and Saint-Germain) to redesign both St James's and Greenwich Parks. In the course of maintenance and alterations within the park, many interesting relics have been found, spearheads, beads, stone implements, even two Moorish vases. The Greenwich Fair, held in spring and autumn in the Park, was a rough-and-tumble characteristic of the eighteenth century, which had its seamy as well as its exquisite side. Dickens, in his *Sketches by Boz,* showed how this fair survived right into the nineteenth century, with almost as much rough handling. Indeed, within living memory the last relic of those capers remained in the excitements of a visit to Greenwich to partake of the shrimp teas at the hotel beside the river.

It was in Tudor days, however, that the Park and the Heath were in the fore-stage of history. Henry the Eighth rode out to Blackheath to meet his bride Anne of Cleves in 1540, having previously had much sport there with his Queen Catherine a-maying. He also sat beneath an old oak tree in Greenwich Park waiting for the firing of the gun that should assure him when Anne Boleyn was safely beheaded. I wonder if it was the same oak under which his daughter Elizabeth sat and signed the death-warrant of her more handsome cousin Mary of Scotland.

Where the Park joins the Heath, along the top of the hill, still stands a perfect example of the domestic architecture of the brothers Adam. It is called the Ranger's House, and was built by the Lord Chesterfield, who wrote the famous set of letters to his son in one of its rooms; the letters that were so characteristic of the morals and manners of the eighteenth century, or at least one aspect of it; the morals which Dr Johnson stigmatized as those of a whore, and the manners as those of a French dancing-master. But Johnson's pride had previously been hurt by the Earl at the time when he petitioned him about the patronage for the famous Dictionary, and had been kept waiting in the anteroom without seeing the patron, or rather the non-patron. The house now belongs to the L.C.C. who maintain it, and serve teas there to the public.

I dare not allow myself to say much about the Observatory, the Royal Palace, and the Naval College (one of Christopher

Wren's most magnificent buildings). If I did, we should never get away from Greenwich; and like Chaucer, we "have, God wot, a goodly field to plough." So let us leave the Park and its bounty of memories of kings and scholars and mathematicians, to travel further down the river Kentwards to Woolwich and Eltham, merely pausing to note that Blackheath was the first place where golf was played in England. James I introduced the Scottish game in 1608.

Woolwich lies east of Greenwich between Shooter's Hill (over which Watling Street, now the Dover Road, passes) and the River Thames. It has long been a centre for boat-building, and remains of Roman vessels have been found. But its fame as a naval dockyard and arsenal was set by Henry the Eighth, who built his war galleon *Harry Grâce de Dieu* there (1,000 tons, a colossal weight for those days), and thus laid the foundation of our British Navy. The building of wooden naval vessels went on there until the middle of last century, when the introduction of ironclads carried the work elsewhere. The Royal property, however, was then used to put up buildings for the making of ordnance and ammunition, becoming known as the Royal Arsenal. Throughout the two great wars this Government factory has carried on its terrible but necessary work, though attacked ceaselessly by the enemy from the air. What heroism the workers have shown remains to be told. Day in, day out, through the years of terror, they have gone into those buildings, accepting danger of their own and of the enemy's making with a stoicism that some people would call Roman, but I should call English.

Woolwich is also the headquarters of the Royal Artillery Regiment, and on Woolwich Common stands the Royal Military Academy, a castellated building built in 1801.

Halfway between us on our Crystal Tower and Woolwich by the river lies Eltham. Like West Wickham, which I shall mention in my next chapter, it has been sadly swamped with streets of jerry-built dormitory-boxes during the last twenty years. But the village remains embedded in this adipose tissue of bricks and mortar, like the relics of beauty in the features of a fat and raddled old woman. The eyes remain those of the young girl.

The eyes of Eltham are the Royal Palace and its environ-

ment of period houses. For centuries this little village lay in
the heart of royal life, seething with activity, and the comings
and goings of the great ones of the realm. The Palace was a
medieval foundation, and by the time of the great period of
English life in the reign of Edward the Third, before the
Black Death threw us back to darkness and barbarism,
Eltham was already one of the most firmly established seats
of the Royal Court. While Geoffrey Chaucer, our most joyous
poet, was clerk of works to Richard the Second, he was on his
way one day from London to Eltham with ten pounds in
money to pay certain workfolk. Being waylaid and robbed, he
went back to London, drew another ten pounds from the
Royal Exchequer, and set off afresh, only to be set upon for
the second time, and relieved also of his horse and other
effects. In the Court Rolls there is a memorandum about this,
and I give a translation from the old French. "Richard, by
the Grace of God etc.—To the Treasurer and Barons of our
Exchequer, greeting. Having received a petition on behalf of
our beloved Geoffrey Chaucer, Clerk of our Works, inasmuch
as on the third day of last year [1390] the said Geoffrey
Chaucer was feloniously robbed near the Fowle Oak of twenty
pounds of our treasure, and of his horse and divers goods, by
certain notorious thieves, in the presence of our coroner and
other of our officers at Westminster, in our prison there; as
is fully confessed by the mouth of one of the said thieves, on
this account we are pleased to pardon him the said twenty
pounds, and discharge him in his account to our Exchequer of
the aforesaid twenty pounds; the which petition we have of
our special grace granted and allowed, and we therefore
instruct you that you cause the said Geoffrey Chaucer to be
discharged on his account to our said Exchequer of the aforesaid twenty pounds, and that he be acquitted towards us for
the aforesaid reason. Given under our privy seal at our
Manor of Eltham, the 6th day of January, the fourteenth year
of our reign."

But the Civil Service of those days was much as it has
always been, rather unmerciful in its memory of the short-
comings of one of its servants. This misadventure was chalked
up against Chaucer on his personal file, and in spite of his
useful family connections (he was related by marriage to the

late King's brother, John of Gaunt) he suffered a period of official extinction. This recession of his fortunes, however, was more probably due to the intrigues of John of Gaunt's brother, the Duke of Gloucester, who was striving after power. But that is an intricate story, outside our scope. It is amusing to note that Chaucer never forgot the highway robbery which relieved him of twenty pounds, his horse and gear, at Hatcham on the way down to Eltham. In the Reeve's Prologue, in the *Canterbury Tales*, he makes the host say

> Lo, Depeford! and it is halfe-way pryme.
> Lo, Grenewich, ther many a shrewe is inne . . .

the last line meaning that Greenwich (which included Hatcham) harboured many a *shrew* or rascal.

The great beauty of Eltham was due to King Edward the Fourth, a monarch about whom I have always had much curiosity, for he seems to have been one of the few of our kings who was given to intellectual and artistic interests. He had a library, which was an outstanding eccentricity in those days. He took a personal interest and delight in encouraging William Caxton, that successful mercer from Tenterden who by long residence in Bruges became infatuated with the new art of printing, and introduced it to this country (an action probably more revolutionary than any other in our history). He printed much of Chaucer's work, including the *magnum opus*; and also Mallory's *Morte d'Arthur,* and his own version of *The Golden Legend.*

So this sympathetic king, a man much given to pomp and a handling of beauty, was fortunate in being well related to the trend of the times, the great times of the Renaissance which was spreading its golden dawn over Europe. King Edward was interested in everything that promoted knowledge and civilization, and particularly his royal imagination turned to architecture, for what art is more-appropriate as a vehicle of kingship? It is the crystallized expression of the art of government, which is a king's purpose and right function. Edward rebuilt the great Banqueting Hall of Eltham, and the stone bridge over the moat. In doing so he was freed by the fact that he had no longer to consider the needs of fortification. The days of closely vizored castles were gone, and building on the grand scale could now be married to the graces and expansions of a more civil necessity.

The Hall at Eltham is a monument to all these changes and enlargements of the human spirit. Without being over-decorative, it is superb in its design. King Edward was a true artist in that he loved greatness in simplicity. Here it is in stone. What a man he must have been, and how much one would like to know more about him, and his fair mistress Jane Shore, who I suspect must have been a woman of intellect and character, for could she otherwise have held the love of a man of Edward's fibre? So in spite of Sir Thomas More's slighting words about her in his *History of King Richard the Third,* where he says "I doubt not some shall think this woman too slight a thing to be written of and set among the remembrances of great matters," I feel that Jane Shore prob-ably played a distaff part in the æsthetic history of England, and that her influence was a gentle and civilizing one.

That great Hall when finished, with its wonderful roof (which George the Third many centuries later wanted to remove to Windsor), was the scene of much splendour. Edward entertained on the grand scale, some of the royal banquets feeding two thousand bodies, and lavishly. That odd old priest and poet John Skelton, whose muse loved a hark-back to Saxon measures, alluded in one of his first poems (when he was an unknown youngster, before he became tutor to the young Prince Henry Tudor, afterwards Henry the Eighth) to this lavishness of King Edward. After the king died, Skelton, in a threnodic poem, wrote

> I made Nottingham a Palace Royal,
> Windsor, Eltham, and many others mo;
> Yet at last I went from them all,
> Et nunc in pulvere dormio.

which is a grim revival of the fatalist spirit of the Middle Ages cropping out in the somewhat political bitterness of Skelton's genius.

Another interesting historical association is that Edward's tournaments for the year 1469 were run by Sir John Paston, member of the family which has since become famous through the survival of a mass of letters whose exquisite privacy and period character have revealed the spirit of that age more than any reconstruction by later historians could possibly do. Here is an extract from one of those letters written to the knight by his brother, who is much concerned about his appearance at Court :

" . . . if so be that you send any man home hastily, I pray you send me an hat and a bonnet by the same man, and let him bring the hat upon his head for fear of mis-fashioning of it; I have need to both, for I may not ride nor go out at the doors with none that I have, they be so lewd : a murray bonnet, and a black or a tawny hat; and God sent you your desire. The seventh day of April, 1469. Your John Paston."

For those people who want to study the architectural beauty of Eltham Palace and its environments, there is ample' literature, and I need not enlarge on the matter here. But I must record how the Palace, after the sixteenth century, began to lose favour with our monarchs, Henry the Eighth especially preferring Greenwich. During the Commonwealth, the prosaic Presbyters who ruled the country in so depressingly modern and Fabian a manner, by dull bureaucratic methods, took an inventory of what was now State property, counting every tree and noting its worth in money. They also noted that the deer in the park, and the palings, had been destroyed by the common people and the Roundhead soldiery. What a reminder that is of the slender hold which grandeur and ritual, either religious or regal, have upon the imaginations of the great mass of the people. Thank Heaven that the Holy Grail has never been found.

So the Palace fell into decay, and all its outbuildings perished. But the great Hall remained, becoming a barn, where moved among the cattle ghosts of the kings and queens and poets and fair women who had feasted there since the thirteenth century when Henry the Third established his Court at Eltham.

It remained a ruin until 1933–5, during which years Mr Stephen Courtauld, a typical representative of a family given to creative gestures of this kind, bought, restored, and presented Eltham Palace Hall to the nation. He also safeguarded its environment by presenting the fifty-acre park with the Hall. The place is now a superbly restored piece of

Quebec House
Tally-Ho, Toys Hill

domestic architecture in the Gothic mode. One cannot too warmly record the appreciation which English people must feel toward this family of the Courtaulds, who came to England as craftsmen in the days of the Great Awakening and have prospered here. Their prosperity has never dulled them. Riches, like poverty, are dogged by fear; and fears means caution and pettiness of spirit. But in this family we find a noble exception.

The Gallery, Hever Castle
Chiddingstone

CHAPTER IV

THE SINGING LANES

WE cannot remain for ever on the Tower of Glass, like Simeon Stylites on his pillar. But we can keep our boyhood days a little longer while we take the next stage of the exploration. It will embrace a wider segment, most of which lies beyond the first group of hills upon which we look from our observation post. The only part of that concentric circle which is visible from the Palace is the northern curve of it, coming out in the further distance to the north-east, where the great river plain stretches into the fog and smoke of industrial Kent.

Let us get through that fog and smoke first, for there is nowadays not much to be said for those approaches to the riverside, unless one is curious about factories that stand in market gardens or swamps. But behind this dreary obliteration once lay country of a most pronounced character, estuarial in kind, with land and water scenes mixed in a fine confusion of creeks, tongues of gravel, bird-haunted tide-marks, and the flotsam and jetsam from seafaring vessels. Approached from the river, there is still much to interest the idler; but this interest is hardly characteristic of Kent. It is the kind of fascination that we feel under the spell of all water-side places, where the sea gives up to the fresh-water twice a day. Such matters belong to the literature of saltings, to which Kent contributes an enormous amount, owing to the fact that the whole outward edge of this spread fan whose hinge is the Crystal Palace, is lipped by the sea or the Thames Estuary. But I have already said something in my opening pages about this give and take which perpetually goes on between land and water around the enormous coastline of the county.

I want now to deal with the district which in shape is a miniature of the whole county. It lies in an arc which stretches from Dartford in a curve south-westward up the Darent valley to Westerham. From Westerham, which touches on the Surrey border, we can then follow that border south-eastward

50

to the Romney Marsh and the Channel, thus completing the exploration of the right-hand straight side of the fan.

Dartford lies about three miles from the confluence of the Darent into the Thames. It is flanked by two chalk hills to east and west, while south of it the river valley leads into the heart of the county. Once the lanes wound pleasantly back, in a leafy network, round Bexley, North Cray, Foot's Cray to Sidcup and Eltham. But the less said about that now the better. All this part, up the little tributary River Cray, and even back along the main road through Dartford to London (the Roman Watling Street) grows more and more depressing as one approaches Town. All that it can now offer is a bewildering satire upon our so-called "progress," since during the nineteenth and twentieth centuries England's population began a tumid expansion, sporing factory fodder and office functionaries whose shallow-rooted lives litter the surface of the land in such districts as this south-eastern approach to London. Could Cobbett see that countryside now, he would be confirmed in his obdurate faith that London was a disease, and that the breeding of human beings with no tradition in the soil was only a sowing of dragon's teeth.

Dartford itself is now a place to escape from as quickly as possible, though it has some points of interest. It still keeps an element of legend about it. I have heard that it is notorious for its dark-haired and fickle women. But any generalizations about women are dangerous. This particular saying may have arisen from the fact that Dartford has played so conspicuous a part in the history of the Englishman's assertion of his rights. John Ball, the fourteenth-century Yorkshire priest who may be called the first militant socialist, was imprisoned in Dartford, and released by the insurgents who gathered around Wat Tyler after that honest tradesman's daughter had been outraged by a King's tax-collector. What a nuisance these tax-collectors always have been, incurring the hatred of the rest of their fellow mortals since the days of Babylon and Thebes. It may be this outrage that has made the Dartford women wary, and has thus given rise to the legend of their feminism and distrust of men. It is only natural. Natural too is the little matter of the Dartford warbler or furze-wren, a relative of the great whitethroat. It was first found in this

neighbourhood in 1773, and so named by the naturalist
Latham. It remains here throughout the winter, and is the
only non-migrant warbler in the country. I think that is a nice
distinction for a town to possess; far more valuable than an
opulent town hall or a fat mayor.

Dartford has another distinction, however; it was the first
town in England to make paper. Queen Elizabeth's jeweller,
one Sir John Spielman, set up a paper mill here in the opening
years of the seventeenth century. The industry still flourishes,
now one among many. The cement works, chemical factories,
powder works, and iron foundries stretch out to the river at
Greenhithe, with a relic of former days of watermen and
tillers of the soil half-buried here and there under the fumes
and settlements of dust. One of these remainders, however,
was beautifully restored in the nineteenth century by the architect G. E. Street. It is the church of St Mary, at Stone, by
Greenhithe. Inside especially this church is a beautiful gothic
survival, with work ranging between Early English and
Decorated, reminiscent of the eastern end of Lincoln
Cathedral. There is no clerestory, but even so the church has
an air of grace and lightness that merits the nickname of the
"lantern of Kent."

Edward the Third once held a great tournament at Dartford, a sport which was so successfully demonstrated here that
he established an Augustinian monastery on West Hill, a road
which still has an air about it, and stirs the heart of the passer-
by for some unknown reason. After the Dissolution, Henry
the Eighth lived in the ex-monastery with Anne of Cleves—
but not for long.

But let us get away from all this, and make our way up the
Darent valley to the unpolluted countryside again. My spirits
rise as I head up-valley for Farningham, though heaven
knows there is still not much to write home about. Farningham is now merely a London omnibus terminus amid a wide
expanse of market gardens, full of vegetables and soft fruit.
This long stretch of alluvial soil is one huge vegetable forcing-
ground whose products feed Covent Garden Market day by
day throughout the year.

We soon begin to find more secluded and sheltered country,
however, as we leave the main London to Maidstone road.

The valley takes on emphasis and character as the hills close toward it, amid the first orchards which tell us that we are already on the famous Maidstone ridge, whose soil grows the best stone fruit in the world. On our right, some way along the London Road, lies Swanley Junction, where there was, until its destruction by a bomb in the last war, a college for training young women in horticulture and market gardening.

From Eynsford (where once lived Peter Warlock, the charming composer in musical pastiche, along with a small colony of. musicians) we now find ourselves in true Kent country. The cosmopolitan riverside and industrial areas are quickly forgotten, and we come by one charming village after another, from which walks branch out to right and left to equally delightful and remote places (such as Chelsfield and Lullingstone Castle), until we get to the head of the gap at Otford, where the little valley breaks into the main west-east stretch of the northern Weald, with the gentle rise of the Sevenoaks ridge in front. As we approach Otford from the north, a section of the Pilgrims' Way, that prehistoric path, turns off eastward. But this is a road that needs a whole book to itself. Indeed, I believe that Hilaire Belloc has already written that book.

Otford too is beginning to be spoiled, for during the ten years before the last war an eczema of villas had been spreading rapidly above the village, along what was the most solitary part—the Pilgrims' Way, which here emerges for some miles of definition along its now intermittent course up from Cornwall to Thanet. But still the centre of Otford village remains unspoiled; the green, the mill, the noble old church against which still stands the last remaining fragment of the Castle.

Coming to Otford up the Darent valley, one approaches it without seeing the miserable suburbia. And also one has the advantage of passing through the village of Shoreham, which sleeps on as it has slept for a thousand years. I know of only one disturbance in this tiny place, tucked away in the hills. It took place in the year 1828 when, after William Blake's death, a farm-wagon carrying Samuel Palmer and other disciples of the poet-artist-mystic rumbled into Shoreham. There they settled, and there Palmer did much of his later work, woodcuts with the light in them that shines "on neither sea nor land."

Otford has the magic of Downland about it. Once, with Aldington, it was the biggest manor in Kent, one of the fat attributes of the Archbishopric of Canterbury, from the beginning of the Christian era in Britain. Thomas à Becket had much to do with Otford. In a distinctly anti-Franciscan mood he once cursed the nightingales of Otford for intruding upon his devotions. The Elizabethan historian William Lambard tells the story thus : "As Thomas à Becket walked on a time in the Olde Parke (busie at his prayers), that he was much hindered in devotion by the sweete note and melodie of a nightingale that sang in a bush beside him, and that there-fore (in the might of his holynesse) he injoined that from henceforth no byrde of that kynde shoulde be so bolde as to sing thereaboutes." Nevertheless I have heard them in the groves of the big house called Beechy Lees that stands in the deep recess of the hills behind the village, on the left-hand of Pilgrims' Way.

Becket did something more positive by striking the ground with his staff in order to conjure forth water. The spring is there still, near the ruined octagonal tower of the palace which another Archbishop built, at great expense, three hundred years later in the reign of Henry VIII (a nice plum to fall into Henry's hands at the dissolution of the monasteries). There is therefore nothing to disprove this pleasing miracle.

Between the tower and the church lies the ancient grave-yard, under the shadow of the Downs, and fronted by a row of ancient cottages. It is a scene of peace and gentle recom-pense. It is sacred to me because there lies buried the brother with whom I used to make those rapturous excursions from Dulwich to the Crystal Palace, and later, in schoolboy and bicycle days, with whom I would explore the lanes that make the first network out of London into the Downs. Musician and painter, he led me through the dark bewilderments of childhood by the easy and natural path of unspoken affection. By some means, with which environment had nothing to do, he had discovered the music of Bach by the time he was fourteen, and used to play the Forty-eight to me, as well as

Field's Nocturnes. And from there we went together into the wide continent of music, I always following, being four years the junior; a great subordination at that period of life.

As time passed, and manhood approached, his health dwindled, but without diminishing his enjoyment of life and his unfailing delight in expressing that enjoyment, either in music or in painting. In 1927, when he was thirty-eight, his body would take him no further, and he died at Otford in the little holiday place which he and his wife had built only four years earlier. It was a beautiful site, high above the village, with a view to south, west, and east, over to Poll Hill, Sevenoaks, with the Weald running right into Surrey to Limpsfield and Godstone, and eastward to Kemsing and Scal, whose churches could be seen shining in the sunset.

This holiday home stood on the downland, among these diminutive riches of flower and grass permanently dwarfed by the century-long cropping of sheep and rabbits. Thyme was the predominant element, whose pervading scent filled the air, the cells of the body, the rooms of the memory, the deep recesses of the spirit. It seemed to come up the hill in waves, from the ruined tower. But in fact it was an exhalation from the ground at our feet, the light, chalky turf, springlike and crisp, with miniature blossoms of bread-and-cheese, harebell, valerian, scabious, and stunted hawthorn bushes like cunning Japanese cultures on which years of skill had been lavished. W. H. Hudson, in his *Nature in Downland*, has much to say about this kind of country, with its deceptive bareness, and its intimate secrets, such as the doorway of the wild bee, or the path of the field-mouse, or the firing-site of the grasshopper, that self-propelled rocket.

To this bare downland the dear settlers introduced some shadow, or schemes for shadow, by setting yew bushes and a semicircle of Scotch pine. The latter can now be seen from miles away, by travellers on the Continental boat-train as it emerges from Poll Hill Tunnel along the main line before running through Sevenoaks. And wild or semi-wild bushes (crab-apples, plums), with great masses of lavender more like trees than bushes, and acacias and laburnum—all these have flourished there in that intensity of light and ground aeration, until the few acres have been transformed into a spur from the valley, with rich darknesses and lush spots hidden from the great dome of sky. Everything grown on that chalk soil, quick and savage, takes a double dose of coloration. To look into a flower from that earth is to look into an element of coloured flame, fierce and primordial.

I will not linger there, though the sting has gone out of that loss, and the place now is serene again for me, with its high removal above the noises of the valley, which is the symbol of the world and its fret and fume. On that hillside of lark-song, and dazzling light coming down from the sky and up from the chalk through the pores of the thin surface soil, I have had, in the past, moments of spiritual feast in a companionship so complete that it was wordless.

Following up the Darent valley we reach Riverhead, which is little more than a meeting of roads. Breaking out of the valley southward we should rise steeply to Sevenoaks. But I will leave that exploration until we make another itinerary at a later stage in our parcelling out of the county.

So let us turn off from the main Sevenoaks road at River-head, and try to follow another stretch of the Pilgrims' Way westward. We shall not succeed, for the ancient road will disappear through one of the lodge gates of Chevening Park, the seat of the Stanhopes, a famous family who had their heyday in the eighteenth century. It was in 1780 that a Lord Stanhope worked a little Enclosure Act of his own by which he persuaded Parliament to give him the legal right to prevent any more pilgrims from making their pious way across his handsome park, within sight of the mansion built by Inigo Jones. To-day that racketeering still profits the present owner of Chevening, but the result is to keep a corner of Kent unmolested by motor-coaches and other unpleasant means by which twentieth-century citizens too largely take the road of pleasure. One has to ride round three sides of the park to get to the western gates, for the approach to Brasted. This great country house was the birthplace of the Lady Hester Stanhope, daughter of the encloser, who was an exquisite example of the eccentric English "milady," a type that from time to time recurs in our native manners, much to the amusement of our neighbours on the Continent. Lady Hester quarrelled with her father, left Chevening, and went to act as hostess at Downing Street for her uncle William Pitt. On his death she was given a state pension of £1,200 a year, and with this independence she finally settled near Sidon, in a house among the mountains of Lebanon, where her craving for domination, if not her social wit, could be exercised without restraint. She became a sort of Hippolyte among the natives, and maintained her hypnotic hold over them until her death in 1839.

If we keep to this stretch of the Pilgrims' Way we shall ride high, the Downs up on our right and the long and fertile valley below on our left. Immediately across it, southward, rise the secondary hills on which Sevenoaks stands, with miniature peaks at Ide Hill and Toys Hill after a two-mile climb. But those still remote places I will attack from the southern side, as the approaches to a wide stretch of the hinterland of Kent. At present we find ourselves passing still up the valley, having left the ancient road to turn into the bottom so that we shall not miss Brasted High Street, with its good examples of timbered cottages, inn, and smithy. The valley along here is delightfully contained within the hills; a complete human settlement, with its several villages whose church towers punctuate the parish divisions, while the wooded hills, especially on the southern side, drop steeply to the road. At the head of the valley, in front of us, stands Westerham Church, and we enter the village round a twist of the road which almost islands the house where General Wolfe, the conqueror of Quebec, spent his boyhood.

Having reached Westerham from Dartford, we have followed the whole course of the little River Darent, which travels in an arc concentric, at a distance of about twenty miles, with the south-eastern fringe of London. Thus we have cut off a portion of Kent which, like the whole county, is roughly fan-shaped. I have already explored its hinge-end, the parishes to be seen from the Crystal Palace. From them, out to Westerham, lies a country that used to be one of the most beautiful in the south of England. Rich in woods and commons, with wild stretches of sparsely inhabited hills, it offered to the cyclist and the walker scenes of complete solitude, with superb views outward and southward—and all this within some ten or twelve miles of London. But if I were to return to those scenes, I should not find my way, for where were such villages as West Wickham and Addington, Cudham and Downe, now there are huge dormitory settlements, street after street of featureless villas—a dreary mushroom growth (but what an insult to the delicate structure of mushrooms!) spored over this ruined countryside since the World War No. 1.

So I shall have to return to this part of Kent only by the roads of recollection, for I cannot imagine that anybody will want to read about a jerry-builder's dump, "where late the sweet birds sang."

Let us now assume that the country outward from the south-eastern suburbs of London had been preserved, by some fairyland statute, some impossible Rural Planning Act, from the dreary and squalid fate that has in fact overtaken it. We'll forget the strips of concrete with semi-detached dwellings stuck on them, like mechanical parts on a halted mass-production belt. We'll forget the little façades along what used to be the high roads; shops in the "modern" style (that is, bricks spoiled with cement wash) where "Anne" or "Yvonne" has set up a permanent-wave salon, next-door to a multiple-store branch.

This is of course a folly, an escape from reality; but let us enjoy it. I can already see two boys plugging away on their bicycles up the steep hill from Dulwich village to the Palace. They pause at the top for a breather, and to cool down. Then comes a grand coasting down the eastern side of the Palace grounds. They glide through Beckenham High Street, turn off sharp at Elmer's End, and have hardly another mile to go before they are in the country. The lane comes to a crossroads, above which stands West Wickham Church. We are here at a county boundary, which is marked by a strip of woodland a little way along the road toward Addington. The church and manor house adjoining it stand alone, for no other buildings can be seen up the hill, or along the valley level. That valley, I recollect, always offered a layer of chilly air to us as we went out and again as we came back, and we could never resist the touch of remote, inhuman magic which lay above and below the air-river of mist that flowed each morning and evening above the meadowland, between the enormous elms. Maybe an underground stream cast this emanation of vapour every time the temperature rose or fell. But there it was, always a silver stream a man's height above the ground, whenever we crossed, and at last we looked for it as the line of demarkation between London and the secret country of our boyhood. Its effect upon us was irresistible— not that we wanted to resist. On the contrary, we surrendered ourselves to the plunge as though here were some waters of transformation, a benign Lethe, which for a few hours could make us forget the grim, logical, and exacting side of our frugal Edwardian family life, in which duty figured so largely.

West Wickham seems always to have been a solitary spot, of great antiquity, as its Saxon name implies. Leland the historian speaks of the church and manor house having been built by one Henry Heydon in the sixteenth century. There is nothing particularly outstanding about the church, other than its perfect site on the hill-slope just below the house and overlooking the long valley which runs east-west, fastening the two counties. The lychgate is an old one, and I remember standing, on a bitter cold New Year's Day of the year 1908, making a drawing of the gate from the opposite field, my hands muffled in thick woollen gloves.

The manor, West Wickham Court, has records back to the time of Edward the Confessor. It fell into the rapacious hands of Odo, the very secular Bishop of Bayeux, the Conqueror's greedy brother. It passed from one family to another amongst the gentry of Kent, amongst whom were the Bullens, or Boleyns. Ann Boleyn spent much time here while manipulating the King's passion for her. It seems to have been a rendezvous between his palace at Greenwich and her father's home at Hever Castle. How rightly apprehensive the Boleyn family must have been as they looked on helplessly at the royal intrigue.

A few hundred yards westward along the valley road and we are over the county boundary into Surrey, at Addington, which is a chapel-of-ease of the Archbishop of Canterbury, with a residence. So having, for the purposes of this book, no visa to cross that frontier, we will turn back and, passing again across the front of West Wickham Church, ride eastward to Bromley. Even in those days of my boyhood it was a big place, stained with the overflow from London. But its steep High Street, and its church which contains the grave of Dr Johnson's wife Elizabeth, the "Tetty" whom he never ceased to mourn, are worth a visit. I recollect spending a night there in a gaping, jerry-built villa during the last war, on a visit to a friend who was Excise Officer for the district. One of the heaviest air raids of that war took place that night, and two mobile guns sat down outside the front door and barked up at the sky, their shells screaming over the house and the adjoining railway station. At each volley the brick box yawned open, the windows and door-frames gradually succumbing.

Escaping due south from Bromley, we find by-lanes again and come by these real Kentish ways to Hayes Common, on our route to Keston. Hayes (which means "heath") is a pleasing little common, with the remains of one hundred and fifty neolithic pit-dwellings. They consist of circular depressions, with banked edges, and some of them have mounds in the centre. William Pitt was born, and spent his boyhood, at Hayes Place, and from here Lady Hester Stanhope's mother was married. In spite of the famous picture of the death of the great Chatham in the House of Lords, it was here and not at Westminster that the statesman finally expired. Another interesting item about this place is that in another of the houses adjoining the common, a small manor named Boston House, were discovered under a coat of wash some ancient paintings, dated 1480. They were possibly the first examples of oil painting in this country.

Hayes for me always meant the sense of at last emerging from the town. Beyond it one came at once to Keston, a place of many waters, which consist of three large ponds whose source is a well where Cæsar is said to have camped with his first army when he was rounding up the defeated British.

Near the spring, now known as Cæsar's Well, is another double-circular marking that certainly signifies a camp, but probably one earlier than Roman.

Not far along the road from the ponds, travelling south, lies the estate at Downe where Charles Darwin lived. One can also walk to Downe from Keston by a footpath across the park known as Holwood, another possession of the Pitt family. Under an old oak tree in this park William Wilberforce made an announcement to the Prime Minister which he recorded in his diary as follows : "1788. At length, I well remember after a conversation with Mr Pitt in the open air at the root of an old oak tree at Holwood, just above the steep descent into the vale of Keston, I resolved to give notice on a fit occasion in the House of Commons of my intention to bring forward the abolition of the slave trade."

Pitt was a great lover of trees, and so great was his passion for planting them at Holwood that during his labours there he would have the work carried on day and night, the saplings being set by lamplight during the hours of darkness.

Going up alongside Wickham Court is a narrow by-lane, out of the Addington to Bromley road. It climbs steeply up to a wide, desolate stretch of plateau country, that is grooved with valleys of a slightly ominous character (a feature common with upland valleys). This was the personal country of our boyhood, and we were in the habit of looking askance at any obvious intruder into that secret land, the kingdom of our young imagination, the country of the singing lanes.

This plateau was netted over with a reticulation of these small lanes, and we never quite succeeded in mapping them out to our satisfaction. I doubt if we should have been satisfied had we done so, for the savour was in the exciting confusion with which, week after week, we explored one or another of them, coming out from time to time suddenly upon a bit which we recognized with a shout. There was one empty cottage which joined in the game. It must have been a movable cottage, for it had the trick of bobbing up first here, then there, in the most unlikely and disconnected ways, at all parts of that wide stretch of deserted country. One hot summer Saturday afternoon, after we had been riding around, up and down the sudden gullies, winding round patches of beechwood, through dried-up stream-beds, until we were parched and dusty as millers, we came upon that malignant cottage when we ought to have been miles from it on the way to Westerham. There it stood, on its latest site, with its windows gleaming at us, complete with the same strip of deserted garden where the ragwort stood waist-high, crawling with a horde of tiger-stripe caterpillars all of which must have taken part in the evil transportation.

The sunlight poured down on that mirage house, and on its crawling carpet of ragwort. A stink like that of rotting apples added to the mockery. Partly to test the reality of the scene, and partly from sheer irritability, I took up a stone from the roadside and flung it at the house. We stood appalled at the result. There was at first a small tinkle of breaking glass. But the spirits of the valley took up the sound and carried it against the edge of the wood running along the top. The tinkle grew to a splintering accusation, breaking back and forth across the valley and shouting at us through its teeth. It was a noise that had fingers, pointing at us; sharp glassy fingers, blue as a policeman's brassard.

We fled from that house. We jumped on our bicycles and pedalled, bent over the handlebars, gasping and sweating, until we had rounded the valley and climbed into another kind of country, that had no inlet for the dreadful echo and the guilt it carried. And we did not stop, nor speak to each other, until by a turn of fortune we came to the one wayside inn that stands in the whole of the hinterland between the West Wickham road and the top main road from Warlingham to Westerham, which closes this special private stretch of country on the south.

That inn is called the White Bear. It is completely hidden by foliage, standing back in the angle of a sharp bend in one of the lanes (I shall never know which) in the network. Thus one comes upon it unexpectedly, after a dark passage through a wood. It is really only a cottage with a curious sign. That sign consists of a wooden model, painted white, of a bear. It is about as big as a St Bernard dog, and it stands head down among the weeds and patches of sweet-rocket in the little overblown garden in front of the inn.

But what teas we used to have there! I can recall still the particular tea which we ordered after that incident of crime. We had two boiled eggs each, a plate of watercress, strawberry jam with country bread and butter, and home-made cake. And having recovered from the heat and the guilt, we sat there replete in the gathering dusk, and read in turn from Thomas Chatterton's verse-play *Ælla*, passing the pocket edition from one to the other. I remember still how my conscience, tender after that window-breaking which only the

eye of heaven and the spirits of the valley had seen, prodded
me afresh as I read the following stanza :

When swift-foot time doth roll the day along,
Some hamlet shall unto our fury brende;
Bursting like rock, or e'en a mountain strong,
The tall church-spire upon the green shall bend.
We will the walls and ancient turrets rend,
Destroy each tree which golden fruit doth bear,
Down to the gods the owners thereof send,
Besprinkling all abroad sad war and bloody weere;
But first to yonder oak-tree we will fly,
And thence will issue out on all that cometh by.

I looked up, and saw to my dismay that we were sitting
beneath an oak. That evening, on the return ride to Dulwich,
there was none of our usual singing as we pedalled through
the alternate hot and cold patches along the lanes; through
hot and cold, light and dark, mist and clear, stopping to light
our smelly oil lamps as the bats came out, and then pedalling
on again with the chill on our cheeks and the backs of our
hands, and the ravishing perfumes of summer night rolling
over us as we headed for home.

That was only one of the hundreds of adventures which
we found in that little pocket of Kent which we had made our
own. During all the years of school life and youth that we used
to explore there, we hardly ever met strangers. Why it was
so unmolested I shall never understand. The isolated farms,
hardly more than small-holdings bare and poverty-drab,
would have a man, or a man and a boy, working in a field, or
leading a horse and cart along the lane near the homestead.
But that was all. We were the only lively and detached
creatures there; we and the valley echoes that rose to greet
us as we rode singing and yodelling on those fabulous Saturday afternoons when all the world was young, and all the trees
were green, and every lane was a singing lane.

CHAPTER V

BEATING THE BOUNDARIES

WE have been wandering about among the home regions long enough. Our goal was to be Westerham, so now let us get there, to make it a focal point for further explorations down the Surrey and Sussex boundaries of our Kingdom of Kent. Leaving those boyhood haunts we come out of the singing lanes to a secondary road that has climbed the North Downs from Keston, through Biggin Hill (now a huge depot and airfield of the R.A.F.) to Tatsfield. This last village is one of nature's mistakes. I have always found that villages at the tops of hills or mountains have something dreary, almost sinister, about them. We climb the slopes amid beauty and remoteness, the romantic quality of scene and atmosphere increasing as we rise above the fatness and busy-ness of the valleys and plains. We anticipate that when we reach the top, the very moment of ecstatic revelation, for which all this mounting grandeur has been preparing us, will burst upon us. And instead, we emerge to a flat, bare, chilly, and poverty-stricken top, whose few inhabitants eye us suspiciously from behind doors or windows (when the windows are not too filthy to look through).

Tatsfield is no exception. It is a squalid little collection of small-holdings and corrugated-iron bungalows. What a vile blot upon the face of civilization is corrugated iron! It has spread throughout the world, ousting local materials and local handicrafts, inducing laziness and physical degradation into the lives of the whole human race. But I must not stop to consider all the evil, both social and æsthetic, which the use of corrugated iron has brought into the world.

If Tatsfield ever has a claim to fame, it will be for one thing only; that for a few years it was the home of Rutland Boughton, the composer of that eerie, Celtic-twilight opera, *The Immortal Hour*. For some reason known only to himself, the musician settled in Tatsfield after the success of his opera. Perhaps it was to mortify himself, and to purge away any

vanity that might have resulted from his fame. Another man of character who lived in this God-detested spot for some years was C. E. Lawrence, the gentle novelist, friend of young writers, editor of the *Quarterly Review*, reader for the great publishing house of John Murray, and secretary of the Savage Club. He was a man of abrupt manners, and had a habit of wiping his hand (a singularly shapely hand) over his white hair as though trying to recall something to a mind addicted to absenteeism. He always carried a long woollen scarf, which he wound round and round his neck as he left his daily train at Woldingham, in preparation for the long uphill cycle ride to Tatsfield. His exit from the train was always remarkable, and liable to fill other passengers with anxiety. For he would continue talking to the very last second before the train started, gesticulating with those shapely hands, trying simultaneously to keep the scarf from catching in the door or strangling him, and to gather up a dozen or more loose books which had overflowed from his battered despatch-case. As the train left the station he would run alongside to finish his conversation, while books dropped from him like leaves from an autumn tree.

So much for Tatsfield. I have done all I can for it. I have given it two decorations; two more than it deserves.

Across the plateau, quarter of a mile southward, we come to the crest of the Downs. Unlike the crest of the South Downs, that of the North Downs is mainly wooded. But where breaks occur, the southward scene is one of the most wide-stretched and noble in the south of England. Crossing the Biggin Hill road we come to the by-road that is making its way over the Surrey border from Woldingham. Here, where it passes the top of the famous Oxted chalk-pits, the scene is at its widest and best. Downland supreme! What an exaltation it is to sit here on a hot summer day and to stare out across the whole range of the Weald, over the middle hills of the East Grinstead–Tunbridge Wells–Brenchley ridge, to the far distant and clean-cut line of the bare South Downs. But we are now standing on the very edge of the county, and must not forget the endorsement on our visa for the purposes of this book. Below us lies Limpsfield, one of the most beautiful villages in all England. But it is in Surrey, and

F   65

we must not venture down Titsey Hill, through the fox-haunted wood, to explore that lovely property of the Leveson-Gower family, a vast, flower-drenched estate still largely unspoiled, although its fringes have been debauched by the suburban-minded builder and speculator.

Here we sit in Chalk-land, a world unto itself. I had something to say about the nature of this kind of country in my last chapter. We see that nature here, on the high ridge of the county border, at its best. I must quote a paragraph from a book called *A Prospect of Flowers,* by the dour poet Andrew Young. It sums up the qualities of the chalk country :

"Or it may be the sketch of a chalk-hill. Wind blows cloud-shadows across the Grass that vainly tries to uproot itself and follow. It disturbs the Nodding Thistle in its sleep, but not the Dwarf Thistle that lies too close to the ground, so close that it looks like a beheaded flower. It ruffles Salad Burnet, feeding its invisible body on the cucumber scent, but flees from the mousy smell of Hound's-tongue. Aromatic plants have their perfumes blown about and confused, so that Thyme smells of Marjoram and Basil of Calamint. Cinnabar Moths rock on the Rampion, a strangely beautiful flower like a blue sea-anemone, deserving its unique botanical name Phyteuma, the Plant. The Rock-rose's petals quiver, as though their gold were melting in the sun; even Yellow-wort, a Gentian that appears too prim to admit those marriage-brokers, the bees, bends from its waxen stiffness in the general excitement of the hill."

That magical paragraph from a book that I dare to predict will be of permanent value gives some of the quality of intimate fragrance and colour of the miniature life of petal and wing seething round us as we sit upon the aerated turf, drugged with light and perfume. One has only to shift a hand or foot to bruise some scent-bleeding leaf. And all this tiny universe is the more accentuated in its Lilliputian perfection by contrast with the vast cup of sky, and the vast saucer of the Weald. What a cup and saucer ! Whoever drinks from them, does he notice the myriad decorations, which are almost too small for even our midget eyes to appreciate?

One can sit hypnotized by this scene, while time and light shimmer and tremble, and minutes melt into hours, golden and dust-moted hours that are bee-haunted and shrill with wings. It is dangerous to our punctual task, and we must break away to the shelter of the grove of beech trees that lines the road where it divides, the right-hand dropping down through the wilds of Titsey Park, to Surrey; the left-hand falling more gradually down the back of the hill to Westerham, which we enter from the north-west, by a modest by-road that breaks into the main street amongst some old cottages.

We turn left to reach the centre of the village, which opens out almost to the size of a provincial-town market-place. On the north side, behind a broad and formerly cobbled path, stands a collection of shops and several hotels. One of these, the George and Dragon, is an old posting inn, where for centuries the Courts Baron and Courts Leet were held. At the end of the broad paving, to the north-eastern corner of the Square, stands the entrance to the churchyard, which opens out to the view along the Darenth Valley that I have already mentioned when we looked along the valley from the other, the Sundridge end. Halfway down the valley stands Brasted Church.

Westerham Church is Early English in origin, with later additions. It sits like a hen over her clutch, with aisles almost as wide and high as the nave. The squat tower is dominated by a short spire. The organ I remember particularly, because it is a fine specimen of the work of the Brixton organ-builder, Lewis. I remember it because of a happy incident. On one of our cycle rides from Dulwich, my brother and I decided to linger about the village so that we might have a ride home through the dusk and the dark. The summer afternoon was intensely hot, and we lay for an hour after lunch in a meadow below the churchyard, looking eastward along the valley, and talking together, after dozing, of the families whose memorials we had read upon from the walls of the church; notably the Wardes, lords of the Manor and Squerryes Park (an admirable family of squire-soldiers and sailors, one of whom was the boyhood friend of James Wolfe, the hero of Quebec). Suddenly, amid these historical browsings and cud-chewings, my brother sat up. "Did you notice that the organ was open?" he said. I looked at him guiltily, yet eagerly. I knew what was passing in his mind, and I welcomed the idea.

Without further words we both got up and made our way
into the church. It was cool after the heavy, scented heat of
the valley. It smelt of years, dried and preserved years; a
herby, dusty smell. Nobody was about. The only sound was
the slow tick . . . tack . . . tick . . . *tuck* of the clock. What a
sound that is. It is time itself. To sit in a church and to let it
come upon one like a dropping of water is almost a torture,
for it begins to tell upon the imagination, to stir it to an agony
of evocation, and then to beat it down again into dread and
utter loss of personal identity.

But my brother's project, whose confidence I shared though
no word had been spoken, was not historical. He walked cat-
like up the nave and prowled about the console of the organ.
Turning over the music, he found an organ setting of Gabriel
Fauré's *Requiem Mass*. I sat in a pew halfway down the nave,
and listened to the music. My brother was putting in the voice
parts on one of the open stops, and the effect was ethereal.
Fauré was one of his favourite composers, for by some un-
explainable affinity this London boy, practically self-taught,
had a passion for French music, from Rameau to Ravel.

I can still conjure that hour of rapture : the cool interior of
the church; the tombs and brasses looming sub-aqueous in the
half-light; the windows brushed from outside with fans of
foliage and green sunshine; the music with its French precision
of emotion, lovely and exalted yet always civilized. I can also
recall my blankness of mind and spirit, as I sat there
enchanted, too deeply moved to be able to register the experience. When, momentarily, we become gods, we look like
blocks or village idiots.

My brother was playing the Paradiso chorus, with its wonderful pastoral accompaniment on the harp, when I was
aware of somebody softly opening the door behind me and
tiptoeing up the narrow strip of carpet. I half-turned my head.
It was the vicar ! I felt a creepy sensation down my spine, and
my hair tingled. Now we were in for trouble !

I was paralysed, and could do nothing to rescue my brother.
So he played on, while the vicar sat himself down in the pew
beside me, his face veiled in the dusky light, but vaguely
severe, at least to my apprehensive mind. Quietly the music
faded down to its serene close. The echoes filtered away, and

all that survived was the tick . . . tack . . . tick . . . *tuck* of the clock.

Then the vicar looked at the boy and said, "Who is that?" My voice was mouse-like as I replied, "Gabriel Fauré, sir." I saw his lips twitch, and he stared at me for some seconds before speaking again. "Yes, but who's playing it?" I was now patently terrified, and could only stutter out, "My brother, sir." Then something happened which I shall never forget. The vicar got up, put his hand on my shoulder, and said very quietly, "Thank your brother for me, my boy," and walked out of the church.

The memorial to James Wolfe is in the form of a tablet over the south door. He was born at the vicarage, where his parents were staying in 1727, before moving into the Elizabethan house at the bottom of the village, opposite the Edenbridge road and the gates of Valence. This house, then called Spiers, is now the property of the National Trust, and is known as Quebec House. It is open to the public, and can be appreciated as an architectural treasure as well as a historical monument. I need say little about Wolfe here. Thackeray, if I remember rightly, gave a portrait of him in *The Virginians*, and speaks of "his fine courtesy." But the temperamental soldier's physical appearance did not help him in presenting this courtesy to the world. He was a red-haired, consumptive boy, with receding forehead and chin, and a malformed lip. Yet his character, livened by a touch of genius, triumphed over his bodily disabilities, and lived a glorious page of English history. Everybody may know his mother's recipe for curing him of his consumption. She wrote it down in her cookery book, which was preserved at Squerryes Court, by the Warde family. Here is her formula for "a good water for consumption."

"Take a peck of garden snails, wash them in beer, put them in an oven and let them stay till they've done crying; then with a knife and fork prick the green from them, and beat the snail shells and all in a stone mortar. Then take a quart of green earth worms, slice them through the middle and strow them with salt; then wash them and beat them, the pot being first put into the still with two handfuls of angelico, a quart of rosemary flowers, then the snails and worms, then egrimony, bears feet, red dock roots, barbary brake, bilony, wormwood, of each two handfuls, one handful of rue-tumeric, and one ounce of saffron, well dried and beaten. Then pour in three gallons of milk. Wait till morning, then put in three ounces of cloves (well-beaten), Hartshorn, grated. Keep the still covered all night. This done, stir it not! Distil it with a moderate fire. The patient must take two spoonfuls at a time."

That was the potion which won us Canada, and thus, ultimately, delivered Arnhem and northern Holland from a satanic possession.

Leaving the house where that was written, we leave the village abruptly, climbing southward up Hosey Hill and over Hosey Common. Already we are in wild country, of bracken, bramble, and pines. Dropping into a remote upland valley called Horn's Hill we turn and wind right and left, climbing again, to emerge round a great spur of hillside (once covered with Scots pines that were cut down by Portuguese peasants during the 1914–18 war) upon another aspect of the superb panorama which we studied in those timeless moments from the top of Titsey Hill. At the high point the road takes another sharp right-hand bend, but it offers another path down a by-lane directly off the angle. This road is magic, and is likely to lead us wildly astray. Let us take it.

At first it is hardly more than a ledge on the hillside. Steeply down on our right-hand side the ground drops over a balustrade to a large garden and a hillside house, where lives Sir Percy Mackinnon, once Chairman of Lloyds. His home is in as perfect a setting as could be wished for. Sheltered from north and east by the great bastion of the hill, it looks over Crockham Hill church and village south-westward toward East Grinstead and the wide range of Sussex. The soil in this pocket of the hills is deep and rich, and everything, wild or cultivated by man, riots luxuriously, so that the whole slope has something about it that reminds one of the Riviera, or a grove in Sicily. Theocritus would have been happy here.

The lane turns abruptly left at a corner where stands an ancient cottage whose chimney-tops hardly reach above the road-level. Down beside the garden of this picturesque place falls a course of stone-paved steps, hundreds of them, which give upon a sloping path that leads through the fold of the hill into the valley, to Crockham Hill church and school. This church is recent, built by one of the Wardes of Squerryes Court. It stands snuggled down in the trees and hill-slopes, its square tower almost overlooked.

The cottage, set upon such a prominent corner, was for many years inhabited by E. V. Lucas, the essayist, topographer, gastronomist, publisher, and specialist on Charles Lamb. Lucas was a figure in his day, a shrewd business man behind his whimsical literary façade and his *bonhomie*. I first met him on the occasion when I wanted to put W. H. Hudson's *A Shepherd's Life* into *Everyman's Library*. I remember entering his office and being greeted by a crafty, rather watery eye, and the words, "What wicked trick are *you* up to !" This disconcerting gambit, however, was followed by a charming smile, a friendly conversation as between writer and writer (rather than between publisher and publisher), and a final agreement to part with the copyright of the classic. Later, after long and complicated negotiations amongst several publishers about a complete edition of Charles Lamb's letters, which I wanted Lucas to edit, he said to me one morning, after a happy termination to the proceedings, "Well, having disposed of the Lamb, let us go and eat a saddle of mutton together at Simpson's !" And we did; washing it down with draught Bass fortified with barley wine. A heavy luncheon; but we balanced it with airy conversation.

When Lucas left that cottage he sold it to the American Quaker poet, Henry Brian Binns, a tall, gaunt, shy man who used to frequent the literary gatherings down the hill at Kent Hatch, where Edward Garnett had built his house and called it The Cerne. But we shall walk down the hill to that after our diversion along this easterly lane.

This lane seems to plunge more and more into luxuriant obscurity. One feels that it is leading into the no-man's-land which the tired, romantic townsman is for ever seeking and never finding. Some kind of magic creeps into the scene. We pass an oast-house converted into a dwelling, and then alongside a sloping orchard which rises up the hillside on our left. The sense of something uncanny, slightly Peer Gyntish, increases, and I am tempted to connect this psychological condition of the passer-by with one peculiar to the place. For this stretch of the hills, between Crockham Hill and Toys Hill, to which we are making our way has twice experienced a geological upheaval. In 1596 an area of nine acres of ground at Crockham Hill sank suddenly, for some eight feet, and continued to sink for nearly two weeks. Then in 1756 two and a half acres at Toys Hill came to life, rising into hills and then sinking into pits. These convulsions have thrown up patches of soil that are abnormally fertile. Whatever may be the cause, this stretch of country hillside is almost tropical in its vegetable luxury. Wild flowers and beetles, butterflies and giant ants, make it a paradise for the naturalist.

The lane leads through the gates and across the front of a superbly situated old house called Mariners, which stands secreted by the rising ground behind it on north, east, and west, with a great terraced view across the Weald to the south. As an approximation to a Sicilian existence I could not imagine any life more idyllic than one spent in Mariners. Over the hill behind it stands another ancient seat, once called Atwell after the family that built the original house in the reign of Edward III. It is now known as Chartwell, and is likely to be a historical monument because it is the home of Winston Churchill, the bricklayer, painter, and writer who in 1940 advised his fellow countrymen to fight "on the beaches, in the fields, the villages, towns and streets," should the barbarian follow up the conquest of France by an invasion of England. What a man! He will surely be set amongst our greatest and most loved.

What concerns me here, however, is not his public achievements, for they are in everybody's mind, all over the world. I can delight also, and more particularly for the purposes of this book, in his turns of speech and hand. Before he took Chartwell, renovating it and making it a masterpiece, he had another old manor house called Lullenden, not far away down on the Wealden hills at Dormans. In the grounds of that house, set under the shadow of an outbreak of ironstone rock, stood an old barn. Mr Churchill transformed this into a lodge for guests, consisting of a living-room with vaulted ceiling and a gallery out of which led the bedrooms. The great fireplace in the living-room was designed with just the right taste and sense of proportion. I cannot imagine a more hospitable or genial setting in which to place a guest with work to do, and a skin sensitive to the exhalations of history.

Perhaps Chartwell's elevation to fame was predicted in 1842, when Crockham Hill Church was built by Charles Warde. Its first vicar was a Reverend Cameron Churchill! The gardens of Chartwell, like those of Mariners, appear to have been touched by the painful inspiration of those two geological revolutions. Its roses and azaleas, its araucaria and cedars, and particularly its giant Japanese cedar (*Cryptomeria japonica*) tempt one to look out over the Weald expecting to see the Bay of Naples, with Vesuvius smoking in the distance.

The magic persists past Mariners, as one drops down into a wild, deserted basin called Puddle Dock. From here the little road climbs steeply, still along a ledge of the hills, to come at last to a cross roads and an inn at Toys Hill. Many a week-end have I spent at that inn, in a sitting-room whose window gave precipitously out to the slope of the hill that dropped away to the plain at Four Elms. The Tally-Ho was a modest little place, with an earth-closet, and a tentative water-supply. But it was remote from the world, and a week-end there was a sort of secular retreat as refreshing to the soul as any the Trappists could offer. Nothing happened there. Time stood still. The war and its rumours, at least during 1914–18, passed below it, like the distant sound of a train in the valley. Early morning mists blotted out that great plain, so that the Tally-Ho used to float, each day, for an hour or two of remote isolation as complete as that of Noah's ark awaiting the return of the dove.

Further east lies Ide Hill, with its little church standing up neatly. That is a more popular viewpoint, a National Trust ground with a tiny village. We can go down the camel's back to it from Toys Hill, or we can climb the crest northward over the Chart and so down the other side to the Darenth valley again, which we enter at Brasted.

That is a delightful excursion from our present objective, which is to beat the boundaries of the county where it runs alongside Surrey and Sussex. For that purpose we must return to the top of Crockham Hill and the main road over from Westerham to Edenbridge. There is a fine run down to the church, which we need not explore further. As we approach the hamlet of Crockham Hill we meet a road coming in from a formerly deep woodland over Limpsfield Common from the northwest. If we walk back up that turning for half a mile we come to a gate on the left, which stands against a prolongation of the wood over the left-hand as well as the right-hand side of the road. Opposite it is a secondary road that leads to Westerham. This spot, once a dark and lonely bosquet whose only source of light came from the south, over the dropping land beyond the gate, is called Kent Hatch.

Near the gate stands, or stood until recently a wicked stroke of lightning brought it down, a gigantic beech tree. This tree marks the boundary between Kent and Surrey. If one explores the woods further in this neighbourhood, one will discover sister trees of this giant, many of them so near together that they still constitute an obvious boundary, though hidden away in midforest, their boles set in a dark fosse and draped with all manner of mosses and decayed matter, smelling of the past, summers and leaf-fallings away back in the days of the Druids, when a toadstool had its ritualistic significance, and a spray from the Golden Bough could bring down kings from their thrones.

Passing behind this tree, one could walk along the bottom edge of the wood, with the great panorama of the Weald on one's left hand. There was an ill-defined path amongst the fallen beechmast, but bushes of deadly nightshade, with ominous black berries, frequently obscured it, and carpets of dog's mercury hid it every spring. But still, it made an approach to the house where Edward Garnett held his literary court in the eighteen-nineties and the early years of the present century. There he had to visit him such people as Conrad, W. H. Davies, Edward Thomas, Prince Kropotkin, Stephen Crane, Henry James, Maarten Maartens, and many others. It was a sort of examination centre, a lodge-gate to the mansion of Letters for so many young men and women of promise that it became a place of pilgrimage. In this beautiful spot the famous critic's wife, Constance Garnett, worked for most of her valuable life upon her translations of the Russian classics, notably Tolstoi, Dostoevski, Turgeniev, and Tchehov.

Readers who would welcome a more intimate acquaintance

with this now sacred spot should read a book called *Beany-Eye*, written by Edward's son, David Garnett, who has also made his own niche in the Pantheon. This little book is a study of the queer character of a gardener once employed by his father in the garden of the Cerne.

But we have trodden over the border, and we must return to our own side of it, finding the road again, and following it due south through Crockham Hill and Marlpit Hill to Edenbridge, which is down in the Weald, with its little river, the Eden,.to prove that we have left the valley of the Darenth at last and are now entering, almost at its head, the valley of the larger River Medway.

Edenbridge is habitually maligned by topographers. I don't know why. It is a pleasant little town, with a high street that narrows picturesquely in the middle of the village, to be spanned by the inn-sign of the posting-house, the Crown, which still has a concealed passage upstairs, where used to be hidden undutied casks, from which pipes ran down to the taproom, delivering liquor unsanctioned by the exciseman. Romano-British pottery of the first century after Christ was found in the village in 1912, and this confirmed the belief that Edenbridge, like Westerham (Squerryes), was formerly a Roman settlement. The great Gresham family, originating at Holt in Norfolk, acquired the manor of Edenbridge in the reign of Henry VIII (he had a habit of paying, belatedly, his debts with lands taken from the monasteries). John Gresham, a merchant prince who "lent" money to the extravagant king, was a great financier who instituted the theory of money values, a now classic doctrine of bimetallism, known as Gresham's Law. Its gist is that bad money drives out good. It is a theory, still held by the sinister world of bankers, which overlooks the fact that money is neither good nor bad, but merely mechanical. Like all other machinery, however, money has been allowed by man to rule him and his destiny, and thus it has become an engine of destruction as deadly as the bomber-plane and the Bren gun.

Gresham's coat of arms contains the famous grasshopper, which gave rise to the pretty fairy-tale about his being a foundling, left in a field, and discovered to a passing peasant by the indignant chirping of a grasshopper. But the family when it came from Norfolk was already an old one, with *la cigale* in its coat of arms; so the little creature seems to have sung as vainly in this tale as it did in La Fontaine's parable.

Round about the village are several old manors and farm-houses. Just over the border, in a wood called Staffhurst Wood, I once rented a fourteenth-century house called Comfort's Cottage. This appropriate name (for the house was a sun-drenched old place, on a bit of open common rising out of the wood and looking over to Edenbridge) was said to have been given it in the seventeenth century when a tenant farmer married a Frenchwoman of the name of Comfret, no doubt a notable vagary from the usual local selection of brides. This old dwelling had a doorway in which Roman bricks and stone-shapings were incorporated, probably from a building formerly on the site. I rented the house from the lord of Titsey Manor, Sir Charles Leveson-Gower, a direct descendant of that John Gresham whose grasshopper can be seen carved over the mantelpiece in Titsey Place. Comfort's Cottage was haunted by nightingales, who sang rapturously in the surrounding woods. It was from these woods that the song of the nightingale was first broadcast to the world by the B.B.C.

In order to avoid penetrating into Surrey once again (no easy matter in this district, for the county boundary winds about crazily) we must turn left just out of Edenbridge and ride eastward to Hever along a pretty lowland lane. Here we approach another patch of charmed country, a rectangle roughly about nine miles by six, bounded on the north by the cross-country railway line which runs dead straight (the longest such stretch in England) from Redhill to Ashford. This boundary is extremely arbitrary, for north of the railway the same sort of lowland country reaches up to the downs, where Toys Hill, Ide Hill, and Sevenoaks Weald lie shimmering in the sun. We can thus explore first the lower land below the railway, with its historical treasures so marked, and then go back to the foothills to Sevenoaks so that we can take a look at Knole.

All about this part of the countryside a profusion of small lanes winds about, to bemuse the explorer and to offer weeks of constant discovery of cottages, road junctions, and all such points which pin down the natural beauty with a brooch of man's making. Thus I find it difficult to know how precisely to begin in my descriptions of these approaches to the several great houses which I want to visit. Each of them can be found by so many ways. The best course to suggest is that the enthusiast should stay at Tunbridge Wells, or Penshurst, and give some time to wandering about here, not in a motor-car, but on a bicycle, or by Shanks's mare, so that field-paths and tenth-class roads can be investigated. They all have their surprises and delights.

Hever is about two miles from Edenbridge. It is entered by a sharp angle in the lane, round the Henry VIII Arms and the church. The castle lies down a little, in the moated hollow, which is approached through the park gates. The castle, its outbuildings, the park and village, are all now maintained richly by the Astor family, who bought the ruined place at the beginning of the century and restored it with great care and good taste. The original castle was a fortified place built in the reign of Edward III, when social conditions pre-scribed such architecture. Later it came into the hands of one Sir Geoffrey Boleyn, who in the reign of Henry VI, when comfort and ease was spreading, added to the castle in a more domestic expansiveness. His great-granddaughter was Anne Boleyn, that damson-eyed, vivacious wit who cap-tivated first the poet Sir Thomas Wyatt (our first notable sonneteer), and then a more dangerous prey, King Henry the Eighth, by whom she became the mother of Queen Elizabeth.

She won little from her conquest. Her courtier father was made Earl of Wiltshire and Ormonde; but later, when the king's passion veered, or was doused in political considera-tions, both she and her brother were executed, and Hever was seized by the king and given to Anne of Cleves, who is said to have died there after her short session as Consort. Why the king treated the family so violently I do not know. Kings have such habits; but it is possible that what at first seemed unexampled luck for the family so inflamed their cupidity and spirit of nepotism that they overreached them-selves. The ambitious earl's tomb and effigy can be seen in the church.

On the death of Anne of Cleves the castle reverted to the Crown, and was ceded to the Waldegrave family. Hasted gives a detailed account of the subsequent owners of the castle, and refers to it, in the eighteenth century, as being "entire, and in good condition"; but it subsequently fell into decay, and when the Astors bought it the remains were being used as byres and other farm buildings. The restored palace, and the noble grounds, can be seen to-day by favour of the owner.

Passing through the village, we come to Chiddingstone, two miles along the by-road. This little hamlet is one of England's gems, with a castle standing on a knoll behind its wrought-iron gates, a perfect example of a Tudor inn, a cluster of domestic buildings of the same period, and a chiding-stone where nagging wives were formerly given a dose of their own medicine. The Streatfeild family has owned this castle since the time of James I. The village, with those round it, such as Bough Beech, Mark Beech, Cowden, and Four Elms, stands on the heavy Wealden clay, which suits the growth of the oak tree. All this countryside is dominated by the oaks, which, either singly or in surviving woodland stretches, stand against time like rocks, struggling every year against the Maytime onslaught of the caterpillar plague which so frequently strips them of their first foliage, and causes them to have a bare, silvery appearance for some weeks until the pest has gone, and the victims have put on a second coat. It is most unpleasant, during the visitation, to walk under the oaks, as the caterpillars hang in thousands by silken threads, and swing against one's skin and hair.

The Streatfeild family has been settled in Kent since the Middle Ages, and has intermarried into other noble families in the county, notably the Leveson-Gowers.

Winding our way still along the same by-road, we leave this village (which happily is now the property of the National Trust and cannot be disfigured by enterprising builders or local philistines) and a mile and a half further eastward we come to Penshurst. This place could demand a whole book rather than a paragraph. Poets from Sidney to Swinburne have sung it. Amongst them was Southey, the pedestrian versifier but good prose-master, and his lines might well be emphasized here, to introduce the reverent explorer to Penshurst.

> . . . Tread
> As with a pilgrim's reverential thoughts,
> The groves of Penshurst. Sidney here was born,
> Sidney, than whom no greater, braver man
> His own delightful genius ever feigned,
> Illustrating the groves of Arcady
> With courteous courage and with loyal love.

The mansion is approached through the village, which is rich in timbered houses, and is not disfigured by a modern village hall and clubroom. The entrance to the churchyard and footpath to the back of the house is across a bricked court called Leicester Square, which is enclosed on three sides by ancient houses with overhanging upper storeys. Under the further one is an archway leading to the church. The church is older, at least in origin, than the house, for it dates from 1200, whereas the present house was not built until 1341, when Sir John de Pulteney, a citizen merchant of London, was licensed by Edward III to embattle his new dwelling with walls of chalk and stone. Since then the house has been severally added to, even as late as the mid-nineteenth century, but nothing has been done to spoil its simplicity and dignity. It is a noble place, somewhat austere outside, but within it has a lightness and grace that harmonize rightly with the legend and character of the Sidney family, who have owned it since the time of Edward VI, who on 6 April 1552 granted it to his Chamberlain and Chief Steward, Sir William Sidney.

The church also has been added to from time to time, the present tower and clerestory being Late Perpendicular. Among the monuments in the church is that of Sir Stephen de Penchester, who died in 1299. He was the founder of the house, and gave his name to the village. The first Sir William Sidney is buried there too, but Sir Philip, the great light of the family, whose character as poet and soldier sums up the whole Elizabethan tradition of an English gentleman, is not there, for he was buried in St Paul's Cathedral, and his tomb thus perished in the Fire of London. But his great-nephew, Algernon Sidney, a man of no less grandeur of character, was buried at Penshurst after his execution. He was a republican (like that subsequent and still more famous connection of the family, Percy Bysshe Shelley), and was to have been one of the panel of judges who condemned Charles I to death. But he demurred at the constitution of the court, and walked out before the proceedings took place. This, however, did not keep him from the wrath of the Royalists after the Restoration, and he was falsely condemned by Judge Jeffreys as participating in the conspiracy against the king's life known as the Rye House Plot.

The church was restored in Victorian times by Sir Gilbert Scott, the architect who built that pseudo-Gothic monstrosity, St Pancras station, and would have similarly disfigured Whitehall with his plan for a new Foreign Office had not Palmerston told him to think again, whereupon he produced the present Italianate building.

As we wander first round the precincts of Penshurst Place, observing how it stands in its massive simplicity like a great rock, with the green surf of a sea of bracken breaking against it, let us ponder about the Englishman and Kentish man, Sir Philip Sidney, who by one or two gestures has made himself a permanent place in English history. He was a true son of the Renaissance, for in those days scholarship was narrow but intense. At twelve he could write letters in English, Latin, and French. That seems to me to be a more solid accomplishment than a smattering of chemistry and the ability to make wireless sets and model aeroplanes. For it means a range of civil consciousness and a capacity for subtle self-expression, both powerful elements in the making of a complete, as distinct from a mechanical, man. Sidney was at Shrewsbury School with Fulke Greville, Lord Brooke, who remained his lifelong friend and wrote a biography of him. Greville said : "I will report no other wonder but this, that though I lived with him, and knew him from a child, yet I never knew him other than a man with such staidness of mind, lovely and familiar gravity, as carried grace and reverence above greater years, his talk ever of knowledge, and his very playing tending to enrich his mind, so as even his teacher found something in him to observe and learn above that

80

usually read or taught. Which eminence by nature and industry made his worthy father style Sir Philip in my hearing, though I unseen, *lumen familiæ suæ.*"

And such a light he has remained, a model of graceful scholarship and the promise of statecraft, this last inherited from his father, Sir Henry, who for twenty-six years had been Lord President of Wales, as well as serving several times in a like office in Ireland; both tasks of great administrative strain in those times. The gatehouse which we can see, and the whole façade of Penshurst looking north and west, were built by this Sir Henry, who died of sheer weariness in the service of the Tudor sovereigns. That year, 1582, was a desperate one for the Sidney family. The young poet-soldier was in the Lowlands, fighting under the command of his incompetent uncle, the Earl of Leicester. Soon after the father's death, the mother died of a broken heart, after thirty-five years of happy marriage. While grieving for her from whom he "had had nothing but light," Sir Philip was wounded by a musket-shot at the siege of Zutphen, and lingered for a month at Arnhem in great agony, while efforts were made to stop the mortification of the wound. He was given a state funeral. His younger brother Robert, who succeeded to Penshurst, later became head of the Dudley family, being heir to his uncles, the Earls of Leicester and of Warwick, while his only sister married the Earl of Pembroke. This first Sidney to bring two earldoms to Penshurst married a Miss Gamage, a wealthy Welsh heiress, a capable woman who loved her home at Penshurst. A contemporary writes of her : "My Lady takes great pleasure in this place, and surely I never saw a sweeter. All things finely prospering about it. The garden is well kept." Marriage with an heiress is a good prescription for being able to keep a large garden in good order.

I am tempted to follow the fortunes of this noble family, with its public life, its scholarship and dignified domestic habits, both given such ample scope at Penshurst. The majestic house still reflects the general character of the family. It has a touch of melancholy and remoteness, especially if one looks back at it from the rising ground as the public road leaves the village and park to the south. From that little

G

distance the sea of green seems to be drawing the mansion down, and the formal gardens cannot be seen. The simplicity which is so characteristic is therefore enhanced by this aspect, and one passes out of sight of Penshurst recalling Ben Jonson's lines :

> Thou art not, Penshurst, built to envious show,
> Of touch, or marble; nor canst boast a row
> Of polished pillars, or a roof of gold;
> Thou hast no lantern, whereof tales are told;
> Or stair, or courts; but stand'st an ancient pile,
> And, these grudged at, are reverenced the while.

I am tempted; but I must resist the temptation, for there is already a mass of literature about the house and its family, and the pictures, furniture, and other treasures with which the house is filled. I could stay for months here, looking at these immovable movables of history, building from them a panoramic evocation of times and persons now vanished. The break-away, as one looks back several times from the road northward, is almost physically painful. So much is left unapprehended, undigested. One leaves with the same sense of bafflement as one feels when listening to great music, or gazing out across the Weald from the Downs. But such nostalgias are like drugs : the more we indulge them the more they befog our minds. There is such a thing as too much longing for knowledge.

All the villages round this district, the northern part of my rectangle, are charming, especially Leigh (sometimes spelt Lyghe), with the road almost suddenly spiralling up round the church, in a sharp curve to higher ground as we approach Tonbridge, where there is the famous public-school and also notable specimens of the English posting-inn (the Rose and Crown and the Chequers). Another old house in Tonbridge is the Bull Hotel, the headquarters of the Angling Society which controls the coarse fishing on the Medway, a river without trout, but rich in heavy carp, of which some are taken up to twenty pounds in weight. Tonbridge is a busy town to-day, but its prosperity has not spoiled its attractiveness and character. It is world-famous for the hand-making of cricket bats and balls, at workshops on the Hildenborough side of the town.

We follow up the Sevenoaks road north-west out of Tonbridge, but turn off left before we get to Hildenborough. This by-road takes us under the railway, and will enable us to stop for a meal at a unique place called the Old Barn, set up after the 1914–18 war by a naval officer. We ride northward still along the network of lanes until we reach Sevenoaks Weald, which stands at the foot of the hills rising to the town. It is a village hidden away, far from main roads. At the beginning of the present century, Edward Thomas, the poet and critic who was killed in the 1914–18 war, lent his cottage at the Weald to W. H. Davies, soon after that lyrical genius was rescued from a dosshouse in Lambeth. There Davies lived alone, and wrote his *Autobiography of a Super-Tramp*, which has become a classic. But as it has nothing to do with Kent, I cannot discuss it here. But I must quote a tiny verse which Davies wrote in that cottage, for it sets in the amber of poetry an incident that occurred there one morning while my old friend was at work with pencil and paper on the story of his life. And that incident is one which is most characteristic of the things that happen to people who choose to spend a summer in Kent. He was sitting in the garden at work one morning when his pencil was arrested because a butterfly settled on it. He was never weary of mentioning that incident, for the mystic in him (and the egoist) gave it a tremendous significance. Here is the poem which he made from it :

> Here's an example from
> A butterfly;
> That on a rough, hard rock
> Happy can lie;
> Friendless and all alone
> On this unsweetened stone.
>
> Now let my bed be hard,
> No care take I;
> I'll make my joy like this
> Small butterfly;
> Whose happy heart has power
> To make a stone a flower.

The Weald of Sevenoaks is, or was, a perfect nesting-place for a poet, for it offered joys both near and far, and that is what a poet wants : the intimate and the unattainable, the one for tenderness and the other for aspiration. No doubt V. Sackville-West, a native of Kent *par excellence*, and likely to be one of its best-remembered singers, learned much of her word-music when she lived in a very ancient house at Weald, in the years before she and her husband took and restored Sissinghurst Castle. Edward Thomas loved the place too, for on its southern slope he could sit protected from the north and east (quarters which the poet hates) and watch

> The swift with wings and tail as sharp and narrow
> As if the bow had flown off with the arrow.

That couplet from Thomas's verse commands me to quote another snatch, to complete the atmospheric picture of this spot in the mid-Weald uplands.

> Tall nettles cover up, as they have done
> These many springs, the rusty harrow, the plough
> Long worn out, and the roller made of stone :
> Only the elm butt tops the nettles now.
> This corner of the farmyard I like most :
> As well as any bloom upon a flower
> I like the dust on nettles, never lost
> Except to prove the sweetness of a shower.

Such is Weald, where poets have made gardens and gardens have made poets, interchanging their currencies of songs and flowers, dreams and landscapes.

So we come, by further rises in the road, to Sevenoaks, one of England's happiest and sunniest towns. Even to-day, with the threat of season-ticketholding commuters who built their dormitory villas there and travel to and from London daily, Sevenoaks remains unspoiled. Its position on the ridge, at the top of the steep rise from Tubs Hill station, cannot be touched. Nor can Knole in its superb park, for these now happily are in the keeping of the National Trust, out of the reach of estate agents, those loathsome wretches who live on the prostitution of our English land just as pimps live on the prostitution of women.

You will find good shopping at Sevenoaks, that old-fashioned county shopping at long-established and self-respecting one-man shops, where buying and selling and nice selecting and recommendation are a humane art. There was, and may still be, though I have not explored there for some years, a second-hand bookshop in which one could discover a first edition now and then. The church, not remarkable architecturally, has a monument to Lambarde, the sixteenth-century topographer, whose *Perambulation of Kent* was the first book of its kind, at least in this country. The church lies at the top of the town, and on the opposite, eastern side of the London-Tonbridge road lies Knole.

The entrance to the park is by a narrow drive between the houses fronting the road, and thus it surprises the new-comer, who is led by this approach to expect a somewhat tamed furtherance of his adventure. But the park is some six miles in circumference; six miles of timeless, placeless romance. Here, indeed, is a world unto itself, with its own literature ! Both the park and the house (one of the biggest in England, with its 365 rooms and 52 staircases) have attracted poets and painters for centuries. How could they do otherwise, for here are such riches of nature and human craft that the mine of inspiration would seem to be inexhaustible. Not only the place, but the family associated with it, are sustenance for the imagination. Even to-day there are two members of the family gifted as artists, and both possessed of that simplicity of spirit upon which the most valuable of human relationships are founded.

I hardly know how to begin to write of the house, and the family. Each is as ramified as the other, with time the back-linen upon which the patterns are woven. The marriage between house and family seems to have begun in the reign of King John, when the then Earl of Pembroke built himself a home. Lord Saye and Sele lived here in 1450—he who was executed by the rebels under Jack Cade, who stuck his head on a spike on London Bridge. Thomas Bourchier, Archbishop of Canterbury, who died in 1486, built most of the present fabric, and another prelate, Cranmer, lived in it for seven years. It came directly into the hands of the Sackville family (where it remains to-day by arrangement with the National Trust) when Queen Elizabeth gave it to her cousin Thomas Sackville, whose grandmother was a Boleyn. This Sackville was made Earl of Dorset by James I. He was the first poet and scholar in the family, as well as being the first of the Sackville family to carry the title. His mother was a Bridges, and I suspect that the poetic gift may have come from this old Kentish family, its recent outcropping in Robert Bridges being a notable example of literary inheritance.

Thomas Sackville was a statesman and diplomat, and the only blot on his 'scutcheon is that he married the daughter of one Sir John Baker, the builder of Sissinghurst Castle, whose hideous character I shall refer to when I come in my wanderings to that picturesque ex-ruin. I call it an ex-ruin, because some degree of poetic justice has been done by a direct descendant of that Thomas Sackville. Mr and Mrs Harold Nicolson, the former one of the most graceful and civilized of our contemporary critics and essayists, and the latter a poet whose work I have already written about else-where (it is she, Vita Sackville-West, who is the descendant of Thomas Sackville) have made an earthly paradise of that old castle which was originally built on the blood and bones of English folk done to death by that human vulture Sir John Baker, Bloody Mary's Chancellor, who under the cloak of religious zeal won by torture and pillage sufficient wealth to build his palace. But "all passion drops like summer flowers," and to-day as we gaze upon the octagonal tower of the gateway to Sissinghurst, with its smutched-velvet bricks, we cannot feel any evil survival; nothing but peace, gentleness, and a grave dignity. Listen to this passage from the poem "Sissinghurst," which Miss Sackville-West wrote in an effort to ease herself of the sweet burden of emotion accumulated during her work upon the castle, and her daily life there :

> I am content to leave the world awry
> (Busy with politic perplexity)
> If still the carthorse at the fall of day
> Clumps up the lane to stable and to hay,
> And tired men go home from the immense

Labour and life's expense
That force the harsh recalcitrant waste to yield
Corn and not nettles in the harvest-field;
This husbandry, this castle, and this I
Moving within the deeps,
Shall be content within our timeless spell,
Assembled fragments of an age gone by,
While still the sower sows, the reaper reaps,
Beneath the snowy mountains of the sky,
And meadows dimple to the village bell.
So plods the stallion up my evening lane
And fills me with a mindless deep repose,
Wherein I find in chain
The castle, and the pasture, and the rose.

It is not amiss to quote that passage here, because I believe that the substructure of its beauty was Knole, where the author spent her early life. Certainly the spirit, the genius of Knole is in that verse, and when you have savoured fully those lines, and perhaps referred to the whole of the poem, you will have come nearer to the atmosphere and character of Knole than my prose paragraphs can bring you.

Nearly four hundred years lie between that poem and the blank verse of Thomas Sackville's contribution to the first English tragic play, *Gorboduc* (which I think may have influenced Shakespeare when he wrote *King Lear*). Sackville also contributed to a queer miscellany called *A Mirror for Magistrates*, in which he lamented the death of the Duke of Buckingham, allegorizing the occasion into a sort of aristocratic *Pilgrim's Progress*. Here again the work was most influential upon many writers of our Golden Age. Certainly Marlowe and Shakespeare learned from it how to utilize historical material.

You will note how I am lingering about Knole, utterly undone and therefore hesitant. Truly I cannot begin to describe its treasures, either indoors or out. There it stands, among its monumental trees and groves, with the deer drifting like the ghosts of heraldry over the bracken and under the shadows of the castle walls. You must go there, and go slowly. Explore the park first, and visit the great King's

Beech, a giant tree in the neighbourhood of the house. Then within the house, a museum as well as a present dwelling for the Sackville family (and may it never be dispossessed by drab equalitarian politicians), you will find a collection of pictures, Van Dycks, Gainsboroughs, and Reynoldses among them; with furniture in such profusion that a complete history of English handicraft might easily be illustrated from these examples. Here indeed is the very soul of our England, with its two thousand years of growth. But also Knole represents our affiliations to the rest of Europe during the centuries, especially those of the Renaissance, when the new learning, and its concomitants of hand-skill in the fine arts, swept as a spiritual fire across the Continent, and made England for a time, as it had been during the Middle Ages, a part of the cultural whole of the spacious Greco-Roman civilization— yet always with a difference. That difference, our English-ness, gives the final stamp to the character of Knole, both to its structure and all that is contained within it.

CHAPTER VI

THE WATERS OF PLEASURE

WE are sweeping down, by a sort of whirlpool progress, along the borders of the county. This method brings us, after our wide gyre to include Sevenoaks, back once more to the wooded and unfrequented frontier. We come first to Cowden, worth mentioning because it is a place typical of this part of the county. It is what its name implies (etymologically), a hollow clearing in the woods. The trees about here still have that deep, sleepy, immemorial quality which one associates with ancient forest-land. Cowden is dampish, heavy, and in the summer it is plagued with flies. I have a recollection of always being somnolent there, and moodily smacking parts of my anatomy as I sat or walked about exploring. And in winter it is damp and cold to one's bones. Cowden was once an ironmasters' village, in the great days of the wooden hulls and the iron cannon, and the short-sighted wastage of our precious timber by the industrialists with no thought toward replacement and the needs of posterity. Not only the nineteenth-century industrialists were sinners. The three preceding centuries, during which the iron foundries of the Weald flourished, found the trade and money masters just as greedy and self-indulgent in their haste after wealth. They were quick to spend wealth and labour on enterprises that promoted their own vanity and aggrandizement (such as the noble houses still to be found in our Kentish villages); but they lacked the Promethean virtue which should have warned them that nature cannot be abused recklessly without an ultimate payment being demanded. At Cowden the deafforestation was bad; a sign that we are approaching Sussex, a county under baronial control during the centuries of the ironfounding, and thus more recklessly spoiled of its natural wealth; while Kent, being in the hands of the Church, was used with a more temperate regard for its resources.

We need not stay longer at Cowden, except to note the

handsome steeple of the church (another sign of Sussex approaching), with its remarkably good oak shingles. I remember talking there some quarter of a century ago with the old sexton, who told me that the shingling was done afresh about 1850 and cost just about fifty pounds. To put shingles on a leaking oast-house in 1945 cost me two hundred pounds, and my building is only thirty-nine feet high—an interesting comparison of costs.

There are three graves in Cowden churchyard pointing north to south instead of the usual east to west. The same sexton told me that this was because they were suicides; though I believe that sometimes Dissenters were thus buried.

But I have another recollection of Cowden. One hot summer day, during a family picnic just after the First World War, I was sitting with a baby daughter in my lap, dozing and half-watching the world around me, under the shelter of a copse which had grown out of a wide hedge at the junction of two fields. The sun beat down in front of us, at the foot of the shaded bank where we lay. Emerging from a nod of forty winks, I saw something that made my blood run cold. I tried to cry out, but my lips were frozen. The child had crawled off my lap, and was sitting contented, murmuring to herself with wonder and delight, while groping out with a chubby hand at something that glittered in front of her. That bright jewel was the eye of a gigantic grass-snake, a creature fully three feet long, whose curiosity had overcome its caution. There it lay, looking at the child with a friendly, but dreadful, gaze. I ought to have recognized its harmlessness; but coming to the scene out of sleep gave me a shock that made me leap up. Instantly the sympathy between child and serpent was broken. The monster rustled back into the undergrowth beneath the trees, grass and dried plants crackling as it passed. Gradually my skin grew warm again, and broke into a profuse sweat. I shall never forget that queer incident, as an example of the fraternization between the innocent and the wise. It had about it an Ovid-like touch, and I remember that at the time I felt indeed that I was in a fabulous place, witnessing the birth of one of the classical legends of Greece.

Dodging about the maze of by-roads to and fro across the

border as though playing the old game of Tom Tiddler's Ground, we go through Groombridge, a richly wooded village lying just south of Ashurst. This stretch of countryside gives one an odd sense of old-fashioned modes; of illustrations to Victorian three-decker novels and of family magazines of the period. This is due to the proximity of Eridge Castle, the seat of the Marquis of Abergavenny. The cottages on the estate are built in pseudo-Gothic style, with little lancet or arched windows. A cluster of moss roses round the mullions is all that is needed to complete the picture. Walking through the district recently with my wife, I looked at her half-expecting to see her striding along with her crinoline swinging, and the ringlets straying wantonly from her bonnet.

It is worth while taking a look at Groombridge Place. It is not a big mansion, but it has beauty. Here a French prince, the Duc d'Angoulême, brother of the poet-king Charles of France, spent some years as a hostage, before the Battle of Agincourt. In Tudor times the estate was the seat of the Wallers, of whom Edmund Waller, the Restoration minor poet, was a kinsman. He seems to have been a turncoat and a craven, as well as a verse-writer of doubtful taste. What a witless fool a man must have been to address so dignified and talented a woman as Lady Dorothy Sidney by the apostrophic name of "Sacharissa"! It is not surprising that she took his literary protestations with marked calmness.

Later, this fine old moated house was the property of a Mr Packer, the friend of Evelyn, who visited here and laid out the garden. Evelyn was a great amateur of landscape gardening, and might be called, without exaggeration, a rival of the French professional Lenôtre. He was the first Englishman to write a treatise on trees, their nurture and value in commerce as well as in æsthetics. I always think of him as a wholly representative English gentleman, temperate, cultured, with a passion for gardens and good prose.

But now we approach Tunbridge Wells over the common. I know that many people sneer at Tunbridge Wells, calling it a stuffy Victorian relic, full of retired snobs and ex-professional people whose only amusement is to meet for morning coffee on Mount Pleasant and to be most unpleasant in their querulous frettings over their rheumatism and the disgusting

habits of the younger generation. I know too that Tunbridge
Wells, as a municipality, is affected by the influence of that
somnolent layer of society, and lags behind in its cultural
activity. It has no municipal opera house, or orchestra (which
it ought to have). Nevertheless, I love it.

I agree with the diarist John Evelyn, who wrote of it just
when it was rising to its full fame, describing it as "a very
sweet place, private and refreshing." It still has that quality
of privacy. I know of nothing more pleasant than to sit on a
day in spring on one of the chairs in the Pantiles, in a spot
carefully chosen to catch the sun and avoid the draught.
There one can meditate among the decaying survivals of
vanished frivolities and fashions. Vanished; decaying, I say :
for it is a disgrace to the town that the Pantiles have been
allowed to slip into such neglect as they show to-day. All the
life and sparkle and wealth have moved to the top of Mount
Pleasant, the shopping quarter. The shops in the Pantiles
are quiet and abandoned; some of them empty. The assembly
rooms are stores for second-hand furniture, where the bric-à-
brac hunter may wander for hours. The old eighteenth-
century music-gallery is a cranny now for the wind to fill with
dust, paper, and dead leaves. Yet one great row of trees
remains, and the paving-stones are delightfully set (though
only a few of the original pantiles remain near the fountain
at the entrance to the promenade).

Ghosts move along that promenade at noon, and round
about chocolate time. I have sat there watching them, figures
in Carolean and Hanoverian wigs, shaking their snuff-boxes
and pointing a toe. I remember one day especially, when I
had just bought a clean second-hand copy of Frazer's *Golden
Bough* in the bookshop at the approach to the Pantiles, surely
one of the most endearing second-hand bookshops in England, with its library steps, its ceiling-height shelves, its
spilled treasures flowing over tables, chairs, and floor. There
I sat, and in wartime too, after a bout of influenza. I read
upon Frazer's old-fashioned, Gibbon-like prose, while a slant
of my attention was given to the light on the paving and the
foliage. A pigeon sat crooning above me, and the civilized
odour of roast coffee floated from a shop nearby. I was transported. "Such a little thing, to remember for years; to re-

member with tears." I forgot nations at war, and men torturing each other. I forgot the brutality of those ghosts, with their vile seventeenth- and eighteenth-century manners and social crudities. I forgot, in fact, mankind as he really is, and I dreamed, for an hour, in a world of charm, gentle habits, spiritual enthusiasm, and a sensuousness disciplined just this side of appetite.

That dream might have some sound historical foundations. Tunbridge Wells is a comparatively recent social flower-garden, but a crowded one. It was first laid out, in a very rustic way, in 1606, when Lord North, the hypochondriac mentor of Prince Henry, James I's eldest son, took a rest cure at Eridge Castle, as the guest of Lord Abergavenny. The miraculous effect of the waters in this neighbourhood upon the disordered and much abused stomach of the young nobleman was rapidly publicized amongst the Court set, and from that year the patronage of the great was assured. Every summer St James's spilt out its jaded beauties, its fops, flirts and overripes, to be driven in their painted coaches down to the old town of Tonbridge, whence they camped out on the near-by hills from which the health-giving waters sprang. For at that time there was no accommodation other than what they brought with them. This *al fresco* state of affairs continued until the later years of the seventeenth century. Charles I's wife, Henrietta Maria, came to Tunbridge Wells in 1629 with a great retinue which had to be housed in marquees. The queen, after her first confinement, benefited so much that it was proposed to call the place "Queen Mary's Wells." After this charming but politically dangerous lady, it is rather bathetic to describe the next queen who came to the Wells. Catherine of Braganza, the ugly Portuguese princess, may have been a suitable and complacent wife for Charles II, but there is little else to be said in favour of her character. She lacked both taste and tact; a handicap when pursuing a life of virtue, but fatal when following a career of frivolity and vice.

By 1639 the accommodation in the new spa had become more solid, for at Southborough and at Rustall settlements of huts and primitive cottages had been made, where the nobility and small gentry lodged, and hobnobbed in a democratic way; a holiday custom which the former made haste to discontinue immediately they returned to Town. It was a social axiom that all restraint and dignity should be put aside by the visitors, and the new watering-place became a centre of scandal, horseplay, sexual licence, and gambling. The morning parade up and down the promenade which is now the Pantiles, while the market was held down below, gave the fashionable world of the Stuarts and the Hanovers ample occasion for every folly that snobbery, malice, and affectation could invent. Innumerable legends survive of the practical jokes, pseudo-duels, amatory intrigues, and fantastic pastimes that enlivened the drinking of the waters. Town "spies" abounded, especially in the eighteenth century, those equivalents of our present-day newspaper gossips who chat, often with *double entendre* to the initiated, in our newspapers and society magazines.

Of a somewhat different kind of gossip from these Grub-street "spies" was that infamous scoundrel Lord Rochester, who in addition to his brutal life, exercised a gift for well-turned but obscene verse. Hume called him "a plague-spot of English literature," and rightly so, though some effort was made a few years ago to whitewash him. As well attempt to whitewash the surface of a cesspool. In a poem describing the follies of this midsummer madness which went on annually at the Wells, Rochester says :

Here Lords, Knights, Squires, Ladies and Countesses,
Chandlers, and barren women, Sempstresses,
Were mixed together; nor did they agree
More in their Humours than their Quality.
Here, waiting for Gallant, young Damsel stood,
Leaning on Cane, and muffled up in Hood :
The would-be Wit, whose business was to woo,
With Hat removed, and solemn scrape of Shoe,
Advances bowing, then genteelly shrugs,
And ruffled Foretop into Order tugs.

And so the satire goes on at great length, valueless and boring, except that it paints a picture of the gross manners and habits of the period. The most notorious and fantastic of these courtiers, whose conduct caused the French Ambassador at Charles II's Court to say of Tunbridge Wells that "they may well be called *les eaux de scandale*," was Lady Muskerry, from the neighbouring great house of Somerhill. By the proximity of her home to the Wells she was able to offer entertainment to Royalty and the Court year after year. A completely foolish woman, she exposed her vapid mind and her deformed body to the ridicule of the fashionable world, trying in vain to compete both with the wits and the beauties of the day. She ruined herself and dissipated the estate, so that after her death Somerhill fell into decay, in which condition it remained for a century.

These *eaux de scandale*, however, continued to flow, and in 1638 a covered promenade was built to shelter the visitors in bad weather, so that they might go from the waters to the coffee-houses without wetting their finery or even their dressing-gowns (for it was later the custom to take the waters in *déshabille*).

The doctors of the time profited as well as they could. Indeed, the first signs of popularity were carefully fostered by a certain Dr Rowzee, who published a treatise in 1632, prescribing a régime for the seekers after health. Both he, and another quack called Dr Madan, insisted that the waters could be taken only on the spot, and not transported, though this did not prevent a traffic in bottled water, at least for a time, between the Wells and London. "Waters once removed," wrote Dr Madan, "lose their vivisick spirits in which a virtue doth reside, which afterwards no diligence can restore. Chalybeate waters in long deportation will not tinge with gall." And again he writes, in 1687, "The Tunbridge waters are impregnated with a chalcanthous or vitriolic juice, which, with its sulphureous particles, irritates and moves the belly to a blackish excretion and by frequent drinking thereof, blackeneth the tongue; because this member, being of a spongey substance imbibes some sooty sulphureous minims into its porosity, occasioning this tincture." That is delightful. It makes me hope that some of the present-day writings about the virtues of synthetic vitamin pills, as set out in the literature which accompanies them, will make equally amusing reading in two hundred years to come.

Much of the character and nomenclature of the place was

settled during the time of the Commonwealth. The timber cottages which were the first settled lodging-houses became separate political camps, those on Southborough hill being frequented by the Royalists, and those on Rustal being used by the Roundheads. The latter maintained an armed camp on Mounts Ephraim and Sion for over a year, as an army of occupation following an abortive Royalist rebellion which broke out at Tonbridge. It was also good strategy to maintain a military strength in this part of the country, which at that time was the arsenal where most of the guns and ammunition were manufactured.

The early part of the eighteenth century, during the reign of George II, showed the Wells at the height of its popularity, at least as a place of seasonal pleasure-making. A well-known print of celebrities in the year 1748 promenading on the Pantiles is annotated in the handwriting of Samuel Richardson, the author of the first novel of sentiment, *Pamela*. He names Dr and Mrs Johnson as two of the famous figures, amongst others, such as Mr Cibber (that gibbering little Poet Laureate and bore), Garrick, and William Pitt. Quite recently, however, this matter of the Dr Johnson mentioned being in fact the Grand Cham has been disputed by Miss Margaret Barton in a delightful book on Tunbridge Wells published in 1937. She says that "since Johnson did not receive his doctorate until after Richardson's death, it is clear that the figures are not those of the great Samuel and his Tetty. Who, then, was this mysterious Dr Johnson, evidently a person of some social importance? I cannot advance any proofs of his identity, but I feel confident that he was Dr James Johnson, the future Bishop of Rochester and a man of large private means, whose unmarried sister, known as Mrs Johnson, became in her old age one of the first residents on Mount Ephraim." This piece of protestantism is worth recording here, because the famous print still plays such an important part in all historical reference to Tunbridge Wells. The argument for doubting the long-accepted is rather slender. Malone, Boswell's friend, and editor in 1799 of the third edition of the great *Biography*, had a footnote stating definitely that the Johnsons were in Tunbridge Wells in 1748, making holiday

Knole Park
King James's Bedroom, Knole Park

after the labour of finishing the Lexicon, and that they are portrayed in the picture.

As the eighteenth century wore on, a heavier element crept into the gaiety of the Wells. The blue-stockings descended upon it, like blowflies. Elizabeth Montague, the Mrs Montague who aped the great Frenchwomen of the period, who kept their salons where the wits of Europe competed, came as a girl to Tunbridge Wells and at once contaminated it with her intellectual snobbery and cultural pomp (the worst forms of vanity and pride). What a detestable woman, with her glittering diamonds, her huge income, and her pretended help to hungry scribblers and scholars! Here she captured the professionally gloomy Dr Young, author of the *Night Thoughts*, a poetic rhodomontade of assumed melancholy. Here she took up the poor parson's daughter, Elizabeth Carter, who was in fact a scholar, and a gifted linguist. Another poet associated with the Pantiles was Richard Cumberland, now deservedly forgotten. In his time he was the most successful playwright of the day, and a formidable bore who would insist on reading his plays in manuscript to his friends. On one occasion he even served up a new play under a pie-crust, thus assuring himself of an audience at his dinner-table. He survived this indecency, however, and died on Mount Sion in 1811, thus surviving his slender talent by many years. That talent was buried belatedly, with him, in Westminster Abbey.

Another man who made much out of little was Beau Nash, a queer mixture of character and foppery. Having become the uncontested legislator of social procedure at Bath, he turned his attention, during the last twenty years of his over-long life, to manners in Tunbridge Wells. He purged the place of many of its more flagrant habits of debauchery and gambling, regulating the latter pastime and giving it at least the semblance of decorum. I wish he could have stopped the practice of eating wheatear pie. This was one of the epicurean treats of the Wells, during the eighteenth century. The little birds were trapped on the Downs by means of small horse-hair nets set in holes in the ground.

With the growth of Brighton, and the new enthusiasm for taking sea baths and breathing sea air, Tunbridge Wells

Groombridge Place
Groombridge Village

dwindled as a watering-place, but continued to grow as a residential centre. During the last decades of the eighteenth, and throughout the nineteenth, century, it grew larger and larger, and its present population is not far short of that of Maidstone, the capital of the county. From whatever approach one comes to Tunbridge Wells the contact is one of beauty and dignity. Kent is the Garden of England. Tunbridge Wells is the Garden of Kent. The many great villas, each standing in a substantial garden of many acres, that surround the town on the several heights, are by now matured for over a century. They are out-of-date, unwieldy, and often grotesque in their architecture. How pathetic it is to pass, and see from the top of the omnibus one pseudo-Gothic villa after another, some of them absurd, as though designed from one of the romantic monochromes drawn by Victor Hugo while in exile. They are now obviously servantless and in a state of shabby-genteelism, though by some miracle their gardens still remain kempt, with the gigantic cedars, monkey-puzzles, and red pines slumbering aromatically on lawns punctuated by Victorian flowerbeds like beetroot salads.

In the midst of all this expensive horticultural approach to the Spa there is an interesting market garden, with a superb view, kept by a Dane who came over here when a youth. He belongs to a military family, and his grandfather was a distinguished poet in Denmark, being now one of the national figures. The present horticulturist's father was a military attaché at the Russian Court, where the boy was brought up. He came into contact with Tolstoi at the age of fourteen, and was converted to pacifism. This enthusiasm sent him to England, where he studied horticulture, and where he has since remained. He told me, some few years ago, that he still maintained a correspondence with two of the Russian princesses, a daughter and a sister of the Tsar (one in a convent), who found refuge in this country after the 1917 Revolution. The nursery specialized in rock plants, and when its owner discovered that I was an English poet he charmingly gave me two miniature juniper bushes, which I reverently planted between the York flagstones round my lily pond. Oddly enough, this courteous and gentle lover of flowers and peacefulness reminded me instantly, both in figure and features, of Aylmer Maude, the disciple and translator of Tolstoi.

Have I said enough about Tunbridge Wells to make readers appreciate its present-day qualities? For it is full of them, in spite of a certain lack of municipal imagination in the running of the town as a holiday place for people of good taste and fastidious culture. How appropriate it would be, for example, as a music centre, with a first-class municipal orchestra run at a loss and at the ratepayers' expense. For what a rotten state of affairs we have come to in this modern world, when nothing is thought to be practicable or worth while unless it yields something over five per cent in money profit, while every other form of profit, in mental, physical, and spiritual benefit, is written off as non-existent by the accountants and treasurers. Let us have a little less of the domination of these treasurers and accountants, who believe that financial mechanics are the only true morality and solvency.

Why does not Tunbridge Wells, as a corporation, take the right pride in itself that its superb geographical assets justify? Why does it not maintain a good theatre as well as an orchestra? It has lately built a quite impressive municipal building, which has a good hall at the back. The fathers of the town should see that this hall is used almost daily for music, readings of our vast inheritance of English poetry, and for lectures. The crowds may not come at first, but gradually a worthy taste would be built up in the native public, and the fame of Tunbridge Wells would spread throughout the world, as that of Salzburg has done. Let me assure those accountants and treasurers that in the long run it would be a good and remunerative investment to send the reputation of Tunbridge Wells soaring into the realm of what they might at present call the "highbrow." Gloomy people say that the two wars, and the flood of American films and violent fiction, are destroying the historic culture of Europe, which has come down through the Renaissance from the rich days of Greece and Rome. If that be so, all the more urgent is the need for those in authority in Europe, and especially in Tunbridge Wells, to do something about combating that flood of barbarism. But I think there is as much evidence to prove that since the wars our people are waking up to the great inheritance of music, literature, and painting that makes England comparable to Athens, that other small state which laid the foundations of civilization two thousand five hundred years ago. The demand for books on philosophy, for verse, for the best prose, for pictures and music; the sudden upflow of new music from a school of younger English composers—all these are signs of a new emotional and spiritual vitality in the people. Tunbridge Wells, with its existing reputation and its noble position, has an opportunity to act as one of the most influential co-ordinators of this new force, this renaissance of all that is best and most permanent in our English nature and character. Why do not the governors of the town risk so long-sighted a venture? Why don't they approach a few of the great motor-car manufacturers (who will soon be richer than ever) and openly ask for gifts of some millions of pounds in paper, or bank credit, or whatever fiction this financial jugglery demands, so that they can begin to build up *real* values that will delight the eye, ear, mind, and soul of the hundreds of thousands of human beings who surely will come flocking to Tunbridge Wells as soon as it has something to offer them, something more worthy than a neglected, dusty Pantiles, a dozen commercial cinema-houses, a chancy cuisine, and an occasional concert or dramatic show? But these occasional shows are pointers in the right direction, and so too is the excellent municipal reference library run by a helpful and courteous staff.

Chapter VII

THE CATHEDRAL OF THE WEALD

AT the beginning of this book I promised myself the adventure of following down the Kent county boundary where it runs with those of Surrey and Sussex. I have done it in the past; but over thirty years of wars and sham peace, as well as the making of my own adult life and the rearing of a family, have intervened, smudging out the details, even though the general memory remains. And that memory is one of a wonderful isolation; of being for many days the heir to an island where I and the brother who accompanied me were Robinson Crusoes. For that exploration led us across country, by back ways and sleepy hollows. I can recall now a triolet that I wrote, to pedal-rhythm, as we rode along on our bicycles. I can see now the very place where the words came jogging into my head, soon after we had set out one summer morning to ride southward through Edenbridge, Hever, Cowden, and Groombridge, along the by-lanes. Is it excusable to quote that triolet now, thirty years later?

> O we discovered a magic land
> Over the heath and the heather.
> We followed the path of golden sand
> And we discovered a magic land
> Beyond the west where the young dreams stand
> Waiting the call of the April weather.
> O we discovered a magic land
> Over the heath and the heather.

The golden sand lay on the southern slopes of Limpsfield Common, among what at that time was a wild-land of Scotch pines; giant trees whose red boles and trunks shone husky in the sun, odorous of holidays and idleness and superb health. It was a lovely bit of country, typical of those county frontiers, where armies of giant ants marched and counter-marched, some red, some black, no doubt guarding the customs and political posts between Kent and Surrey against the illicit traffic of blackbirds, and the revolutionary propaganda of the flitting cuckoos and yaffles who are always lingering about those borders, waiting to stir up strife and restlessness amongst the peaceful natives of the hedges and bracken-banks.

I had a friend who lived in a spacious house which he had built in the Nineties on the edge of Limpsfield Common, with a great garden dropping down the hill toward the Weald of Edenbridge, with terraces, bosquets, lawns, and stretches of perfumed flowering shrubs, all designed round the giant pines and oaks originally on the ground before it was civilized. He was an elderly man, very sick with asthma, which made his conversation sound like a series of irritable gasps from a person distracted with cares. But in fact he was serene, mischievously humorous, with shrewd artist's eyes that twinkled behind the agony of his effort to breathe from one moment to another. His name was Lewis Fry, and he was a Quaker whose grandfather had been a Pease, a banker in Norwich at the time when the Norwich School of Painters was at its zenith. The ancestor had bought a collection of water-colours by David Cox as they left the painter's hand, and had put them immediately into portfolios, where I was able to browse over them a century later. Their colours were therefore as fresh as when they were painted. And there the sand and the pines shone, and the rich green of the oaks, vivid as the shouting hues beyond the window of the studio where I was sitting with the portfolio on my knees. I remember looking from my suffering old friend, first at these fragile beauties in water-colour, and then at the scene pulsing under the sun across the Weald; and I recall at this moment how the mystery of life, of the contrast between beauty and pain, the counterfeit of art and the actuality of nature, came down upon me with a great burden of wonder and exultation. What courage, what genius, and what an impersonal source from which to supply these attributes of human nature!

In addition, the old friend possessed copies of Turner's *Liber Studiorum*, and also the less-known volume of the same name by J. S. Cotman. Also his own paintings in the district, amateur work maybe, but none the worse for that, caught much of that infinite source of which I speak. He gave me two of his own pictures, pleasant pieces, influenced by the doctrines of his cousin Roger Fry, the art critic.

What in fact did happen in those distant days, and on those rural rides, was that my brother and I got to Lamberhurst one night completely exhausted. We had intended to go on to Hastings, to join some relatives there; but a head wind decided otherwise, and we fell off our bicycles at the Chequers in the middle of Lamberhurst village, where we gave our machines to an ostler (there *were* ostlers in those days) and sat down to a good dinner and a bottle of hock that I can still enjoy to-day. For the palate of youth is a generous one, and will make little difference between an ordinary *vin du jour* and a vintage wine. I remember that I had with me a volume of Keats's poems, and there we sat, slightly fuddled with bodily tiredness, a good meal, and the strength of the wine in our young heads, while I read snatches of the marvellous young doctor-scholar to my brother, who was sound asleep in the chair opposite me in the deep bay window of the room jutting out into the street. I recall too that we examined the visitors' book, and were excited to find there the name of Ellen Terry, who praised the inn for its hospitality, as I can praise it now, somewhat belatedly.

I have never forgotten that lovely village, the inn, and the magical night of youth spent there. It is a happy chance of fortune that has, in my later years, brought me to live only five miles from that scene. Here I am now, writing in a lofty workroom set in the top of an oast-house on the southern slope of a hill that looks along an upland valley westward to Lamberhurst. It is a vantage-post for these parts. Across the valley, silhouetted against the sky between two gigantic elms, stands the square tower of Goudhurst church, whose peal of eight bells comes with Tennysonian melancholy across the two and a half miles on Sunday evenings, to put the signature of our long English history upon the scene and the special moment of the week, that moment when the people become most corporate; serene, if somewhat saddened, with recollection of that other world which religion, and time itself, conjure upon their hearts.

Beyond the other, eastern end of the valley, at the end of

a stretch of woodland five miles deep, and a park that has been truly described by the county historian Igglesden as the most varied and enchanting in the whole of England, stands Cranbrook in its ring of hills. One drops down into it from every approach. Driving to it from Goudhurst along the ridge, magnificent views spread to right and left; northward, on the left, across the real centre of the hop country to the Maidstone ridge, with Lynton, Sutton Valence, Boughton Monchelsea, and Boughton Malherbe stationed along the hilltops ten miles northward, the distance growing more and more remote to the eastern head of the great run of the Weald, with Egerton and Pluckley dropping down to Ashford twenty-odd miles due east of us.

The view on the right hand is little less extensive. It takes the eye to the Sussex boundaries running south-east to Rye and Romney Marsh. Some people say that one can see the Channel beyond, either from here or the continuation of the ridge between Cranbrook and Hawkhurst. But I have not seen it yet. Perhaps this is because my eye is too busy appreciating the configuration of hills that makes this scene so enjoyable. It has a sort of classical quality, with its fold upon fold of wooded or open slopes, studded with kilns and red roofs, the mansion of Bedgebury rising out of trees with its stable spire like a minaret; the larger spire of Hawkhurst's chapel-of-ease emerging from another wood ahead. The whole composition is so patterned that it seems to sum up, in a perfect cluster of symbols, the nature and tradition of our English life. There is at first the intimate, almost cosy quality suggested by the signs of man; the farms, oasts, barns, country seats and churches, ricks and trim hedgerows. Then from that emerges a faint emanation; it is the ghost of Anderida, the medieval forest of the Weald, that once stretched for over a hundred miles between Winchester and Ashford, so dense that only swineherds and huntsmen could inhabit there. Something of that darkness lingers still over the scene, like the haunting overtone above bell-music. It gives an atmosphere such as we find in the background of the first easel pictures painted by Giorgione; an air of other-world, and a breath of terror coming at midday to taint the sunshine.

But I am already shooting past Cranbrook. That is the danger, for there is so much to see in the circle around my present home that I become like a dog let out as soon as I begin to explore. I want to describe everything at once. To calm myself down I will walk the whole five miles from here, my poet's observation post in an oast-top, to Cranbrook. It is a walk that hardly touches a road. I go down our hairpin-shaped lane from the house, take a footpath behind the neighbouring farm two hundred feet below us, and begin to climb slowly alongside a long hop garden, through a copse with a stream trickling through it (a great place for prim-roses and windflowers in April), and across a number of meadows that during wartime have been ploughed and sown with corn.

There is always a special emotion that takes one's heart when walking through a cornfield, no matter what the time of year. I might call it an Old Testament feeling. It has a sober and moral quality, and religious humility tinges it too. Tennyson must surely have been influenced by this emotion when he wrote that lyric :

> As thro' the land at eve we went,
> And plucked the ripened ears,
> We fell out, my wife and I,
> O we fell out, I know not why,
> And kiss'd again with tears.

It is just that; a sort of intense quietness that goes too far back down the prospect of human life for anger or fret to disturb one. And when the wheat is ripe and its heavy, formal ears swing by their millions on their stalks, the picture has a classical cast, as though the Goddess of Plenty were come out of Greece, and were almost visible, to fill us with a worship more ancient than the faith that built the village church towards which we are making our way as the vision comes upon us.

But that church is not yet in sight. We have first to come out, after passing through more oak and chestnut woods, upon the ridge road between Goudhurst and Cranbrook, which we cross to enter a lane past Dogkennel Farm, now a private house whose oasts have been capped with copper snuffers and balls, that glow with their arsenic green most Slavonically in the sunshine. Now we enter Angley Park, which is the one described by Igglesden as the most delightful in the country.

He does not exaggerate. Never have I seen such variety and wildness so near to civilization, displayed in an enclosure of a hundred and fifty acres. It is richly wooded, with ancient trees of which some are said to be survivors from the royal forest of Anderida. Paths wind their way through miniature ravines and over hillocks, among bracken and carpets of pine-needles where in midsummer the giant ants keep up a frantic traffic. Though Cranbrook is only a mile away, it is hidden by the configuration of the ground. We look down to an old mill, beside a pond that is said to have been inhabited by a fabulous monster whose partiality was for the flesh of unfaithful lovers. Somewhere near it is the burial-place of a smuggler, a local man, who was shot during a struggle with the Excise men in the days when Cranbrook and Hawkhurst were notorious centres for the romantic commerce in contraband. Passing through a long wood, we leave on our left a lake with islands that might be a water from the west of Ireland, so remote and desolate does it shine.

We now pass the site of the demolished house. This place is no loss, for it was built in 1869, a date when the whole of Europe was possessed by the demon of ugliness. Not even ancient blood could resist the contagion, for this house was the work of an owner named Tomlin, member of a family that had been settled in Thanet since the middle of the fifteenth century. Leaving the park reluctantly, we approach Cranbrook by an upper road, and a footpath that brings us out behind the church.

What a noble church it is; rightly named "the cathedral of the Weald." Both inside and out the church is at once remarkable for its clean-cut character and the way in which it seems to diffuse light. The stone of which it is built has a warm glint, so that the square tower appears to be as soft as an old russet apple. The body of the church is a hundred and fifty feet long, with the line of its roof broken pleasantly by an octagonal turret. The tower, ninety feet high, is also

surmounted by a turret, and a fine weathervane. The building is rich in gargoyles, and it has dripstones to the eastern
windows, with corbels in the form of angels bearing shields.
The oldest part of the church is the south porch, which has
a handsome groined roof, and an old oak door with fine
mouldings and shafts. This porch is probably six hundred
years old, if the conjecture is true that it belonged to the
original church which was built here in 1291. A hundred and
forty years later, however, in 1430, the rich Flemish weavers
settled in the village decided to have a more impressive
place of worship, worthy of their money-bags. Further additions to this noble example of bourgeois pride were made in
the suceeding centuries.

Inside, the dignity and spaciousness are at once apparent,
for the interior is flooded with light. The only church that I
know comparable in this matter is that of Saffron Walden in
Essex. But Cranbrook is less denuded by Puritanism, though
it has a singular survival of that spirit in its famous total-
immersion font, or baptistry, which is to be seen just inside
the south door. It was built there by an incumbent in 1707,
one John Johnson, who was also a somewhat contentious
theologian, one of his treatises being called *The Unbloody
Sacrifice*.

Above this oddity (odd at least in a parish church) is the
entrance to a room over the south porch. It is known as
Baker's Hole, because here in the reign of Mary Tudor, that
sallow-faced zealot whose passion and religion combined to
warp her judgment, a certain Sir John Baker, who was her
Chancellor, imprisoned and tortured Protestants before burning them at the stake. He seems to have been a Nazi-like
monster, who out of his plundering and murdering of his
neighbours in the name of religion built himself a showy
Tudor palace at Sissinghurst, two or three miles away beyond
the village of that name. Two hundred years later, in 1752,
Horace Walpole summed up what remained of its preten-
tiousness in the following words : "You go through an arch
of the stables to the house, the court of which is perfect and
very beautiful. This has a good apartment, and a fine gallery
a hundred and twenty feet by eighteen, which takes up one
side : the wainscot is pretty and entire; the ceiling vaulted

and painted in a light genteel grotesque. The whole is built for show; for the back of the house is nothing but lath and plaster." During the Napoleonic wars French prisoners were kept in this place, and they hastened its decay. To-day, however, the remains have been restored by the present owners, the two interior courtyards being made into formal gardens, and the walks beside the moat developed into a fairyland with profusion of briars brought from Persia, and masses of iris. The court that Walpole praises is still whole, overlooked by an exquisite tower-keep containing a room where one of our most valuable contemporary poets works. If beauty, and good taste, and gentleness of spirit are an acceptable currency, then the present owners of Sissinghurst Castle have propitiated the sins of the original builder of the place.

Looking back at the remains of the castle from the nutcopse down by the moat, across large flotations of colour from the Persian briars, one is possessed by a sense of utter peacefulness and serenity of spirit. I know of nothing comparable, unless it be the lakes behind the ruins of Fountains Abbey in Yorkshire. What a gift is this faculty of vivid historical consciousness, which has enabled the owners and rebuilders of Sissinghurst to touch every brick, stone, and the very soil around them with a restorative hand; more than restorative indeed, for the original builder could not have made his gaudy palace, built of his neighbours' bones and blood, symbolize the quality of character and culture with which its present owners have endowed it.

But we must return to Cranbrook, taking a back lane that leads us past one of the oldest houses in the district. Coursehorn, or Cowshorn, is a fine example of those firstfruits of middle-class wealth of which I have already spoken. It is a weaver's house, built by one of the Flemish immigrants, or his descendants, in pre-Tudor times. It stands a mile from the village, but when Queen Elizabeth made one of her periodical itineraries of Kent, and accepted certain ceremonies at Cranbrook, she walked from the George Inn at the centre of the village along a path of locally woven broadcloth. It looks therefore as though Sir Walter Raleigh's gesture, in throwing his cloak over a puddle for the queen to pass dryshod, was not an extravagant action to curry favour, but merely a custom of the times !

I have not been inside Coursehorn, but I fancy that I should be able to describe it by comparison with one of the three similar houses on the Goudhurst side of Cranbrook, where we shall come to on our walk back. These weavers, the "Grey Coats of Kent," had an opulent sense of domesticity, and their house reflected their outlook, with its substantial pride, its dignity, its respect for craftsmanship, its love of sober proportions.

We had not long begun to examine the monuments in the church when I was drawn off by contemplating the unlovely character of Mary Tudor's Chancellor. Having exorcized that ghost, I can look once more with intense delight at the unusually ample records of a family which has been settled at Cranbrook since the reign of King Richard the Second. But earlier than that, in the twelfth century, the family came to Kent from Annandale in Scotland, the adventurer from the north being called William Rookehurst. He seemed also to use the name of Roberts, which has been the family name ever since. He settled at Winchet Hill, a secret pocket in the Weald uplands, behind which lies the hidden valley where I am sitting at this moment.

Here the family remained for nearly three hundred years, though it seems to be impossible to-day to trace the exact spot where their home stood. There are two existing houses which are claimed to be the site of the medieval settlement, and one of them was the birthplace of the poet Frank Kendon, whose family settled here a century ago. That story is another interesting one, though of a different temper. It is told in the poet's prose book, *The Small Years*, the record of a childhood in the Nineties, when this place was utterly remote from metropolitan life. The little book is now a classic, written in prose like a glass of well water, clear and icy, with frosty films on the outside of the glass that catch and break into prismatic gleams the light that seeks to stream through. Listen to a passage from it, one which describes the remoteness of the place. "Our very remoteness made us a world to ourselves : we were as self-supporting as civilization would allow; my father bought flour by the sack and coal by the fifty tons; but our gardens could keep us in potatoes; and we often had some of last year's apples still to eat in this year's May. As children we knew next to nothing of a reputed world; the kingdom of our wanderings was not ten miles across, and the kingdom of our eyes, from one horizon to the other, not more than twenty in the clearest weather; but these two circles encompassed enough to occupy all our faculties, until one by one we grew foolishly ambitious. Our neighbours were the original salt of the earth; and though our meadows were our counties and parishes our nations, our little world was quite large enough to get lost in. Ulysses could say no more."

But I can. I can add that by some miracle, or freak in the gyrations of modern society, this corner of Kent remains to-day as it was nearly fifty years ago, in the description which I have quoted. Throughout the war it has kept its character for remoteness, and even the activities of the Home Guard on the ground, and the conflicts which reached such intensity in the air in 1940–1 and again in the latter half of 1944, served only to emphasize the unbreakable continuity of the time-dream in which this little valley and its hamlet are bound, and have been bound for the past thousand years, during which time they emerged like a sleepwalker from the shrinking forest of Anderida.

Cranbrook Church is rich in relics of the Roberts family. Among banners, arms, and pieces of armour, there is a most original memorial. It is a genealogical tree on the wall of the south aisle, placed there (some say painted by her own hand) by a daughter of the house who against her parents' wishes married Nell Gwyn's bastard son, the Duke of St Albans, who inherited most of his royal father's faults and none of his virtues. But more of this family in a moment, as we shall make our way back to Goudhurst and in so doing shall walk along the upper bounds of Glassenbury Park, still the seat of the Roberts family.

We cannot leave Cranbrook without a look at the famous windmill and the school. The mill, built in 1814, is said to be the largest in England, and it is still in full turn. What an exhilarating sight it is to stand on a windy day in Stone Street and to watch the great sails milling round like a small

boy boxing. I always expect to see Don Quixote come rattling
through the village with his squire far behind, slowed up by
the need of passing the George Hotel. The mill is built of
wood, and is octagonal. The sails are elaborate, with out-
ridings of mechanism that give it an aircraft-like appearance.
It would be better compared with a modern sailing-ship, for
it also has auxiliary engines to drive the millstones when the
wind is unfavourable.

The school is one of England's smaller public schools, and
has yet to produce a Prime Minister, a Poet Laureate, or a
President of the Royal Society. But it has the quality of its
neighbourhood; dignity, serenity, and a fine calmness which
inspire confidence. It was founded in 1574 by one William
Lynche, no doubt from wealth garnered from the great
weaving industry which had flourished in Cranbrook and the
surrounding villages (notably Biddenden and Goudhurst)
since Edward the Third invited Flemish craftsmen to settle
there. Fuller, in the seventeenth century, said that "Kentish
cloth at the present keepeth up the credit thereof as high as
ever before."

Queen Elizabeth granted the school a Royal Charter (the
original engrossment and seal being still in existence). Not
only that, but the queen in person laid the foundation stone
of School House, a noble building which is now the head-
master's house. In the dining-room is a table given by the
queen. It is a fine piece of furniture, with a scoop and carvings
in the centre. Elizabeth had a pleasant habit of giving tables.
There was a superb example in the table of Middle Temple
Hall, a single piece of wood that stretched right across the
width of what was one of the finest halls in Europe; both
hall and table being destroyed during the war.

We must leave Cranbrook without having found what I
would give Shakespeare's "second best bed" to have found;
the cottage near Cranbrook where Daniel Defoe, while in
hiding for political reasons, wrote *Robinson Crusoe*. But I do
not despair; indeed, I cherish the disappointment, for what
a purpose still to have left in one's sedentary latter years!
No doubt one day, when I am least intent on the pursuit,
some half-illiterate villager will let drop a hint of what he
heard in his infancy from the then village idiot, and by this

clue I shall be able to trace the immortal cottage where the
real, as distinct from the *actual*, Alexander Selkirk was con-
ceived and born, to be henceforth the prototype of all boys
between the ages of eight and eighty. I like to foster the
superstition that the cottage may be the same in which the
Victorian poet Sydney Dobell was born in 1824. The builder
of the mill in 1814 was named Dobell. Sydney Dobell was
one of the very minor stars of the sky wherein Browning and
Tennyson blazed; but he turned a good sonnet, and his kinsman Bertram earned a vicarious immortality by rediscovering
the seventeenth-century poet and mystic Thomas Traherne.

Or failing that, would the cottage have been at Wilsley
Green, up the hill from the village on the Goudhurst and
Staplehurst road, where Douglas Jerrold, another famous
Victorian writer, was taken from his birthplace in Soho to
spend a happy childhood. In his *Chronicles of Clovernook*
(distinct from *Mrs Caudle's Curtain Lectures*!) he sets out
"to show every green lane about it; every clump of trees,
every bit of woodland, mead and dell." And that place-name
is only a thin disguise, revealing by concealing the Cranbrook
where his mind lingered so nostalgically over his infancy.

I have already mentioned Wilsley Green as a rich example
of the settlements of the Flemish weavers. Wilsley House is
a rare specimen of their handiwork and tradition in domestic
architecture. It was built about 1470, with heavy gables and
leaded windows whose glass is old, some of its panes
scratched with verses and emblems by French prisoners of
war who were immured there a century and a half ago. In
the spandrels of the doorway over the original main entrance
can be seen Tudor roses. The timber of the interior is impressive, especially the great king beam across the hall,
which is on the first floor, and is rich in linen-fold panelling.
One can still see the old hook from which hung the scales for
weighing cloth. Such massive oaken timber, as hard as iron
and much more elastic, is a reminder of the wealth of trees
that still survived from the medieval forest as late as the
Renaissance days, when industry and commerce were beginning to alter the face of our land. Michael Drayton, in his
epic poem in hexameters, *Polyolbion*, published in 1613, referred sadly to the changes that were already taking place.

The Pantiles, Tunbridge Wells
Lamberhurst

In view of the further degradation of the countryside which is happening to-day, and is likely to continue if speculative builders, small-holders, and other mongers of ugliness have their unsocial, philistinish way, it would be well to quote a few lines of Drayton's neglected epic :

"Could we," say they, "suppose that any would us cherish,
Which suffer every day the holiest things to perish?
All to our daily want to minister supply,
These iron times breed none that mind posterity.
'Tis but in vain to tell, what we before have been,
Or changes of the world, that we in time have seen;
When, not devising how to spend our wealth with waste,
We to the savage swine let fall our larding mast,
But now, alas, ourselves we have not to sustain,
Nor can our tops suffice to shield our roots from rain.
Jove's oak, the warlike ash, veined elm, the softer beech,
Short hazel, maple plain, light asp, the bending wych,
Tough holly, and smooth birch, must altogether burn.
What should the builder serve, supplies the forger's turn;
When under public good, base private gain takes hold,
And we poor woeful woods to ruin lastly sold."

Thus spoke the trees of the Weald through the lips of that gentle-minded scholar who was a friend of Shakespeare. The industrial circumstances have altered, for the iron and wool have gone northward. But what an ominous topicality has that line, "when under public good, base private gain takes hold." How it fits as a description of what still goes on (and will go on so long as human nature remains the same) under the guise of social service, municipal government, and public welfare.

Leaving the Green we come to Wilsley Pound, where the actual pound may still be seen. The cross-roads here lead on the right to Sissinghurst, straight on to Staplehurst which is down in the plain, and left along the ridge to Goudhurst. We take the last, and see before us a wide view of the northern half of the Weald, with wooded heights amid which shines the white mansion of Linton, the home once of the Cornwallis family. But that is twelve miles away. We pass another Flemish weaver's house on our right at Whitewell,

I 113

A Kentish Valley near Hawkhurst
Sissinghurst

in a dip. It is called Frizley, and we have no time to explore it, having already examined its contemporary at Wilsley.

Climbing slowly we come at last to the northern fences of Glassenbury, stopping for a glass of well-handled beer at the free house, the Peacock, whose host has the right English gift of hospitality, and with his wife keeps the house spotless, and the beer superb. Their great pride is a fine dark oak table made from local wood and as firm as a rock. Standing before the open fireplace, which is hung with copper pots and pans, it has a baronial warmth along its polished single-piece top.

We will turn left to the park gates and lodge. What a noble place we are approaching! The drive drops steeply down, amongst giant limes and oaks. Turning to the right it opens to a circular drive, on the right of which is a brick bridge over the wide moat. Across the courtyard stands the house, disfigured by a nondescript Victorian facing that ought to be removed to reveal the fifteenth-century stone-work behind it, thus making the front and the back of the house harmonious.

Across the moat to the left of the house (which lies in a cup of hilly ground), where once stood the chapel, is the opening of a gigantic lime grove, paved with moss. It is a Gothic, awe-inspiring walk, rightly associated with the ghost of a daughter of the house who, over a century ago, was bereaved on her wedding day. As she and her bridegroom rode away along the avenue after the wedding feast his horse reared, threw him, and he broke his neck. She is said to haunt the grove every anniversary. And why not? Did not Marie Antoinette appear to two distinguished English schoolmistresses some years ago, when they were lunching in the open air behind the Petit Trianon at Versailles, on the anniversary of the day when the queen suffered her agony in the garden, being arrested by the mob? We dare not dogmatize about these matters that hover over the borderline of material experience.

The back of the house gives directly on to the moat, which is wide, with its waters lipping the great stone wall and throwing up, when the sun shines, thousands of tiny reflections that play a colour-symphony over the surface of the stone. Mullioned windows open across the moat, from rooms that comprise the most ancient part of the house. To stand across the water, a few yards along the lime avenue, and to contemplate this scene, is to feel the slipping back of time over several centuries. Here is feudal England again, with the manorial system still at work, and each man in his place in the social frame. Round about one the great trees tower, making a rampart against the twentieth century, with its sordid levellings, its insane speed, its easy scepticisms. The past surges back, cleaned of its indecencies and cruelties. All that remains is the grace and the melancholy.

Inside the house this conjuring with the time spirit becomes even more dominant. Immediately after entering the great entrance hall one is transported through the years. Behind the hospitable hostess tread her ancestors, six centuries of generations of them, starting from the walls, the furniture, the suits of armour. It would be an uncanny sensation were it not tempered by the sense of generosity and simple friendliness which is the spirit of the place. The past is not a charnel emanation; it comes upon one in this hall with a warmth, an amplitude, carrying so many ages of culture and good living for which it can now find little outlet. It greets the understanding guest therefore with gratitude, and offers all it has.

The hall is heavily panelled from floor to ceiling, with the family arms used as a decoration for the panels. On the right is a highly ornate mantelpiece, with more armorial decoration and the date 1571 and the initials "W.R." and "F.R." The furniture in the hall is all ancient, standing in the places for which it was made; oak chests, a great table originally built for shuffleboard (a sort of primitive billiards), chairs with fine needlework covers on the seats.

The portraits here, as well as those in the dining-room, are a pictorial history of the family, as well as of English art. The early ones are dim primitive pieces, with conventionalized faces and garments. Amongst them are two portraits of the Duchess of St Albans, before and after her unfortunate marriage. The contrast between the two emphasizes the fact that grief is time's rival in its ability to etch the human features with the acid of experience.

On the dining-room table stands a silver bowl decorated with coins of the time when it was given as a wedding present to one of the daughters of the family by the great Emperor Charles the Fifth, who played such a conspicuous part in the history of the Renaissance, uniting at his birth the dynasties of the Hapsburgs with those of Burgundy, Aragon, and Castile. This piece of surviving actuality shook me deeply as I sat before it. By one of those chance vagaries of boyhood I had once picked up, for a shilling, Robertson's four-volume history of the emperor, which I read during a summer holiday from school. It was a good leader toward the greater pages of Gibbon. It woke me to the passion for history, and the application of the historical method to every interest, either in art or science; and it did so at that formative time when the foundations of the mind's character are being laid. Impressions received during those days are never forgotten. That is why I stared at this piece of silverware as though I were hypnotized. Could it be true? I *felt*, rather than *thought*, that this object had been touched by the warm, living hands of that emperor who had played fabulously upon my imagination over a period of forty years. The intensity of this luncheon-table experience was too much. I stared until my attention dulled. The emperor faded back into the past, and I found myself baffled in the same way that one is baffled by a vast stretch of landscape, or a contemplation of the night skies when the stars are at their full station along the perspective of the Milky Way. We stare at those prospects, earthly or sidereal, and we see nothing. Our minds boggle, and all that we can achieve is a sort of vague longing, a sullenness, those "fallings from us, vanishings" that Wordsworth experienced as he sat contemplating the *Intimations of Immortality*, and as I sat looking at this piece of Renaissance silverware.

Perhaps the choice corner of the house at Glassenbury is the tapestry bedroom, whose walls are covered entirely in needlework done in blue and cream embroidery. In such a room one might imagine Keats's Madeleine "unclasping her warméd jewels one by one," while the hidden lover watches the play of the warm gules of colour over her garments, hair and skin. What a room to have for one's privacy! But I think, if I were invited to make a habitation in this noble house, I should choose a larger room right at the back, with long mullioned windows in the wall dropping direct into the moat.

Here American officers were housed during the war, when most of the house was taken as a hospital, with the park occupied by great marquee tents. I saw this room just as it had been refurbished after the Americans had gone over the Channel. It smelt of the linseed oil with which the panelling had been restored. That smell is the smell of history itself. I suspect that if I were to encounter old Father Time, with his scythe over his shoulder, groping his way along the corridors of the ages, I should take from him a whiff of linseed oil.

This room was rather low for its size; but it would be warm, and its space would permit of it being used for work in the day and sleep at night; a self-contained den for a scholar. Were I to make my workplace there, I dare say that within a few months I should find myself writing in black-letter instead of normal script. It might be dangerous. Gradually I should recede from the modern world, to inhabit one of dreams and ghosts, sunk in this dell among the giant trees, with the opiate murmurings of the waters of the moat against the wall beneath me. In such a setting I might at last fully call up the significances of that silver bowl on the dining-room table, and meet the Emperor Charles the Fifth in person. But after that, should I be fit to return to the highroad of the twentieth century, and the normal purposes of my life?

After that memorable luncheon we strolled across the bridge (once a drawbridge) and turned up the lime grove. At the entrance to it was a small obelisk, to mark the spot where lay buried Napoleon Bonaparte's famous white horse Jaffa, which had been brought home after Waterloo by one of the sons of the house who was in Wellington's entourage. The dynasty of Glassenbury survived the innovations of the French Revolution and the upstart of Corsica. It remains to-day, with much more insidious and universal tides of change creeping towards that haunted moat and grove of limes. Is it doomed, with all that it stands for, to join the

Emperor Charles the Fifth, and to make way for the un-splendid and irreverent society, the society of the lowest common denominator, with which we are threatened in the post-war world?

CHAPTER VIII

A STONE'S-THROW OF HOME

THAT round trip from my workroom-oast leaves us with yet another to make south-westward, across a diameter of five miles to the county boundary. And here is a June day for it, a real Kentish day, when time stands still because the sun has entranced himself. A kind of faint, blue haze has hung over the countryside since dawn, and increased toward midday, although a breeze has sprung up, coming inland with a tang of salt in it, and occasional little boisterous bouts that catch the swelling fruit trees and toss up their skirts with a rousing chuckle.

What exercise of a long-standing self-discipline has been needed to keep me at work indoors all the morning! Satan, in the form of a yellowhammer's lazy song (the very essence of luxuriating summer), has thrown up temptations to me through the open windows. But now I can resist no more, and I'm off, this time by bicycle, the itinerary being too big for walking and too small for a car.

We drop down into the bowl of our little upland valley that runs west-east, with a small tributary of the River Teise flowing through it westward, ultimately to join the Medway. On the northern slope the soil changes to gravel and sand, with the result that beech trees appear and rhododendrons. From here southward and eastward, right across country far from railways and main roads, the evergreen Greek rose tree often lines stretches of the roads for miles, so that in early June one walks along avenues banked in purple.

With the inspiration of this lighter soil, a neighbour at Ladham House, just below the approach to Goudhurst, has been able to develop a magnificent garden of heaths, gathered from all over Europe. It is a most pleasant relaxation to wander along that end of his park, among Portuguese heather bushes six feet high. Indeed the whole of his park is delightful, for its flowering shrubs are finer even than those at Kew. I have seen a cream-coloured rhododendron standing up some fifteen feet, one great, unsullied cone of colour blazing against a blue sky, like a fantasy by van Gogh.

But the gardens all around the citadel of Goudhurst are superb. There is another, also on the northern slope before reaching the village, called Frogshole, whose setting and constellation are perfect, for the whole little estate is contained in a jealous fold of the land, opening out to a view right across the Weald northward to Maidstone and Ashford. In this garden the wind seems never to blow, for it is sheltered completely from the prevailing south-westers, those hooligans in the gardener's life. In such a retreat as this one could be philosopher and lover together, leading the life that Andrew Marvell yearned for but never attained. He never attained it because he was a human being. Who, since Adam's mistake, has been able to do so? We make our gardens, but we wander in them as strangers, ticket-of-leave creatures, watched by conscience and cares. I think we possess other people's gardens more than we possess our own.

I know that often I look across the valley from my own terrace to the roofs of my friend and neighbour at Frogshole, and I fancy I see in that paradisal setting the haven of peace that I, in common with all men, crave to discover. And he, no doubt, looks in my direction, compelled by the same illusion.

Before climbing up to the main cross-country road between Goudhurst and Cranbrook, let us look back along the almost private valley which we have just crossed. Within its seclusion exists a handful of families who have been there for centuries, a little community unto itself that is a miniature society fully representative of England as a whole (except for the urban; unless I, the newcomer, may stand as a sample of that). A half-dozen of surnames covers them. And a visit to the old graveyard on the hilltop will repeat those names; so will the parish registers.

The valley is filled and overflowing with riches. Apple and cherry orchards and hop gardens, with an occasional meadow (during and since the war the meadows have been ploughed and given to corn-growing, with more picturesque as well as utilitarian results), are varied by patches of surviving woodland. Over on the right begins a wood that stretches for five miles to Cranbrook. Along the course of the small stream in the bed of the valley there frequently hangs a scarf of mist. Sometimes in spring and autumn it grows from a scarf into a long, rolling quilt, above which the ridge projects like the further bank of a great river two miles broad, along whose course my imagination has often raised sail as I gazed from my workroom window.

Goudhurst is responsible for the term "hop garden," as distinct from hopfield. In 1341, when the manor belonged to the monastery of Leeds, the vicar of the parish was paid from the monastery in kind; "lambs, wool, cows, calves, chickens, pigs, ducks, apples, pears, onions, and all other herbs sown *in gardens*, and hay." The vicar pleaded that hops, even then one of the most remunerative of Kentish crops, were grown in gardens, and he went to law about it. After a long suit, the Abbey of Leeds won. Nevertheless, the memory of that plea has lingered on in the traditions of Kent. No doubt the minds of Kentish men have kept that term "garden" instinctively, with a view to future contingencies. A farmer wastes nothing.

The village has a perfect situation. It stands on the top of the hill, and has views all round the compass. Northward it looks right along the main course of the Weald, over the Maidstone ridge with its string of prettily named villages, to the further and higher North Downs, behind which lies the Thames estuary, twenty-five miles away. Five miles to the west lies Sussex. Southward stretches another inland valley similar to that which we have just left, but larger and even more wooded. Most of it is occupied by the great Crown estate of Bedgebury, once the seat of the Beresfords. The big house, now a girls' school, stands like a French chateau among a group of superb lakes. It is a decorative place, built in the nineteenth century when Hausmann's rather heavy grandeur dominated the reconstruction of Paris, and hence affected the architectural taste of the rest of Europe. The stable spirelet rises above the trees, with a gleam of water. The woods are maintained by Kew as an experimental station for raising conifers and deciduous trees from abroad.

The dominant feature of Goudhurst village is the noble old church, set on the highest spot, between two gigantic elms. Its wide ragstone tower is a landmark. It must have been even more conspicuous centuries ago, for it once had a spire rising from that already lofty tower. In 1637 the church was struck by lightning one hot August night. The steeple was burned down and the bells melted in the heat. Before the Civil War the tower was rebuilt and an Italianate decoration set round the west door. Purists condemn this, but I find it pleasing enough, especially as it is half-hidden by a gigantic archway of yew. The base of the tower evidently escaped, for if you examine the mouldings of the lower course you will see parallel grooves where the villagers habitually sharpened their arrowheads. And that must have been earlier than the seventeenth century.

During the war, and Home Guard duties, I got to know that tower intimately, for we had our most important observation post on its leaded roof. What memorable sights we saw from there; actions in the Battle of Britain, and during the doodle-bomb episode in 1944, that will gradually sink into the local folklore, becoming more and more fabulous as time dries out the reality. That is the trouble with history. It is worthless without the rekindling by imagination, and our imaginations are never powerful enough to recapture more than a fragment. It is the same with this vast landscape which we can yearn toward as we look out at it from the battlements of Goudhurst's church tower. We look and look, but somehow it remains baffling, not quite real; it is remote, a vague generalization. So it is with history, until a small thing suddenly connects it up with actual people and events of our own time. For example, I can see just south of us on the next rising ground a quarter of a mile away (the hill drops precipitously south of the village) a group of farm buildings belonging to a family called Stringer. In the parish records for 1638 to 1640, during the rebuilding of the tower, there is the statement that the work was under the charge of John Stringer, churchwarden, of Trigg's Farm. I shall give another instance in a moment of this continuity which alone can bring history to life, and make our minds *and spirits* grasp the reality that once was warm, moving and living, aching and hoping, behind these two-dimensional records in parish books and on the stone monuments in and around the church. The whole authority of age lies in that power to evoke the past as an actuality, and so to dominate the imaginations of a younger generation. As we grow veteran in our memories, we become unconscious historians, and to that extent are oracular. "Were you there?" is the awe-stricken question. "And did you once see Shelley plain?"

The church has suffered badly from a landmine that almost destroyed the near-by vicarage (a modern, shoddy villa). All the windows went, but as they were Victorian stained glass we are better for the loss. What scope the village has for a magnificent war memorial! The tower could have a new spire put on it; and local craftsmen could design windows that would commemorate all that happened to the village during the war. Planes, bombs, doodles; all are objects that lend themselves to the conventional shapes of stained glass. I like to think of a window showing Christ standing in front of the children of the village while a diabolical doodle-bomb (hell's travesty of a Cross) rushes overhead. How much more vital and commanding would such designs be than the vapid commercial stuff sold by the leaded foot. I would have another window showing the local farmers (and their faces would be recognizable too!) bringing their wartime tribute of corn to feed the nation. Such windows would be significant, and increasingly valuable, as the years covered up the actual events in the dust of time. This was how, in the Middle Ages when Christianity was at its most potent and creative strength, our ancestors made their memorials; they seriously and passionately intended them to be fortresses against oblivion. But we are too self-conscious in our generation. Is it really possible to believe that the feeble, mass-produced memorial windows put up by a London contractor will perpetuate the events and characters of the five years during which Kent stood in greater peril than at any time in her history; five years of sweat, and blood and tears, as Mr Churchill promised us? No, we want the men and women who did the job, the fighting, the labouring, the watching, to turn now and to make the monument of that vigil. It may prove to be clumsy, amateur work; but it will be *ours*.

The interior of the church is magnificent, for it has some of the finest tombs in the country. The difficulty of talking of tombs and their occupants is that immediately one is carried out of the church into the neighbourhood where once those sleepers, now in effigy, were quick; as gay, as sinful and as full of humbug as ourselves. So let us first look at the fabric of the church, which dates from 1119. Not much purely Norman work is now to be seen, however. The five arches of the nave are pointed, in the Early English tradition. The south aisle is particularly wide, and has a separate high-pitched roof, with good gables to east and west, and a coved ceiling with ribs and bosses and tie-beams. These are worth examining, if you are interested in architecture.

The large west window, of three lights, in the tower is a replica of that in St Catherine Cree, Leadenhall Street. This suggests that mass-production was already in its infancy in 1638, when the tower was rebuilt by a London contractor.

The most conspicuous and noble tombs in the church are those of the Colepepper family. Like the Sidneys of Penshurst, the Colepeppers are well rooted in Sussex and Kent. Their principal seat was at Bedgebury, long before it came into the hands of the Beresfords. They were full-blooded enough, and played a large part in the history of England. A Lord Colepepper was Master of the Rolls to Charles the First, and was a statesman of great acumen. He engineered, behind the scenes, the process of bringing back the exiled Prince Charles after the death of Cromwell's son and the end of the Protectorate. Catherine Howard, Henry the Eighth's fifth wife, was a Colepepper. She was also as vivid an amorist as her royal husband, and amongst her several lovers was her own cousin Thomas Colepepper, who lived at the beautiful village of Hollingbourne, which we shall visit later.

In the seventeenth century there were sixteen Colepepper families in Kent. But the Civil War broke them up and many emigrated. To-day, in the island of Antigua, in the West Indies, there is a Colepepper living on his estate, and it is called Bedgebury! One of the founders of Virginia and Carolina was a Colepepper.

The largest monument is in the south aisle. On it lie two almost life-size effigies in wood (a rare material for such a purpose). They are Sir Alexander and his wife, 1537. The painting of their dress and armour is still in lively colours. A more elaborate Colepepper monument is on the south wall of the chancel, where the lord and lady are kneeling on their cushions, while below them, in separate panels, the huge family, boys on one side and girls on the other, kneel also in devout symmetry, all looking like miniature adults rather than children.

Bedgebury, the original home of this family, is one of the oldest manors in the country, for it has a deed of gift dated A.D. 815 when Kenwulf, King of Mercia and overlord of Kent, gave it to his thane Count Suithnoth. It has had a comparatively peaceful history, lying there in that southern country under the protection of the Goudhurst ridge. It is extremely fertile and well watered. Behind the house stretches a mile of waters, and behind that four miles of thickly wooded parkland as far as the county borders at Flimwell. Like Angley Park, its neighbouring estate, of which I wrote in my last chapter, Bedgebury has a touch of wild, primeval character. One can wander there and for a few hours become a recluse or a pioneer, according to temperament. To sit on one of the narrow necks between two of the lakes, among the wild fowl, while a breeze comes down off the pine trees on the hills behind, resinous with the perfume of all the escapades and holidays rolled into one superb, natural pomander—this is indeed to know happiness.

One of the lakes is known as Hammer Pond; another as Furnace Pond. Such names indicate what industry was once carried on here. Guns for the fleet that fought against the Spanish Armada were forged on Bedgebury estate, and it is probable that three centuries ago the park was less a retreat than a Chatham, with its furnaces, the sound of woodmen's axes felling fuel, and the constant traffic in culverins.

During the war a devastating fire destroyed many acres of the woodlands and the pine nurseries. It was started by land-girls who threw their cigarette stubs down among the dry undergrowth. It was put out by the soldiers stationed in the neighbouring villages, who with the local Home Guard turned out that night and fought for twenty-four hours with besom and hose.

Another picturesque family commemorated in the church

is that of the name of Campion. I tried to establish that Thomas Campion, the Elizabethan song-writer, was one of this family, just as I tried, equally unsuccessfully, to discover that Nicholas Culpepper, the herbalist, was a Goudhurst man. The Campions lived at Combwell, on the site of Combwell Abbey, founded by a Robert de Thunhan, whose son Stephen accompanied Richard Lionheart to Palestine, and was given the dangerous responsibility of bringing home Queen Berengaria of Navarre and her sister Queen Joan of Sicily. After many and long adventures he got them safely to the royal castle of Chinon in Poitou, where the king had his headquarters. What an Odyssey that must have been, as full of fables and monsters, delays and temptations, as that taken by Ulysses two thousand years earlier, over almost the same route.

Combwell, also richly wooded, runs with Bedgebury, and the lonely road between them is like a carriage drive rather than a public thoroughfare. The woods, with high boskage of rhododendrons, overhang it, and in June the way is a way of flowers, with the blown blossoms underfoot and the great ramparts of purple on each side.

North of Combwell, and lying nearer to Goudhurst, is the estate of Finchcocks, with a house whose tall front can be seen from the High Street. It was built by the Bathursts. Two other ancient houses on this southern side of the village are Pattenden and Twissenden, both dating from the time of Edward the First. The single-line railway that branches off from Paddock Wood and runs through Horsmonden, Goudhurst, Cranbrook to Hawkhurst passes close by Pattenden, but as the single rail is rusty from infrequency of trains, the slumber of the ancient house is not disturbed. As the ending of their names implies, these houses grew out of clearings in the great forest, and for centuries they must have remained isolated and sylvan, socially comparable to farms in the forests of Russia or Finland to-day. They still have about them a self-contained air, like hens dozing in the dust on a hot day. Their great doors, their overhung windows, and the heavy panelling and beams of their interiors—all these features hand-hewn and therefore superbly proportioned— have the effect upon a visitor, as indeed upon a dweller, of timelessness. To live in such houses is to be insignificant and humbled.

> Time like destiny came down and shook
> Their hearts with fear, turning their pride to dust.

The economic history of Goudhurst is an epitome of that of much of the county of Kent. Edward the Third in the fourteenth century invited Flemish master weavers to come to England, to teach their craft to his subjects, and to settle here themselves. He thus intended to increase the value of our principal export trade in wool, by converting it to the export of broadcloth. He succeeded, and had not the Black Death intervened, the effect would have been immediately discernible. As it was, that continent-wide disaster put back the results of his statesmanlike act for over a century. By 1725 there were thirty looms established in Goudhurst alone. When it is realized that each of these looms employed eighteen women spinners, as well as several men, such as quill minders, scowers, scribblers, and sorters, those thirty looms will represent a considerable industry. Wealth came rolling into these now sleepy villages, and much of it settled down into the form of real estate and merchants' houses. These houses, built by the master weavers for their work and their habitation, are noble pieces of domestic architecture. Each of them has a great hall as large as a small chapel, where the looms were established. Now they make studios or music-rooms for the people who have the taste and the means so to adapt them.

Disease was a frequent interrupter of this prosperity. The church records show that the plague visited Goudhurst again in 1658. A hundred and fifty-nine people died in three months. Soon after this disaster an Act of Parliament was passed, one of those cart-before-the-horse efforts with which financial experts and middlemen (those non-creative parasites on the body of society) love to encumber the Statute Book, whereby it was laid down that all subjects of the realm should be buried in wool. It was cunningly assumed that death and the necessity for shrouds were fairly widespread, and that the woollen industry would accordingly benefit. In 1795 an affivadit was put in at the Maidstone Assizes that

"W. Wickham, Victualler, was not put in, wrapt or wound up or buried in any shirt, sheet, shrift or shroud made or mingled with flax, hemp, silk, hair, gold or silver, or other than what is sheep's wool only." Such a device is characteristic of the rodent-like minds of those brokers and jobbers who seem always to get the legislative and administrative power into their hands. I suppose the men who *make* things, the true workers, are too busy to concern themselves with such coercions and restrictions.

That is an interesting affidavit, not only as an economic record, but also because it gives us another example of the continuity of history, and the osmosis of past record (the dried, the flat, the unreal) into present flesh and blood. The Wickhams are a flourishing family in this district of Goudhurst to-day, with numerous farms, notably Combourne, a holding typical of West Kent. It stretches through our upland valley, and comprises a little of everything; cornland, pasture, hop gardens, apple and cherry orchards; all kept in apple-pie order. The Wickham family once held Gore Court, an old yeoman foundation on the northern drop from the village, a mile from our Courtesan Green, whose charming name was doubtless due to the fact that on this spot, where the lords of Glassenbury were first settled before they went to the next hill and built their moated house, one of those lords must have set up an auxiliary *ménage* for his leman; a practice which puritanism later forced underground, so that it became furtive and shamefaced. The nineteenth century, in its prudery, even altered the name of the hamlet to Curtisden Green; a piece of etymological dishonesty. It is an odd thing that prudery will often go with complete æsthetic unscrupulousness.

Another interesting little titbit of economic history at Goudhurst is the record of the battle with the smugglers in 1747. All these villages within twenty miles of the coast and conveniently situated near the wild Romney Marshes were hotbeds of smuggling, almost up to the middle of the nineteenth century. Nobody loves the exciseman. As Burns said, "the Devil's awa' wi' the exciseman." Customs duties, and all the spider-nets of tariffs, are more examples of these fear-born tricks of the financial jugglers, activities that benefit the

Cranbrook Mill
"The Peacock"

human race not one whit. On the contrary, they breed dishonesty, because they have no foundation in common sense
and constructiveness. But I am approaching very near to the
arguments of One-Tax Henry George; and they are debat-
able matters outside my scope.

Ignoring, therefore, the morality of these matters, at least
in their origins, we can contemplate the history of the
nefarious illicit trade that sprang up as soon as tariffs were
high enough to make the risks worth while. We have the
same activity to-day, with black markets corrupting the whole
economic life of Europe. Like all gambling ventures, this
illicit trade attracted the bolder and more ruffianly characters. Hawkhurst was one of the centres, and the "Hawkhurst
Gang" under its leader Kingsmill became notorious, for not
only the King's revenue but also the lives and property of
private citizens were endangered. A native of Goudhurst, an
ex-soldier named Sturt, organized a local militia, swearing
them in and training them in professional style. So successful
was he that the gang advertised their intention of attacking
the village in force. This piece of Nazi-like bluff did not dis-
hearten the volunteers, however, and the boast had to be put
into effect. The interesting thing is that Sturt set about the
establishment of his defences in exactly the same way as did
the Home Guard in 1940, except that he lacked the fire-
barrels for throwing jets of flame across the approaching
roads. But then Sturt had no prospective Tiger tanks to con-
tend with.

Fortifications had been dug and erected against the eastern
high road coming in along the top of the ridge from Cranbrook, and surely enough the Hawkhurst Gang approached
from this side (as we had anticipated that the main body of
Germans would have to approach overland). On the very
spot where the Home Guard made their last, farewell parade
after four years' active and enjoyable service, the militia
met the smugglers and routed them, killing several and cap-
turing more, who subsequently were hanged. There is a
legend in the neighbourhood that some of the defenders were
stationed at the windows of the ancient hotel, the Star and
Eagle (then called the Star and Crown). This fine old
hostelry, however, which nowadays is restored architectur-

Glassenbury
Goudhurst

ally and is in full swing as a hospitable hotel, is connected with the vaults of the church by an underground passage, whose purpose has always been of a dubious reputation. It may be that some of those snipers with their muzzle-loading muskets and home-made shot fired high rather than damage the men who they hoped would bring more profitable consignments after dark. Kingsmill's body was hung in chains at the junction of roads by Gore Court. Bad laws breed bad characters.

Outside the church, along the road where this battle took place, there stands a long line of low-built houses, all under one stretch of roofing, which are the most conspicuous relic of the wool trade in the village. Another survival stands opposite the Star and Eagle—a handsome house, with good panelling inside, where the Home Guard had its battalion headquarters during the war.

The view northwards, from the lower Tunbridge Wells road, is one of the grandest in the south of England. For me, however, looking north always gives a sense of being in exile. I am looking away from the sun and the Mediterranean—the centre of civilization and right living. I am looking toward the darkness and the cold, the regions where obduracy and Calvinism flourish, like moss in caves. To be on a hillside facing the sun at midday I am at home, and the youth of the world and of the human race lie before me. I hear the tread of Homer's men, and the voices of his women as they sit weaving behind the walls of Troy. I sniff the wines of France, and listen to the cadence of its superb prose. I said this one day to a commercial traveller who joined me in a glass of beer outside the inn at Kilndown, which stands in all its newness (it and its church are little more than a century old) on a height south-west of Goudhurst. The traveller had just come across from the village store, and was lamenting the wartime shortage of groceries and how he hated to disappoint the small retailers. From the question of shortage and restrictions we moved rationally to a discussion of the weather and the sun, the source of all groceries. This led me to relieve myself of my prejudice against looking north. He agreed fervently. Holding up his glass of beer to the light he declaimed with

some dramatic emphasis, "O for a glass of the warm south."
Rather snobbishly, I corrected his quotation. "O for a beaker
full of the warm south," pointing out that the epithet "full"
contained the essence of Keats's philosophy of life, and that
to leave it out was little short of blasphemy. He agreed
readily, and took no offence. Indeed, he carried the matter
further, and said that his careless substitution of the word
"glass" for "beaker" cut the subsequent pre-Raphaelite
Movement off from its source. I in turn agreed with him.
We then discovered that we were both confirmed borea-
phobes. This called for another libation, and we shook hands
at parting, he to continue his travels to the village shops of
Kent, I to my desk. Such encounters are the musk of life.
They give it a savour and a bouquet.

CHAPTER IX

ALMOST OUT OF BOUNDS

STANDING on that height, in front of the lonely little pub at Kilndown, the Kentish man is almost out of bounds. What a delightful thing to be! I don't know whether or not it is a fact, or whether or not it is due to some mental kink in my own nature, but I am always struck by the increased attractiveness of the ends of gardens, the corners of parks, the no-man's-land of battlefields, the limits of parishes, and the boundaries of counties. Perhaps it is because they are usually the neglected places; the wild flowers beyond the bonfire patch; the bit of road that two rural district councils each swears belongs to the other, so that its surface is never made up or tarred.

Kilndown has that quality. One feels that here the old spirits of the locality have found a last hiding-place, before modern human society, with its deadly efficiency and scientific, Fabian organization, will ferret them out and put them to good use, instead of letting them play their pipes and seduce the wild flowers and the smaller winged creatures in sweet and mischievous idleness.

I am in danger, however, of becoming Barrie-like if I linger here, so with one last look back to see Goudhurst standing like a conventionalized medieval village on its sugar-loaf hill I will move on towards the equally beautiful village of Lamberhurst and its two outriding grandeurs, Bayham Abbey and Scotney Castle. I have already told of my boyhood adventure of a night spent so happily at the Chequers, Lamberhurst, under the influence of youth, poetry, and half a bottle of wine. It is absurd, but whenever I go through that village nowadays I glance at that old hotel (so old that it is sunk just a little into the earth) and see a ghost. And like all the ghosts of one's own past, it makes my bones to ache, and a cold wind of finality to blow through the chambers of my mind, slamming a distant door.

Northward lie a number of interesting villages, but they

lead away from the borderlands, and so I shall leave them until I turn more particularly to the interior of the county. Coming now to a cross-roads along the ride towards Tonbridge and the Wells, the most direct route from Goudhurst, I turn left and almost immediately drop steeply into Lamberhurst. The church lies up at the top, hidden away in a small park, near Court Lodge, a square Jacobean house handsomely placed. A footpath leads past the house to the church, which surmounts a sloping graveyard richly shaded with trees, that stand islanded in the surrounded parkland, with an almost stage-like effect, as though posed there. During the summers of the war the Home Guard had a camp there, and I recall one hot summer day when we were engaged in an exercise on signals, carrying small radio sets and flags. The dot-dashing went on all the morning, with much tramping about and concentrating of attention through eye and ear; lively work, and most enjoyable in the company of good fellows. But this was followed by a heavy Army meal of stewed meat and boiled vegetables, ladled out in bulk. After that we resumed our exercise. I found myself stationed under the great trees below the bank of the church. I set up my radio, tuned in, and prepared for the afternoon's work. But suddenly, and incredibly, there burst from within the church the sound of a good piano, well played. Now even a bad piano acts upon me like a strong liquor. I can pass a villa in the suburbs and hear a child practising scales on a dud upright piano with an under-damper action, and even at that I have to stop and listen, gradually disengaging myself before I can proceed on my way, just as though the sounds were floating spider silks. But when a *good* piano, played by hands that know what it all means, comes upon me with what Shakespeare called "that falling sound," then I dissolve. First my limbs falter, so that I collapse and lie along the ground, like old Adam in *As You Like It*; then my mind floats off from that supine figure and hovers about in the fourth dimension. There I remain, with my bats outside my belfry, temporarily out of action.

That is what happened that summer afternoon. The world was very quiet, because there was no wind and the trees were still. The player went from one Beethoven sonata to another, playing with a certain rough and ready clumsiness, as though out of practice, but knowing what he was doing and bringing out the shape and structure of the superb masculine music. Some three-quarters of an hour passed, and I then noticed frantic flag-waggings from across the park. Inquiries were being made about my signals post. I slowly spelt back, on my buzzer, the message "Have contacted Muse." Then my curiosity would brook no more. I took French leave, stole over the fencing, and looked into the church. There sat a soldier at a grand piano just under the lectern, playing for himself, with no audience to be seen. He was now working his way through an adaptation of the Tchaikowsky Fifth Symphony. The faults in his playing emerged more distinctly while I was in the same building, so I went back to my post and listened from there for some minutes, to be disturbed by a heated sergeant who had crept up under cover. "What the hell do you . . ." he began, and continued for some time until he too heard the music. Slowly his jaw dropped, and he looked uneasy. "You see!" I said, demurely. He looked at me in disgust, then turned and made his way back across the park. Shortly after that I was promoted.

Such is my recollection of Lamberhurst church, an ancient place, with two of its piers out of the perpendicular. It is said that Edward the First came here in 1299, and made to the parish a present of seven shillings when news was brought to him that his negotiations for marriage with the sister of the King of France had been successful, and that a treaty of peace between the two countries could now be made.

We continue down the hill to the village, which lies in the deep river valley with a bridge over the Teise, and a hotel on each side of the bridge. The further one is the Chequers, where I spent that memorable but uneventful night so many years ago. It has been an inn since 1412, and during the days of coaching it was four hours' journey from London. I have never had the courage to ask to see that front room upstairs, with the huge double bed, where the shy youth slept more than thirty years ago. No doubt the maid who turned down the coverlet and gave him a quizzical glance, half-amused and half-informative, has long since matured and gathered in her harvest. Nor have I ventured to research in the visitors' book for that year, to find out if the over-many lines of rhymed couplets written there by that youth were discreetly removed by the landlord. It is the legend that matters. The facts are trivial enough, like most of the facts in early life. But how tremendously they loom, how novel and world-shaking, "when all the trees are green, lad."

Lamberhurst is a quiet enough place nowadays. It was once the most busy centre of the Kent and Sussex iron-founding industry. It was from the Gloucester Forge (named after one of Queen Anne's short-lived children) that the railings of St Paul's Cathedral were produced. They weighed two hundred tons and cost eleven thousand pounds. I believe that only part of the original Kentish iron survives in London, much of it having been pulled down in late Victorian times and sold to Canada. Another product of the Lamberhurst forges was the fireback, a piece of domestic commonplace now fetching high prices. I remember being with a friend in Caudebec, in Normandy, who bought in an antique shop there a fine example of a fireback, with a design based on the mystery of the phœnix rising from the flames. Years later I bought one in Cranbrook, and the design was almost identical with that on the Norman piece. Is this further evidence in favour of my argument in the opening chapter of this book that Kent and Normandy are an identity?

The iron-smelting went on for centuries in this part of the county, but all that survives to-day are numerous "hammer" ponds and "furnace" ponds. With the discovery that coal could be turned into coke for smelting, the industry suddenly, in the latter half of the eighteenth century, changed its locality, thus saving the last of the southern trees, which had been rapidly vanishing, without replacement. The Lamberhurst forges alone consumed some two hundred thousand cords of wood a year. The get-rich-quick iron forgers, like the American farmers to-day, had no long-term policy and cared not a damn for posterity. They cut down the forest of Anderida to feed their furnaces, and left the wounds for nature and the patient Kentish farmer to heal. I know of little industry carried on in the village to-day. Before the war a Dutch weaving house settled there and produced some beautiful fabrics that were retailed in the West End of London. Opposite the weaving shop is an ancient house called Coggers Hall, another survival of the earlier days of the weavers. It has a fine hall and much wealth of panelling. Beside it runs the River Teise, emerging from the bridge which carries the main London to Hastings road.

Branching right from that road in the centre of the village, and rising steeply, a secondary road runs to Wadhurst and Tunbridge Wells. At the top of the hill, by three ways, we take the right-hand for a mile and then turn down a by-lane that brings us to another century, and almost to another world. It is the approach to Bayham Abbey. This place is one of those which I find difficulty in writing about. Its beauty is absolute, like that of Fountains in Yorkshire. The situation is not dissimilar. Indeed, many of the great abbeys of England appear to have been sited according to a prescription. There is always a ridge above them; always a sheltered valley; always a string of lakes opening from a small river which waters and refreshes them. Bayham has all these specifications. The hillside by which one approaches is heavily wooded with old oaks, thickened with younger timber of beech, conifers, lime, and elm. All is wild-flowered and seized with bines and bryony. "These are the woods of Westermain, enter ye who dare." Well, we dare, and our reward is a rich one.

The park is entered by a gate, with a Gothic lodge standing in a rose and vegetable garden, all rather subdued under a proud umbrage of trees. The drive drops steeply, with dells on the right hand, round which the road curves, planing down to the level and the open park. There stands a little church on a bank of raised ground, with swampy levels beyond it, marking the course of the River Teise, which has just fed the string of lakes before flowing round the site of the abbey. We approach that site across the flats, and over a bridge to the ruined gateway, a fourteenth-century entrance to the abbey. The main arch still survives, with a few decorations rubbed by the weather. All is heavily overgrown with bushes and trees. Beyond the gateway the precincts are spacious, open lawns leading on the right hand to the rushy edges of the biggest lake, and on the left to the main ruins.

These are impressive still, though sadly neglected. A locked gate shuts off the nave, but one can look right up it, to the massive chancel arches, which are broken off abruptly just where they begin to fan out to span the ceiling. The church must have been a noble piece of Gothic work. The nave is narrow, very long and very high. Before its destruction the church stood 257 feet in length. In addition to the church there was a presbytery in the form of an apse, with four transepts and four lady chapels. The chapter house and remains of the cloisters can still be seen to the right of the chancel remains, and a few fragments of the domestic quarters. All periods of Gothic are represented, for the abbey was founded in 1200 by Robert de Turneham and Ela de Sackville, who dedicated it to the Virgin Mary. It housed a community of Premonstratensian Canons. These were a strict Order, a reformed sect of the Augustinians, who in the twelfth century, under a German prelate called Norbert, settled in a remote place in Aisne, near a village called Prémontré, which gave its name to the Order. Bayham must have been one of the first of the settlements of this Order in England, of which there were thirty-five houses when Henry the Eighth dissolved the monasteries. The main work of the Order was to try to convert the Germans to Christianity in the country around the Elbe and the Oder. Recent history shows how far they succeeded.

The English branches of this Order were called White Canons, from their thick woollen cloaks of undyed material. It must have been a picturesque sight to see such figures working about the abbey in those medieval days when the settlement was hidden away here far from the traffic of that savage world of men, a brooch of gleaming gardens and well-fed lakes sunk into the bosom of the Wealden forest that stretched, primeval still, all along the county, and north and south to the Downs. Here indeed was a strict retreat, where probably no strangers came during the entire year, other than fellow members of the Order from headquarters at Laon in France, or Newhouse in Lincolnshire. The place is silent, isolated and serene to-day. The set of the valley and the wooded hills around it gives the visitor a sense of solitude that is persuasive to moods of intensive self-searching.

The present setting of Bayham Abbey is an instant and positive remembrancer of immortality, with all that it implies of self-responsibility, and the innate loneliness of the human soul. What must it have been like when the abbey was in full life, under an isolation that was absolute! The imagination can hardly rebuild such conditions. Only a hint comes upon the mind to show how here, as all over the country, were ways of life, and differences of environment that, could we return to them, would make us feel as though we had come to a strange planet, of vastly greater surfaces, and a human life pathetic in its littleness, imprisoned in its own huge freedoms; with so vast a possibility of ranging that it dare not set out.

It is not surprising that legends survive of a procession of whiteclad and tonsured figures to be seen at certain times passing down the nave of the abbey. Where the inmates once trod is now a green sward, and ramblers climb here and there among the stones. Swans and moorhens inhabit the ponds, cutting their little patterns of idleness on the waters, and making the reeds rustle as they disappear amongst the osiers and wild lilies to find their nests. Standing in the body of the church one can look westward at the waters, and see, on the summit of the rolling parkland hill on the right, the great mansion built for the Marquess Camden in the nineteenth century by the architect David Brandon, who restored Chilham Castle at about the same time. The stone of which this pseudo-Gothic house was built did not come, as might be expected, from the ruins of the abbey down below. It was quarried at Maidstone. The family, whose name is Pratt, came to Kent from Devonshire in 1700, settling first at Wilderness, a lovely spot near Sevenoaks. The marquisate, with the earldom of Brecknock, was created in 1812. William Camden, the historian, was a member of this family, and I believe he lived here.

It is a remarkable thing that this solitude can be found, with such substantial recollections of the medieval world, within fifty miles of London, and only a mile or two from the main London to Hastings road. It is miraculous that there should be such another survival, possessing even more suggestions of romantic solitude, within the same parish. Yet that miracle is to be found at Lamberhurst, for Scotney Castle lies on the other side of the village, on the semi-private road that runs back through superb valley scenery to Kilndown and Goudhurst, via the park of Finchcocks. This little road is one of the most delightful in the county. It makes its way, tortuously, along the valley dominated by the façade of Finchcocks, whose fine Queen Anne front sets the time signature for the adventure. Here we are in the late seventeenth or early eighteenth century; patches of neglected woodland giving upon isolated fields of corn or paddocks that open a view to the ridge on the left, and open stretches on the right (if moving from Goudhurst). I know that whenever I take this by-road I half-expect to meet John Constable at work, sketching a lane-end, a barn, or a venerable tree whose misgrowth has taken his fancy. A green day in July is the most harmonious, for if one goes earlier the riot of colour from the massive banks of rhododendron and azalea grouped up the hill is too gay for the historical weight they should carry. But in July, when the merging greens combine into an English melancholy, and the birds have stopped singing, the ride through this valley is almost ghostly, even at midday. Finchcocks stands about halfway along the valley, before it begins to take on the humours of Broceliande. The house, with its tall, narrow windows, its baroque porch, its large recessed medallion above the porch where stands a statue, its general effect of curves and pomposity, is a stylish place that one feels would suitably house a spinsterish connoisseur such as Horace Walpole, or the poet Alexander Pope—men of exquisite taste but dry and waspish hearts.

Passing Finchcocks, the road instantly becomes wilder, and the trees closer and more hemmed in with tanglewood. There are giants among them, enormous limes and sweet chestnuts, the former at this time of year throwing out auras of perfume that come upon one like music. This perfume grows more insistent as one approaches the modern Scotney Castle from the side, for thick shrubberies of box and yew add a slightly French (Royal France, not the Fourth Republic!) suggestion, increasing and not subduing the nostalgia of the lime-scent.

The house, built in 1837, overlooks the deepest part of

the valley, with the ruined medieval castle in its moat lying directly below, as a background to the dropping gardens and walks among the ornamental trees and shrubs. Earlier writers have claimed that this is one of the most beautiful gardens in England, and they do not exaggerate. I think that to-day, with the grim new economy that has overtaken the country landowners, Scotney Castle garden must have lost its horticultural smartness and finish. But it is all the more in keeping with its setting and the wonderful relic to which it leads. It has a sadness now; the sadness of grass lawns that are slightly in neglect (like all lawns in France), of trees that here and there have to bear the burden of one of their number fallen and leaning against them in death, under veils of creeper; the sadness of bosquets where nobody comes to sit in youth or in the prime of life. Courtyards lead to the house, giving upon each other through tall gates that stand permanently open, and indeed could not now be closed because great wistarias have coiled themselves about the gateway. Crossing the lawns before the front of the house we disappear into the dropping shrubbery and follow one of the many paths beneath more giant limes until we come to the moat, now thick with water-lilies. Islanded by it, the ruin stands against a background of rising hills and woods. Its beauty, with all its undertone of vanished life and power and rich circumstance, takes such a hold on the imagination that it is difficult not to be somewhat overborne. It is like an excess of music, as I have suggested, part of that symphony in which the scent of the lime trees plays a sort of *basso ostinato.*

It is difficult now to reconstruct in the imagination the castle as it originally filled the island within the moat. Standing in the water is the remains of the oldest part, a fourteenth-century circular tower, which has since been roofed in with a witch's hat of tiles. The early crenellations and dropholes remain round the top of the stone walls, broken only in one patch where the tower runs into the shabby remains of a dwelling-house built into the middle of the ruins. This nest of brickwork and plastered bay-windows is Elizabethan, though there is a date 1849 graved in the plaster under one of the windows. But this is probably an indication to record when the windows were replastered, and not when they were set in the house. Several outside stone staircases remain, the masonry thrust awry by gigantic wistaria trees that have taken a permanent hold upon most of the ruined building, and are now supporting what they first helped to destroy. By walking through the archway in an outer wall one comes upon an ancient bowling green, facing which is the remaining wall of a later addition to the castle, with an Italianate doorway dominated by a coat of arms. I have heard that Inigo Jones was responsible for this seventeenth-century aggrandizement which was never finished. It was to have been a big banqueting-hall.

The castle was named after its founder, Walter de Scoteni, who built it in the thirteenth century. He was afterwards hanged at Winchester for taking too active a part in the royal family squabbles, by poisoning the brother of the Earl of Gloucester, to whom he was steward. The castle was subsequently sold to Chichele, the yeoman Archbishop of Canterbury whose tomb can be seen in the cathedral. It passed from him through his niece to a family named Darell, who remained Roman Catholic after the dissolution of the monasteries, and therefore had to adopt the expedient of making a secret priest-chamber in the house. It served its purpose in 1598, when the Jesuit Father Blount took refuge here and used the hidden chamber while the queen's officers searched the premises in vain.

The castle remained in the possession of the Darells until 1720. After that, little record was kept until the Hussey family bought it in 1778. They still own it, and permit visitors to see it. Having, I hope, seen it, those visitors can now follow my route out to the high road alongside the county boundary again, through the fine woods of Combwell and Chingley, to the high cross-roads at Flimwell, where for a mile we have broken bounds into Sussex. Turning left, we re-enter the county and after a run along the ridge, with wide views still to north and south, we reach Highgate, the binary village with Hawkhurst. This is a most pleasing district, richly varied in timber, with many large houses and gardens planted with exotic pines during the nineteenth century, and now therefore odorous and shady. This gives a southern quality to the place, especially as the cottagers have a liking for hydrangeas, which grow luxuriantly here. Every garden is filled with these litmus-like blossoms of fading blue.

Another fact that gives Hawkhurst a southern quality is the food. There are two hotels in Highgate both of which offer excellent meals. The Royal Oak and the Queens are both old posting-houses that have kept up the pre-industrial and pre-puritan tradition. Even during the war and the rationing period, they managed somehow or other to offer a substantial meal and an occasional bottle of red wine. Lying between the two inns is a row of old-fashioned shops with a charming colonnade that runs for at least a hundred yards. It has a Regency atmosphere, and the buying of a tube of tooth-paste at the chemist's, or a packet of seeds at the iron-monger's, takes on almost unconsciously a touch of cere-moniousness most pleasing to the jaded modern mind. Good manners are a characteristic of Hawkhurst, and therefore it is always refreshing to go there. Maybe this habit of cour-tesy is a survival of the fierce resistance which Hawkhurst, along with Goudhurst, has been used to put up against the intrusions of democratic control, in the form of excise duties and customs levies. Most of the old houses in the neighbour-hood have underground cellars and tunnels, formerly used by their owners to further the flourishing business of smuggling. The little town maintained an illegal army of some two hundred men to run and to protect the trade. Light carts, drawn by dogs, were specially built for the night flittings between Hawkhurst and Rye, where the kegs of liquor and bales of silk and lace were brought in. The inde-pendence of outlook which that dangerous trade fostered has become a parochial habit, and I feel that it survives to-day, betraying itself in an odd gesture, a phrase, a gleam of the eye, in one's dealings with the present natives of this attrac-tive place. One has only to mention anything to do with the Government to see a faint smirk pass over the face of the native, as over the face of a cat who has stolen the cream. The most likely place to observe this psychological inheri-tance is the post office. I have stood here quietly watching, to distinguish the true native from the visitor or the resident from outside. The two latter behave in the normal way, with that impatient resignation which we all adopt in post offices. But the deep-rooted Hawkhurst man, woman, or child enters the post office as though it is enemy territory. A certain watchful insolence colours their voices as they ask for a stamp or the old-age pension. I almost imagine that I see their dull modern clothes bulging where a muzzle-loading pistol is hidden, as a matter of old habit.

The Germans, haters of individuality, made a special effort to destroy Hawkhurst during the war. Out of a thousand houses scheduled in the parish, eight hundred were damaged, and a direct hit from a doodle-bomb practically destroyed the old church in the more ancient part of the village on the further hill nearest the county boundary, the part known as the Moor. Why the bombs could not have left this noble old church, and taken the Victorian pseudo-Gothic one at Highgate, only the god of Philistines knows. That god was a hard-working one during the war, for he seemed to protect all his monuments in our ancient towns and countryside, and to divert the bombs as often as possible to the beautiful and historical buildings by which our country is recognizable.

We leave Hawkhurst, still licking its wounds, with mounds of broken glass and plaster piled up on the roadsides by the local builders, who are working, months after the end of the war, to repair the damage done to these old smugglers' homes. Riding off along the ridge, with the great view southwest over Sussex before us, we take up once more our purpose of following the boundary down to the sea. The first village that we come to suggests by its name that this purpose is nearly accomplished—Sandhurst. This place, a pre-Norman settlement, is clustered around four roads, and characterized by many weather-boarded cottages, and a charming little Nonconformist chapel (I should think it must be late Georgian) set among trees by the roadside. Off the village, along the Benenden road, is an exquisite example of Tudor architecture, called the Mill House. But all these domestic features, which in another village along the Weald would hold our attention, are dwarfed by the excitement which grips us. For we have come to a complete change in the nature of the countryside. The heavy woods, the lushness which was so particularly marked at Hawkhurst, suddenly stop. The high ridge drops southward, and before us we see a great expanse of flat meadow and marshland, ribbed by gleams of silver where a network of streams and dykes drains into the river eastward and south to Rye and the open sea. We have come to Romney Marsh, and that is a continent unto itself.

Bayham Abbey
Finchcocks

CHAPTER X

THE CONTINENT OF THE MARSHES

CONTINENT is the right word. Romney Marsh, which includes Walland Marsh, although part of Kent geographically, is a land unto itself with a law unto itself. Wherever one drops down to it, from Newenden (as we shall enter now), from Appledore, from Bilsington, Bonnington, or West Hythe, the effect is the same. The intruder begins to fidget in his pocket, groping for his passport, while trying nervously to recollect whether or not he was foresighted enough to get it visaed for this remote, slightly hostile country.

Why this large triangle of land, pushing its apex out into the sea, should have so self-contained a character it is impossible to say. Maybe it is due to the fact that the inhabitants have been working at frantic speed for the last two thousand years building dykes of brushwood and rock, and cutting their way through choking intrusions of sand and shingle in strangled riverbeds. This preoccupation has kept them facing one way—seaward, with their backs to the rest of the land and the community of the Weald. It has made them, perhaps, somewhat impatient of interruption. Another reason may be that for a great while, all through the Middle Ages and up to the time of the dissolution of the monasteries, the Marsh was Church property, mostly belonging to the See of Canterbury, and was governed according to ecclesiastical law. When, later, this handful of fertile and well-watered hundreds passed into lay hands, the great necessity still remained : the sea *must* be kept under control. And for that purpose funds must be available. The most outstanding fact in the economic history of the Marsh is its principal tax, the "wall-scot," charged on the owners protected by the dyking and draining, a craft in which the marshfolk were the most expert in Europe.

That labour also gives the key to the historical beginnings

Scotney Castle
St. Mary's Church, Stone, and its Mithraic Altar

of life in the Marsh, which extends, one-twentieth part of the county, from Rye to Hythe west to east, and from Dungeness to Tenterden and Aldington from the sea northwards. Belgic tribes, in prehistoric times, settled here. They were already skilled in embanking, from the necessity of their lives in the Low Countries, and by the time the Romans arrived these Celts had already begun the struggle against the vagaries of the tides and currents which play upon this shifting coastline. The Romans at once brought their engineering genius to work upon the problem, and threw a paved way (*stratum*) across the Marsh from Durovernum to Portus Lemanis (Canterbury to Lympne).

Meanwhile the River Rother (which we are now approaching in our attack upon the Marsh from Sandhurst) continued to writhe in its struggle against the sea and to the sea. All through the ages the conflict has been like that between a nursling and its rich-breasted but reluctant mother. The river has groped blindly, its mouth seeking like a baby's for the nipple, and always being half-denied. The frustration has led to strange and contorted processes of land and water. Nennius, in his ninth-century *Catalogue of British Wonders*, says: "The first marvel is the Limen Marsh [the old name for the Rother], for in it are 340 islands with men living on them. It is girt by 340 rocks, and in every rock is an eagle's nest, and 340 rivers flow into it, and there goes out of it unto the sea but one river, which is called the Limen."

The Saxons built a wall from Appledore to Rye, and called it the Rhee Wall (which means merely a watercourse). This work, some eighty feet wide, reclaimed 24,000 acres. It is probable that the Marsh, thus first made possible as a sound and profitable habitation, was named from a Saxon worthy, one Presbyter Romanus (a sort of local Prester John).

For a long time the Marsh was a separate kingdom, Merscwari. In the eighth century Offa, King of Mercia, invaded Kent, and granted Orgarswick (near Dymchurch), Agne (now in Old Romney), and Ruckinge to the Church. The Danes, in Alfred's time, came up the Rother, burning the monasteries and churches already established in the Marsh. Michael Drayton, in his *Polyolbion*, says:

Those Danish louts whom hunger starved at home,
Like wolves pursuing prey, about the world did roam :
And stemming the rude stream dividing us from France,
Into the spacious mouth of Rother fell by chance,
Which Lymen then was called.

Like most flat countries, this district was subject to the
tides of war as well as of water. King Harold stood at
Appledore before the Battle of Hastings; and throughout
the subsequent history of the Marsh its people have gone
about their daily life with their weapons near at hand; and a
firebrand too, for their knowledge of the dangers of the sea
has not made them squeamish about luring fellow mariners
to destruction by false fires. There are numerous records of
wrecking activities. One of the most picturesque of them was
made in the reign of Edward the Second, when the men of
the Marsh plundered a vessel named the *Blessed Mary of
Fonte Arabia*, wrecked off their treacherous coast while outward bound with a rich cargo for Gascony. What a picture
that conjures, with all its historical implications in the background ! What was that rich cargo for Gascony, and to whom
was it consigned? What would be the load on the return
journey; garlic, and red wines, and perhaps a learned
missionary from Rome, with the honey of scholarship and
subtle laws under his tongue?

The Marsh quickly became prosperous. In Domesday
Book mention is made of salt works, on ponds or pans,
lying along the coast, where the salt was evaporated and
collected for export from Romney, which became a thriving
port thick with traffic. In the archives of the Kent Archæological Society there is a vivid picture of Romney as "a
flourishing town possessing a good, sure, and commodious
harbour, where many vessels used to be at road; where Earl
Godwin and his sons entered and led away all the ships they
found in the port; where a part of the Norman Conqueror's
fleet were repulsed; where kings and princes rested in their
travels; where at the Norman Conquest a large roll of burgesses was to be found, with privileges since granted, as old
as if not older than existed in the City of London. As a proof
that this was not a thinly populated place, it is recorded

that in a crowd of people assembled in the town in the reign of Henry III one Lauretta le Pontier was trodden under foot and stifled to death."

But in front of Romney to-day stretches the great nose of Dungeness, a Slawkenbergius land that is ever growing larger, the shingle advancing out to sea at the rate of twenty feet each year. Romney's prosperity declined suddenly after a series of terrible gales over a period of years during 1238 to 1287. A Royal Charter in 1252, in the reign of Henry III, laid down certain embankment laws, and incidentally referred to "ancient and approved customs" by which Romney Marsh had been governed "time out of mind." While the Charter thus emphasized the antiquity of local practices, the laws it framed could not provide adequate protection against the malpractice of nature during those violent years, when Winchelsea, Broomhill, and many other places then near the sea were destroyed, and the estuary of the Rother was diverted from Romney through a nearer passage to the sea at Rye. This finished Romney as a port, and gradually the life there has dwindled, so that to-day the only way in which "one Lauretta le Pontier" could possibly be done to death would be by the trampling weight of boredom. Nothing remains of the Church's trade in wool. The only reminder of that huge export industry, which made England's wealth in the Middle Ages, is the present number of the famous Romney Marsh sheep that still graze over the Marsh. They are to be recognized by their white faces, wide heads level between the ears, and coal-black noses.

It is more difficult to recognize the human folk of the Marsh, for they have a technique of invisibility. I have never known such a social reticence. Certainly the flats are sparsely populated, and one would not expect to meet many people in these wide grazing areas; but here and there are cottages, huts, larger settlements that might almost be called farms, and occasionally they coagulate into hamlets and villages. But they appear all to be deserted. Do the natives go indoors and barricade themselves against the passing of a stranger? I suspect that is what happens, for seldom is one of them encountered face to face. I once met an old man standing by a bridge over the Rother, on the way to the Isle of Oxney.

I asked him if I were right for Stone-cum-Ebony, which I
knew from the map to be at the blunt head of the island, an
island from which the sea has long since receded, leaving it
surrounded by gently heaving waves of grass, and fleets of
sheep. The old marshman dropped his head somewhat, so
that the sunbleached brim of his felt hat hid his eyes. Then
he turned aside and spoke over his shoulder a few syllables
heavy with suspicion, "Cross the bridge." Nothing more
would he say. He thereupon became part of the bridge, a
weathered inanimate object of stone or timber, frozen into
an absolute inscrutability. That is practically the whole extent of my converse with the people of Romney Marsh. Yet
they are not always so latent. There are historical records
of their truculence. All through the troubled centuries they
have been at fisticuffs, and an occasional knifing, with the
visiting fisherfolk and mariners from East Anglia, the Humber, Picardy and Normandy. On one typical occasion a brawl
took place at Romney between the natives and a parcel of
Yarmouth boatmen. In the course of it a marshman was
killed. This led to proceedings by the Crown, and to the
hanging of the leader of the visiting team. Further, a perpetual fine was laid upon the community of Yarmouth, consisting of an annual payment of a number of barrels of
herrings to Windsor Castle. I like such royal gestures; they
have a fine acquisitive indignation about them. This incident,
an example of how *ex parte* justice works, may have led
to the folk-image about dragging a red herring across the
path.

It is odd, too, how a people so conspicuously, or perhaps
one should say inconspicuously, shy should have been famed
in the Middle Ages for their histrionic gifts. The Passion
Play, an annual event at Romney, was of national fame. All
over the Marsh the acting of miracle plays was popular. In
1463 the jurats of Romney, out of their common chest, paid
to Agnes Ford the sum of 6s 8d for the play of *The Inter-
lude of our Lord's Passion*. This surely must be one of the
earliest records of a woman dramatist in our country.

Much coming and going took place in the pursuit of this
folk-drama. Companies of players from other villages came
to the Marsh, from as far afield as Herne. That may not

seem to be far to-day; but one has to recollect that in those times the almost impenetrable forest of Anderida lay north of the Marsh, and that from Herne a company of players would have to cross it, and brave its dangers of man and beast, with the burden of their stage properties and their lives. And those stage properties were considerable. The Chamberlain's accounts for 1560 show how the plays were produced at Romney with some splendour. On the Whit-Tuesday of that year the large sum of £12 5s 6d was collected from the audience. The expenditure had been lavish. The deviser of the play received £4, and the Common Clerk wrote out the playbook on parchment, and the parts on fourteen quires of paper, for about £2 per play. From the jurats of Lydd, copes and vestments were bought for £9; from London came stuff for dresses costing £4 11s 5d, and for making the garments many pounds were charged. Special mention is made of John the Baptist's coat, the cotton coat of Judas Iscariot, and twelve sheepskins for "godhalls coats." Beards and wigs were hired for four "ban cryers" and a beard for the Fool. Three wainloads of bows; escutcheons costing 20s, dozens of goldskins, and sheets of goldfoil, pounds of glue, brimstone, red lead, red ochre, verdigris, rosset, florrey, and nails; a gross of points; ells of buckram, a paschal lamb, which was dressed; a shoe, set on the centurion's horse; a wayte, a drummer and minstrels"; all these were provided for four performances at Romney that year. What extraordinary sophistication is revealed when we begin to inquire into the details of life during those ancient times. The tendency is to view the past just as one looks at distant hills, with a false simplification. Seen along the vistas of time, our ancestors appear to us to be childlike and primitive, whereas in fact they are merely somewhat different from ourselves in habit and fashion. We are no subtler, and no more experienced in worldly wisdom and politics, because we now enforce our interests and opinions with the bombing-plane instead of the stake and the rack.

But that again may be a matter of opinion, and will not move us along our road from Sandhurst down to the entrance to the Marsh. In order to reach the Marsh after leaving Sandhurst and Newenden, we have to transgress somewhat into Sussex, crossing the Rother which is the boundary between the counties, just before going over the railway, at Northiam and Beckley station. It is a busy little spot here, with mills and warehouses picturesquely grouped. We turn off left along a by-lane, towards Peasmarsh, so that we may get back as quickly as possible into Kent, by recrossing the Rother over the bridge where I once addressed myself so unsuccessfully to the local spirit.

In front of us now lies the whole reach of the Isle of Oxney. It is a whale-shaped ridge that begins to rise a mile back from the river, with lovely falls of parkland and wood, relieved in its softness by timbered houses and farm buildings. To the right hand, surmounting the outward flow of the river toward the estuary, the ride mounts, to end abruptly, almost cliff-like, with a thick, rounded head. We are making for that head as soon as we reach the top of the ridge.

It is a magnificent scene, with a fine contrast of flats and heights. The river winds along the valley, turning sharply south at our right hand, toward Rye and the sea, thus creating a funnel-shaped gap through which we glimpse the levels of Walland Marsh. From our present low vantage they appear to ride higher than we are, like the sea seen from water-level. But now we climb the southern face of the isle, and reach Wittersham.

It is a sleepy village, standing 214 feet above the surrounding country. Hence it has wide views on all sides. The church is a landmark for marshfolk from miles around. It presides over the larger of the two parishes into which the isle is divided, the other being Stone-cum-Ebony, surely one of the most odd and picturesque names in England. The view southwest from here, across Rye, Winchelsea, and the further stretch of the Marsh to Fairlight behind Hastings, is one of constant variety because of the play of waters along the Rother below. In winter, when the floods are out, the whole of the valley is afloat, and the setting sun burnishes it and sets the landscape blazing. It is a memorable sight, a sort of Hallelujah Chorus in colour. They get the breath of that chorus too in winter, for the gales blow here from all sides like Old Fury himself.

The church is a twelfth-century foundation, with a tall,

cleanly designed Perpendicular tower on top of which once stood a beacon for carrying the news inland from warnings at Fairlight. The interior contains a beautiful little modern chapel to the memory of Alfred Lyttelton, one of the Souls, that group of æsthetic intellectuals who, at the end of the nineteenth century, tried in vain to stem the tide of squalid business men which was invading English political life.

This pleasing memorial is in ironic contrast to the hideous bathroom window which stands behind the altar. Two other pleasing items in the village are the row of old buildings which juts out into the roadway beside the church, thus creating a sort of miniature Booksellers' Row; and a fine old windmill which stands in the garden of the house where Forbes-Robertson, the Shakespearean actor, lived.

From here we can look northward to see the noble tower of Tenterden, which we shall look at more closely on our pryings into the interior villages of the county. For the moment, our way lies in the opposite direction, eastward to the head of the isle, rightly named Stone Head. That bare name, however, does no justice to the luxuriance of this little, inland promontory. One might be in Italy here, overlooking the Central Sea. Approaching Stone along the ridge, we pass one after another of ancient houses, each with an idiosyncrasy of structure that makes it unique and memorable. One in particular, called the Stocks, that stands at the cross-roads before we begin to drop over the nose of the promontory, through Stone down to the Marsh, is a superb example of Early English domestic architecture. From there we plunge into the heart of the luxuriance, under great oaks and nut trees. This little gem of Italian temper set in England is well described by the late A. G. Bradley in his book, *An Old Gate of England* :

"It traverses a deep cut, picturesquely embowered in copses of hazel and oak which are radiant at the first bursting of their leaves in spring in a spangled carpet of anemones, primroses and bluebells. In no country known to me do primroses riot with greater luxuriance, or with richer colouring than in this network of deep and sheltered lanes that all about here connect the high roads and are as hospitable to spring flowers as the more famous ones of Devon. Being of more generous breadth and often bordered by high copsy slopes, they at any rate display their wares to much greater advantage than the rigid wall-like west country banks."

The road curves down corkscrew-wise, and on its first bend, under a wilderness of green, we come upon Stone Church, beside which stands one of the oldest dwellings in the county. It leans at an angle, under the weight of heavy, frowning eaves, and the side nearest the church seems about to sink into the ground. The two relics of human passion— the home and the faith—there they stand side by side, pathetic in age, defiant still by their very position at the head of the isle, of the never-ceasing assault of nature. The sense of obstinate clinging to an obsolete dignity is increased as we walk up the little churchyard cut out of the cliff, and enter the church. It smells of damp, and down the stones of the pillars stand beads of water, which are set like jewels on tiny cushions of mildew. I know of no smell more evocative of the passage of time, and of the brevity of our human story. Perhaps it was this smell that touched the nostrils of Shakespeare, when, at the end of his pretty comedy of *Twelfth Night*, he dropped the curtain and made Feste the clown sing that heart-breaking little song about "The rain it raineth every day."

Such was my mood as I explored the small church at Stone. This sense of things vanished was accentuated by a startling discovery which I made of an object standing in the dim light of the interior of the tower. It was an ancient, pre-Christian altar, a survival through the Romans, who set it up on this headland in the second century A.D., of the Persian worship of Mithra, that lighter cult of the sacred Bull, that terrible worship with its phallic emphasis that preceded the more spiritual sanctification of the Ram, Aries, later to be made the symbol, through the Lamb, of the Christian faith. This altar, hacked and battered, still has a bull carved on its side. In the indentation, the saucer shape, on its top, some discoloration suggests that it was a sacrificial altar. What a significant piece to find in this grim old Christian church! It served to link up, ominously, in my imagination, the darker background of our history upon which the light of Greek thought began to play as Christianity took up the purer and more ethical aspects of the esoterics of the classical world of the Mediterranean, and infused into them the novel idea of the value of the individual soul, and of its responsibilities.

In all places where nature is dominant because of some outstanding characteristic of weather or land formation, the institutions of the humans settled there are always coloured decisively by that feature. So it is on Romney Marsh. Though Christianity spread over the Marsh at an early stage in our history, and though the Church had temporal sovereignty over the Marsh for so long; the sea winds, the sands, the shifting ground and subtle waters, it is these, rather than the gentle admonitions of the Gospels, that have moulded both the worship and the worshippers of the people of the Marsh. The dripping piers in that little church, and the minatory altar-piece carved with the labyrinthine sign of the Bull, struck me at once as being the right symbols of the religion of the marshmen, these shepherds, wreckers, and dealers in contraband.

Dropping down at last from Stone to the Marsh proper, we meet the Royal Military Canal, which was made during the invasion scare when we were at war with Napoleon. Had we made this descent in Roman times we should have come to the sea, which is now over ten miles away, at the tip of Dungeness, though only six if we cut due south to the Camber Sands. But I advise the fastidious person to avoid Camber Sands, which are now little more than a car park and a fairground, a dump for waste paper and empty bottles. It would be delightful to take boat up the canal to its terminus at Hythe; but disuse (indeed, I believe that it was never used, being superseded immediately after its construction, when the railways were built) has choked its course, and I doubt if a boat could get through. Its route lies just under the hills that frame the Marsh, along past Appledore, Kenardington, Warehorne, Ruckinge, Bonnington, and Lympne. There is a road alongside the canal, good for walkers and bad for anything on wheels. But it is enchanting to the eye! The hills on the left hand, the distant view forward, with the south-eastern bend of the Downs on their way to Folkestone, showing the great break at the Ashford gap, the groups of large trees in contrast with the horizontal items of the Marsh (gates, flood-rails, stretches of water and pasture), all combine to offer a paradise to the water-colourist and the etcher.

Appledore is really the gateway out of the Marsh. It stands on the first rise, with Shirley Moor behind it, as a step before the next rise to Tenterden and a complete change of character in the countryside. For Tenterden belongs to the Weald, along with Cranbrook and Goudhurst, although in the past it had its tiny port at Small Hythe, three miles away, which once stood in the backwaters round the north of the Isle of Oxney. It is incredible to think that such conditions obtained within historical times.

Although Appledore is really on the Marsh, in character it is one with Tenterden and the other rich villages of the medieval weavers. It has a broad high street like Tenterden, and many perfect examples of half-timbered houses and shops. Go into the baker's shop and look at the carving on the central beam. The position of Appledore at the head of the northern channel round the isle made it an important place in those days when the water reached it. The Danes sailed up to it from Boulogne in the year A.D. 893 with two hundred and fifty ships, and found it already fortified with a Saxon castle. They occupied the town until King Alfred with his golden tongue persuaded them, but only temporarily, out of it a year later.

A guide-book, intent on doing its duty, would now direct you from Appledore swiftly across the Marsh in a south-easterly direction to New Romney and thence to Dymchurch; less than half an hour's run in a car. But to hurry in that way would be to lose all the character of Romney Marsh. One needs to walk or cycle across, and round and about within it. Only gradually does its unique quality begin to seep into the wanderer's consciousness. I do not know how to define that quality. John Davidson, the late Victorian poet who died (by walking deliberately out to sea) in 1909, the same year as Swinburne, caught something of the spirit of the place in his poem called "In Romney Marsh," of which I will quote four stanzas:

As I went down to Dymchurch Wall
I heard the South sing o'er the land;
I saw the yellow sunlight fall
On knolls where Norman churches stand.

And ringing shrilly, taut and lithe,
Within the wind a core of sound,
The wire from Romney town to Hythe
Alone its airy journey wound. . . .

As I came up from Dymchurch Wall,
I saw above the Downs' low crest
The crimson brands of sunset fall,
Flicker and fade from out the west.

Night sank : like flakes of silver fire
The stars in one great shower came down;
Shrill blew the wind; and shrill the wire
Rang out from Hythe to Romney town.

That strange, arrogant man was once seen by a friend striding about, under a heavy frown of thought, on Victoria Station. When the friend stopped him, he looked round scornfully on the crowd and exclaimed, "I have discovered that I write for an audience of two only. They are Shakespeare and God!"

It needs some such spirit as that to appreciate fully the remote, self-contained nature of Romney Marsh, and that maybe is why Davidson wrote a poem to celebrate it. Like flew to like. Romney Marsh, like Davidson, shrinks away from the mob, turning unto itself and the ceaseless music, æolian harp music, that seems to hover above it in the air. The poem has remarked on that strain; but during the war the emphasis would have needed to be heightened, because of the thousands of additional wires that were hung, in a loose, untidy network, between Hythe and Rye by the Army, R.A.F., and Civil Defence. They made their music too, adding a more throaty strain to the shrill "ringing, taut and lithe" of the telegraph wires.

There is, however, an even more subtle. wind-music in the Marsh. It comes from the ground when a smart breeze is leaping over Fairlight, and coming to ground, because it is fresh and cold, over the warmer Marsh. It stoops and runs its fingers through the hairy grasses and weeds, and the result is a steady siffling, sighing rustle, rather like the hum of a swarm of gnats, or a dynamo, with the rhythmic little flick aside that both occasionally give. It is a music that creeps into the mind and gradually hypnotizes it into an indifference to all else in the world. The hills recede, time stands still, and the listener, like John Davidson, finds himself alone "with God and Shakespeare," no other personalities being sufficiently elemental, and at the same time subtle, to bear company in this light-haunted, air-haunted country, through which the water creeps snakelike to the sea, tended by a myriad beetles, sea and land birds, butterflies, and a vast choir of wild flowers and grasses singing an unceasing insect-song; a choir only ankle-high, but faithful and finally dominant over all things foreign to the Marsh.

It is not really easy for the stranger to make close contact with these intimate aspects of the Marsh, for the surface is often treacherous with bogland, and mostly below road-level. But the visitor can spend a few hours in solitude, or with that one person who can make solitude even more inviolate, sitting on one of the banks sloping down from the road to the land-level, choosing the sun-side or the wind-side. That session will be a mystical experience !

Having thereby imbibed at least a little of the spirit of the Marsh, he can then go on down the cape to Lydd, a queer, remote village lying just behind Dungeness. With Broomhill it was an auxiliary to the Cinque Port of Romney. All of the Cinque Ports had such subsidiary ports to assist them to cope with the excess of trade. As we approach Lydd across the most desolate and houseless part of the Marsh, we have a sense of rising gradually toward the sea. This is odd, but correct, for in fact the Marsh drops from the seafront and is higher there than at Appledore. Lydd is seen from afar off as a massive church tower sticking out of a mound of green foliage. That mound is a wind-barrier of elms. By making one's way to this oasis that on a hot day seems to stand mirage-high, shimmering in the light, one realizes that the word "marsh" is a misnomer, a survivor from fifteen hundred years ago when the district first began to dry out through man's reclamation. The way is over a skein of dykes that parcel up the patches of grassland where the sheep in thousands drift about in a year-long somnambulence. Little bridges, trampled into hoof-pocked mud, join one to the other of these squares. Occasionally a willow or a thorn tree stands in the level, with an old crow huddled there for a rest, while listening cynically to the enthusiasm of hundreds of larks shouting and wasting their energy up in the blue.

So we come at last to Lydd, to find the distant mirage real enough. It is a large village, with one or two fine old houses, notably the manor house of Westbrooke, a secondary seat of the Dering family. The embattled tower of the church stands 132 feet high, and the periods of the church pass through Norman to Perpendicular, though in the north-west corner of the nave there are the outlines of three arches that were most probably Saxon, and suggest an earlier building on the site. The High Street runs down to the shingle now, and looks to the sea across a waste of ground given over to artillery practice. The village lost its function, along with its parent port of Romney, when the Rother suddenly changed its course after the great storm of 1287, which choked the mouth of the river, causing the stream to turn right-hand at Appledore and to flow down to Rye. For five centuries previous to this, however, Lydd (called Hilda by the Saxons) prospered as a port and as a military base. The little town, in its first Charter granted by Edward I, was given all the privileges of a Cinque Port (it then faced Romney across the estuary of the Rother), and it shared in a substantial revenue from the complicated medieval taxes, among them being that on the fish marketed in the two towns. I like Hasted's description of its thousand inhabitants : "some few in a better situation in life but the generality of them are such as follow a contraband trade with France, or fishermen who have cabins on the shore with a common dining-room, where they spend the summer months."

To push on from the village to the point of Dungeness is indeed to push hard, for the going is over loose shingle. The scene grows more tarry and ropy, more like old Peggotty and his upturned boat. Huts, fishermen's sheds, boathouses, a few bare-looking inns, a lifeboat station, and a lighthouse; these are the features of this no-man's-land that has crept up out of the sea since the Middle Ages. The natives often move about with bits of board tied to their feet, like snowshoes, in order to ease their passage over the shingle. They are called "backstays" or "baxters." Everything looks so flat, so shallow, that it is a surprise to find, when reaching the sea, that it is blue and deep quite near shore. Vessels of some size can approach and anchor there, sheltering from storms.

It is unreal indeed to stand in this strange no-man's-land, watching the piled-up waters of the sea, deep and powerful and menacing, as it carries to and fro a constant traffic of ships, swiftly and deftly; ships of all sizes, ships of all shapes, from the sailing wherry to the ocean liner. It is like being set, miraculously, as the Jews were in their crossing of the Red Sea, on the scoured bed of the Channel, waiting for the awful moment when the waters shall break their unnatural tension and come tumbling back, meeting in one colossal buffet and swirl hundreds of feet above one's head. In this hollow land that sense of tension is always present, for the puny human being who ventures here cannot realize that it is the land which is gaining on the water, and that the ocean-threat is merely the distant growl of a receding storm, an echo from millions of years ago. I have never been on the Dungeness when a gale is blowing; but I imagine what it must be like. There can be no signs of recession then! The wind and the walls of water must surely come raging in. making the shingle shriek in terror. How the few little human erections survive it I cannot understand; the post office, the Dutch Consul's house, the untidy fishing-sheds, and even the lighthouse with its massive bastions of concrete.

The lighthouse is about a hundred years old, and is manned by four keepers, two of whom are always on duty, responsible for the two lights and for the fog-signal horn which is housed nearby.

Growing in the loose shingle are all manner of sea-plants, though I have not seen samphire here, that herb of St Peter which makes a good pickle. Maybe it has always been gathered the day before! But on one visit I saw a charming juxtaposition—a hare sitting up beside a great sea-thistle, preening himself and gazing out to sea. The queer plant, with its glaucous leaves, the green salted down to grey, and the flower-head a touch of faded royalty; the squatting hare slightly grotesque with his long Little Tich feet sticking out in front of him, the wind ruffling his white belly and the tiny flames of fiery fur along his back—this picture enraptured me, and I lay on my stomach, watching, while the heavens wheeled over me, and the shadowy traffic of ships drummed past; lay watching in that timeless enchantment. I could see the little drawn mouth; the smart whiskers that moved from time to time in an oarlike motion; the unsuspecting eye, a huge, milky moon so luminous that I knew, if I might dare to creep nearer, I should see the lighthouse reflected in it. What was that unaccountable creature, no longer maddened with spring, contemplating as he gazed out to sea? Was there some thought of suicide in his shallow mind, such as the lemmings propose when they gather in thousands on the coast of Norway and are stirred by primeval longings to visit the lost Atlantis?

The spell was broken by the rumble of a Dungeness cart. A tremor shook the squatting animal, he fell to his feet, loped through two or three ungainly strides, and was gone, leaving the thistle to face the sea alone. These carts have wheels that replace the usual felloe by broad ones over a foot wide, so that they look like paddle-boats floundering about over the loose surface of the ness. These carts play a great part in the lives of the few inhabitants. They clack their way along the wooden paths (made of railway sleepers) between the houses and sheds, carrying fishing gear, soil for the gardens (brought by the railway trucks that take away ballast), seaweed, and other odds and ends of marine commerce. I cannot imagine how these people make a living; but they appear to do so, and to thrive sufficiently to make that life attractive. They dig into the shingle and find delicious fresh water. That is miraculous enough, and maybe it is a symbol of other vouchsafements by which their habits are enriched. I should not be surprised if they have a technique for extracting honey from the sea. Where does that fresh water come from, since Lydd has the lowest rainfall in England?

Fairfield Church, Romney Marsh
Dungeness

Wildfowl of all sorts inhabit Dungeness. It was once a breeding-place for herons, in the days when an ancient holly copse, called the Holme, was more prosperous than it is now. But herons still come singly to bask along the water-edge, their vanity urging them always to choose a spot where there is a mirror of wet sand or a pool where they may contemplate themselves, standing with sunken head and neck, gazing smugly down their beaks. It is a grand sight to watch a heron take off from this static state of self-congratulation, for all is suddenly quick, fluid, and effortless. Down comes the second leg, hitherto tucked up, the wings open and shut, as though being tested, then they begin to beat, and the whole cargo of vanity is in the air, gliding along above the water, increasing pace and height, streaming along from beak-point to tail-tip, a grey and opal vessel of gracefulness and power.

Have I said enough, in this mere piece of impressionism, to bring to the reader something of the peculiar nature of the Marsh, and of the head of Dungeness in particular? I do not know how else to do so, except by throwing time to the winds, and settling down to write a book by the microscopic method, borrowing the genius of W. H. Hudson, and the over-sensitive fervour of Richard Jefferies. Still half-hypnotized by level things, the eye-fixing little parallels of wavelets and sand ripples, of sea-grass bent horizontal, of natives lying full-length under the shelter of longboats, of smoke from "salt-caked smoke-stacks" making a smudged perspective line along the Channel mid-distance; still under this spell I turn and look inland across the whole depth of the Marsh, to the rising ground of Appledore and the prow of the Isle of Oxney. On my left hand are the ramparts of Rye, on my right the turn of the Downs to form the cliffs of Folkestone and Dover at Shakespeare Cliff. Beyond that high ground is the heart of Kent, a rich and lovely region that from this fantastic water-level seems utterly remote. The only factor that unites the two is a legend; a legend and a piece of tainted history; the tale of the smugglers and their courageous crimes, their traffic under hooded lanterns. Such were the guilty paths that once united marsh and upland interior. Now it is ended, this clandestine industry, and the separation

Kingsnorth Gardens, Folkestone
Dover Castle

between the two parts, the two *natures*, of the county is complete. But I forget one bond that still remains. It is the annual trek of the sheep from the Marsh to the fruit orchards inland. Every year a large number of them are moved off the Marsh so that its pasture shall not be too closely consumed; and the precaution benefits the cherry and apple orchards of the Weald and the Maidstone Ridge, because the sheep-droppings fertilize the fruit trees.

Now, having tasted Dungeness, let us make our way up the eastern beach to New Romney, the first of the coastal towns along the Channel.

CHAPTER XI

BEATING UP THE STRAITS

COMING from Lydd to New Romney, we have crossed a fertile stretch of ground that was once the open estuary of the River Rother. The first thing that strikes one after leaving the bewildering economic aspect of the wastes around Lydd is the fat and ample evidence of agriculture in which Old and New Romney stand. Here again is a country of yeomen, squires, burgesses, among their accretions of substance through the centuries, in the form of orchards, ripe fields, farmhouses, and manors. We are back too among trees; ash, willow, thorn, and elm, whose green bosoms and shadowy skirts bring again a maternal quality to the scene. Here once more is a true mother-country, deep in kindness.

The character of Old Romney church adds to that sense of fullness. The hamlet lies back from the sea, along the road running north-west up to Appledore, and we may explore up here before looking at New Romney. Old and New are dubious epithets, coined vaguely around the time when the great storms in the thirteenth century changed so much of the geography and therefore the economics and social habits of the Marsh villages. New Romney is very old, like New College, Oxford! There stand the two villages to-day, like almswomen sitting in the sun, and it would be quite impossible to say which of the venerable sisters is the elder.

They sit in the sun against the Rhee Wall, the first of the dykes built towards the reclamation and preservation of the Marsh. "Rhee" is an ancient word, probably Celtic, which suggests that the wall, and the channel which drained the waters held by the wall in front of Appledore, was an engineering work earlier even than Roman. The Belgics who came over and settled here before the Romans were experts in such work, owing to the necessities of their life in the Lowlands. Rhee, or Rye, means water, and it crops up plentifully in our place names. I say it is probably Celtic, but it appears to have a widespread etymological root. The River Rhine, by show-

ing a Teutonic association of the name, does not confound
the theory of a Celtic origin. Rather it hints at pre-Gothic
settlements of Celts on the mainland of Europe before they
reached Britain. Another inspiring speculation about the
origin of the word is to recall that the Greeks named the
mother of Zeus, father of the Heavens, Rhea, which comes
from *rheo*—anything flowing. Rhea was the goddess of ferti-
lity, the water-deity who brought saving moisture to the earth.
The word "rheum," from which comes rheumatism, has the
same origin. All this is a fascinating little channel of etymological research, for it shows so vividly how words are crys-
tallizations of experience, embalmments of our past history,
sometimes holding within a syllable the closely packed record
of thousands of years. Words are thus indeed magic, as the
ancients believed, and their power to sway individuals and
whole peoples comes from this fact, that they contain so much
in so small a reservoir.

So this Rhee, or Water Wall, ran along the line now
followed by the road between Romney and Appledore for
some six miles, holding back the sea from forty thousand
acres of land which is now among the finest cornland in the
world. Cobbett remarked in his *Rural Rides* that the whole
of North America had no place where such rich and nutri-
tious wheat could be grown as in Romney Marsh. In Saxon
times this land was already a fat prize for marauders, for the
Saxon Chronicle tells us that in A.D. 796 the King of Mercia
sailed down the North Sea and through the Straits with his
longboats and entered the mouth of the Rother, which was
then the furtherance of the channel draining the reclaimed
land. He laid waste all around there. The same thing happened in A.D. 838 and 893, when successive waves of Danish
pirates (or as we should call them now, colonizers) sailed
right up the Rother to Appledore, and settled there.

The study of the fluctuations of these various waterways,
all dominated by the sea from without and the Rother from
within (and the wrestling match between the two), is a confusing one, because it is like watching the behaviour of a living
creature whose next movement is unpredictable. The give
and take between land and water determined the whole
economic, social, and legal forms of the communities that

peopled the Marsh. A society whose daily existence is threatened from hour to hour must necessarily have some form of government on the spot, who should be capable of quick decisions and the enforcement of those decisions. Thus it is that Romney Marsh stands unique in this country. The government of that part of the Marsh still holds its sessions in Dymchurch, in the New Hall (a name which time once more has made a misnomer). This government, known as the Lords of the Level of Romney Marsh, rules over the district between the sea and the Military Canal from south to north, and Hythe and Appledore from east to west. The other Levels of Walland (west of the Rhee Wall) and Denge (between Lydd and the lighthouse) are administered by a Crown Commission.

The Lords of the Level maintain a court consisting of a bailiff and jurats whose authority is constitutional and ancient, as well as being proved by numerous Royal Charters from time to time as disputes with the Crown have arisen. Practically its whole surviving function is the maintenance of the fight against the sea. For this purpose its powers are unusually great. It levies a tax throughout the area of its jurisdiction, and in order to collect this tax it takes precedence even before the Official Receiver in Bankruptcy. It can also take sand and soil at will from any landowner within the area, for the repair of the sea-wall. Such is the government of this miniature northern Campagna, which remains a pocket of ancient customs, capable perhaps of promoting a course of study comparable to that begun by Frazer in the Alban Hills of the true Campagna, work which resulted in *The Golden Bough*. But a similar research in Romney Marsh would have to begin with some occult recollections of the demigoddess Thetis, rather than Diana, because of the part played by the sea in the customs and superstitions of the natives of the Marsh.

Further up the road from Old Romney we come to Snargate, where a great manipulator of superstitions once lived as a vicar, before removing to London to be a Canon of St Paul's Cathedral. Richard Barham was a Man of Kent, being born in Canterbury in 1788, and inheriting the small manor of Tappington Everard from his father. He was a scholarly antiquarian, and the expertly rhymed verses which made him famous as "Thomas Ingoldsby" were the efflorescence of that scholarship.

Returning on our tracks along the Wall we reach New Romney, after a look into Old Romney church to see the baroque square pews and the double-decker pulpit, of opulent woodwork that symbolizes the fat countryside around. At last the noble tower of New Romney church, which has been looming up over the flats since we started out from Dungeness, begins to draw near. We are in the most picturesque of the Cinque Ports. Romney was one of the original five ports (the others being Hastings, Hythe, Dover, and Sandwich) which by their number gave the name to this old corporation of local naval strength set up as the first essay toward a national defence machinery against the risks of invasion from foreign enemies. These five towns, to which from time to time others such as Rye and Winchelsea, Deal and Reculver were added, undertook to provide a fleet of armed ships to patrol the Straits. In return for this the Crown gave the Corporation considerable powers of self-government. A citation of those powers makes picturesque reading to-day, and here again may be found a museum of old English institutions and customs. It is charming to hear, for instance, of the jurats of these ports having the right of sac and soc, tol and team, blodwit and fledwit, pillory and tumbril, infangentheof and outfangentheof, mundbryce, waives and strays, flotsam, jetsam, and ligan, amongst other juridical and legislative rights. A definition of those quaintly named rights may be found by the reader who is sufficiently curious in the matter. I will not give it here, for we are lingering already overlong on the Marsh, and are in danger of an attack of rheumatism in our feet. The Cinque Ports' organization of a coastal defence persisted until the Tudor kings saw its weakness and its dangers, and substituted a national machinery—the Royal Navy. But the Lord Warden of the Cinque Ports still is an office that is ceremoniously filled, and the holder of it is concurrently Governor of Dover Castle, and until 1903 had another official residence at Walmer Castle.

New Romney gives the effect of standing on a corner, as

indeed it does. For a look at the map will show how the road
in from Appledore, across the middle of the Marsh, turns
up abruptly north-eastward along the flat coast to Dymchurch and Hythe. This part of the journey is the longest
run through the Marsh, but it is somewhat less characteristic
owing to the fact that the road runs along the seashore and
thus shares qualities held by many other roads along flat
beaches on the English coast. Unfortunately, one of those
shared qualities is the disease of bungaloid growths. All sorts
of shacks and squalid erections disfigure this coast road. It is
a strange thing that whenever human beings come within
sight of the sea they lose all sense of personal decency and
become déshabillé, both domestically and in their clothing.
But outraged architects and town planners have already said
enough about that without my weighing in. Nevertheless, I
have always found it a matter for wonder that most of the
seaside holiday resort towns in England represent philistinism
rampant, with every form of shoddy, mass-produced, and
banal amusement, flaunting itself with depraved and shameless gestures before the face of nature, and all that is dignified and graceful in our national character. Maybe this
degeneration takes place wherever excessive numbers make
discretion and good taste impossible, for our inland beauty
spots too are mostly made horrible by the same depravity—
Belsens of pleasure instead of cruelty; and there may be no
way of curing the disease so long as mob psychology—what
one might call in Shakespeare's words the mentality of "the
sweaty nightcap"—lags so far behind the growth of individual consciousness.

New Romney stands almost unspoilable on this coast road,
with its noble church and a cluster of old buildings round it,
survivors of a little town that was a flourishing port when
the Normans came to England. It furnished a number of
ships to augment King Harold's fleet that withdrew into the
Thames and never fought (due probably to William's Fifth
Column strategy). The administrative Brotherhood of the
Cinque Ports used often to meet here during the years before
the Rother changed its course and robbed the townlet of all
importance. Unlike Richborough and Dover, New Romney
has given passage to no famous characters in our history.

Once Thomas à Becket tried to escape to the Continent from there, during the course of his long-drawn-out disputes with the Crown on behalf of his Roman master. But adverse winds drove him back, and he returned fatalistically to his palace at Canterbury, to await whatever might be the outcome of other, political storms. The little town's chief concern seems to have been to maintain its fishing rights and its prerogatives within the Corporation, as opposed to the elbowings of the representatives from Yarmouth who sat as visitors to protect the seasonal activities of the Norfolk fishermen who came down to the Kent coast. The rivalry was edgy, and often resulted in street fights, to be followed by displays of outraged dignity on the Bench. There remains in the town a long curved horn of brass which used to be blown at the opening of the herring fairs, both at Romney and at Yarmouth.

The road out of Romney passes a golf course running alongside the sea, in a triangle that closes to an apex where the Dymchurch Wall begins. This wall is the principal barrier that forms the central frontier against the sea. It is three miles long, and now consists of massive concrete cast in a concave form twenty feet high, with a bonework of outriding groynes to break the force of the waves at this most exposed part of the coast. During the making of it, remains of the earlier Roman dyke were found. As it stands to-day, the wall cuts off the sea from the vision of the traveller along the Hythe road. During the war it formed the basis of formidable fortifications to protect a vulnerable area forbidden for five years to the general public. Strong-points and heavy-gun emplacements punctuated every few hundred yards. The wall, thus decorated, gave the effect when seen from below of being the barricade of a closely besieged fortress. Indeed, it was so, especially during those uneasy years of 1940–2.

There is not much to be said for Dymchurch to-day. It is still the seat of the government of the Marsh; but its historical interest is sadly overlaid by the fact that the stretch of sands beginning here have attracted so many holiday-makers that the familiar bungalow-disease has fastened like a tumour on the village and distorted its earlier form and character.

So we carry on to Lympne, the old Roman Portus

Limenus. How this little village has come by its confusing way of spelling its name I don't know. Perhaps the device was an ingenious effort by an early resident who hoped to make the public too shame-faced to attempt to pronounce the name of the place, and thus to shun it as a holiday-camp. Approaching the village, we realize that we are at last reaching the edge of the Marsh. Before us rises a bastion of what once were sea-cliffs similar to those of Folkestone and Dover. Now they run inland, and are covered with woods, while below them runs the Military Canal. Lympne stands on the now green-carpeted slope, with the tumbled remains of a Roman fortress scattered over an area of some ten acres. Excavations have brought to light many coins and funereal inscriptions, the latter mostly personal ones, inscribed with the names of soldiers and their wives stationed in this northern outpost of the Roman Empire, saddened by their fate at having to live and die in a provincial military head-quarters.

All this stretch of hillside, rising suddenly from the Marsh, is nostalgically beautiful. It is surely the sunniest spot in England, and in consequence has a subtropical quality. It is not surprising that the Romans settled in the district like a swarm of bees on a southern wall. It must have been a little Italy for them, a solace in exile. The road connecting Lympne with Canterbury, known as Stone Street, is a Roman highway that in the heyday of the occupation was lined with handsome villas. In an earlier chapter I have already described the dimensions and appearances of such villas. They made a suburban landscape much more dignified, spacious, and massive than the pinchbeck congeries which disfigure our country roads, as signs-manual of the shoddy period of the first phase (already lasting over a century) of the Machine Age. It looks as though, by sheer evolutionary process, we are in for something more under control, more significant in design, as the machine is subjected and given resilience as a tool, comparable to the human hand. And this improvement will carry politics and economics along with it, and will not be a result of their influence.

The Roman remains on the hillside at Lympne have been given a Saxon name, Studfall Castle. That has not prevented them from being pillaged to provide stone to build the fortress erected at the brow of the hill in Henry V's time. This place is now part of a private dwelling, near the church which is supposed to be the chapel built by Archbishop Lanfranc, who came from Normandy with his bureaucratic master, and tempered somewhat the harsh Civil Service rule of that administrator with a touch of humanism.

Excavations made here in the middle of the nineteenth century revealed the foundations of a villa adjoining the fortress, and an altar to Neptune erected by Aufidus Pantera, a prefect of the fleet. Part of the walls of a building conjectured to be a barracks was also unearthed. The coins found, all of the third century, suggested that the station was flourishing round about the beginning of the fourth century, just before the Romans left England. The strength of the surviving stonework is remarkable. It consists of limestone in double courses, with occasional periods of Roman tiling.

Lovers of the romance spirit, the spirit that was the seed-bed of the songs of the French *trouvères*, and produced such apple-clean, April-clear legends as the story of Aucassin and Nicolette, will want to pay a visit to Westenhanger while they are so near, for it was here that the Fair Rosamond is said to have lived before she was removed to Woodstock and her little labyrinth of love. Rosamond Clifford was the daughter of an old Norman family named FitzPonce, and her beauty was fabulous. She seems to have been one of those flowers of humanity which from time to time emerge, a perfect harmony of body, mind, and soul. Henry the Second, a king of pious character and great ability, whose statesmanship was frustrated by an unlucky accident, devoted his life to Rosamond, whom he loved. When his Queen, Eleanor of Aquitaine, conspired against him with her sons in the rebellion of 1173, he openly acknowledged his fair mistress and imprisoned the queen. That is always a dangerous step to take. This flouting of convention ended in the death of Rosamond, some say by poison at the instigation of the queen. Another unconfirmed part of her story is that she had a son by the king, who afterwards became the Earl of Salisbury.

It is tempting to linger among the recollections of the mistresses of kings, for the English aspect of this inevitable relationship is clouded in reticence. Who knows much about this Fair Rosamond, for example, or the gentle Jane Shore, Edward the Fourth's lady? I have always had the ambition to create a tale about her name, in spite of the contumely with which Sir Thomas More mentioned her in his phrase : "I doubt not some shall think this woman too slight a thing to be written of and set among the remembrances of great matters." But was this contumely? Was it not rather a wistful desire to linger with her shade, a minority observer in the fields of history? How different these few women of the English courts appear to be from the dominant mistresses of the French monarchs !

So we leave Westenhanger, with its faded tapestry of a king's love, and come back to the coast road, and the flash of the sunlight on the southern waters of the Channel. All is life and movement again. We are leaving the lonely Marsh and are approaching a miniature Riviera. For I think that Folkestone has as much claim as any of the Cornish villages to call itself the English Riviera. We come first to Hythe, a quiet, pleasant little place, where the Military Canal begins. It lies under the approaching hills that now crowd down to the sea and shut off the Marsh, though there is a tongue of flat littoral running eastward through Sandgate to the sudden rise into Folkestone.

Both Hythe and Sandgate have a character of being hand-maidens to a fairer creature, though many people must prefer to stay in them for a summer holiday, rather than to face the crowds that in normal times of peace wander up and down the top promenade and the network of paths amongst the Leas of Folkestone. If I were a parent with a carload of children I should certainly choose one of these two villages down by the sea-edge, with no cliffs to negotiate every meal-time. And the canal is an ideal toy for youngsters. They can wander up and down it in rowing-boats or canoes and be in no danger of drowning. They can land at frequent intervals, and play at Redskins, or "Bevis," or become Amazon explorers working their way into the untrodden interior. And their parents can doze safely meanwhile in the shelter of a hawthorn tree.

As we approach the cliffside road into Folkestone, we see the hills looming across the narrow strip of flats that finally ceases at the foot of the climb into the town. Cæsar's Camp and Sugarloaf Hill stand just outside the town. They are turf-covered hillocks, the former showing the indentations of ancient military works, which historians are inclined to attribute not to Cæsar but to an English king a thousand years later. The two hills are steep-sided, and in their higher reaches have to be climbed on all-fours, and with the help of the sheep-runs which wind round them, giving a quaintly medieval aspect to their slopes. The view from their windy tops is magnificent, and it is tinctured with the smell of thyme. I recall now that it was on the northern shelter of Sugarloaf Hill that I slept out in the open air for the first time in my life. I must have been about seventeen years old, that age when the sky is filled with trumpeters and heralds, when every bush has its nightingale, and every flower its drop of ichor.

I left the town one golden evening in early September, with a friend who had been playing in an orchestra there. We took nothing with us, except raincoats, for the days had been intensely hot for a week past, and every evening the heat had come up out of the ground in great waves of luxury and indolence. It was a starry night, and a young moon was dropping down westward over the Marsh. Pastel shades, of opal, shell-green, and coral, smeared the sea. People were crowded on the Leas, lingering after the music. Beyond the town the world seemed to be deserted. We two were townsmen, unused to the solitude of night in the country. We climbed slowly, rich in friendship (as only the young can be), while the turf gave springily beneath our feet, dry and aromatic. As we rose, the warmth gradually dropped away. Chilly little fingers of air touched our cheeks, and tapped our knuckles. We reached the top of the hill, and stood watching the moon go down and disappear. Then our attention was attracted by a white procession of vapours creeping up the Channel. They came serpent-wise, writhing in their progress, and spreading like a ghost-tide a few feet above the surface of the sea. Their backs were sprinkled with star-dust, a phosphorescence like the gleam of mackerel. We looked, and we wondered—and we shivered. Somehow the warm summer perfume of thyme had vanished, and a wistful odour of burning wood and autumnal dampness had taken its place.

Far away we heard faint sounds of humanity coming from the town. Then the lights began to disappear, and the sounds died away. An enormous silence came down over the world, broken only by the chirping of crickets and the occasional sigh of air passing through the turf at our feet. The mist had grown thicker, and it now veiled the stars, so that we could no longer see the Milky Way. Even the larger stars and the planets were dimmed. We felt the backs of our hands and our cheeks damp. And we shivered again. Turning away from the sea, we groped round the side of the hill toward the north and inland. Here we stumbled upon a small hollow where the air lingered more warmly. Below us the darkness lay intense, and on exploring we found this to be due to the presence of a small clump of hawthorns. Gathering dead wood we lit a fire, which burned smokily and lit up the mist, so that we sat in a room of shining silk, like a chrysalis in its cocoon. We had brought a thermos of hot Bovril and some biscuits. Consuming this nourishment, we lay feet to the fire, trying to shrink ourselves into our raincoats. And there we froze, being afraid to build the fire larger lest it should grow beyond control. We dozed, and sometimes talked bravely, in half-whispers, our voices flickering with cold. When at last "out of night earth rolled her dewy sides," we collected our stiffened limbs, sorted them out and fitted them again into their sockets, standing up to greet the sunrise. That was the greatest and most welcome sunrise that I have known.

Did we catch colds or pneumonia? No, we went down into the town, to the fishing district by the harbour, and found a rough eating-house already open. At seven o'clock we were embracing a huge dish of eggs and bacon and washing it down with strong tea. And all the day we felt like sleepy gods who had fed on honeydew and drunk the milk of paradise.

I am inclined to think that it is impossible to be ill at Folkestone. The air is magical, and the spirit of the place is benevolent. The holiday-makers' part of the town, lying behind the Leas, is inoffensive enough, while the shops are distinctive. That general good humour which is a characteristic of the people of Kent is heightened at Folkestone into a positive kindness. This quality of whole communities is a most unaccountable thing. Why one town should be good and another evil is something outside the range of moral science and the measuring-rod of the psychologists. Folkestone is an entity, as complete as that of a charming woman. It has grace and beauty. The Leas, with the deep Undercliff, are a feature of Mediterranean grandeur. Here is certainly the finest marine parade in England, and probably in Europe. It is a mile and a half long, and the Undercliff rises from the sea to some 120 feet, richly covered with flowering shrubs and tamarisk, through which many little paths wind down, with occasional level platforms or gazebos, where the idler may rest on the up or downward climb and gaze out to sea, or along the great bay south-west toward Dungeness, or eastward to Shakespeare Cliff, across the front of the town and the Warren (that miniature wilderness) beyond.

It was from one of those platforms that I first saw the coast of France. That too I remember, like the night on the hills, as a landmark in my life. Already, at that early age, I had begun to look at Europe (through the covers of good books) as the great mother-presence to whom sooner or later I should have to return, as through the estrangements of several incarnations. History, the arts, languages, the mighty genius of France—these had begun to come upon me as tangible forces, I might almost say as personalities, as the mysterious entity of God comes upon the imagination of the religious mind. I had realized how Englishmen, for hundreds of years past, had gone for enlightenment across the Channel, to make the Grand Tour, or as wandering scholars, or to live amongst the artists of Paris or the literary self-exiles of Florence and Rome. I had learned how Milton, Shelley, and Browning had reacted to the riches of Italy. These new ideas, bookish contacts coming like fire upon the passion of boyhood, were burning behind my eyes when I looked out one summer day from a sheltered seat below the Leas at Folkestone, and saw on the horizon a faint line of smoky grey that broke suddenly into a streak of vivid white, to fade again to grey. It was the mainland of Europe! I remember that a complete suspension of all thought and feeling took place in my mind and heart. Here was something bigger that I could experience. I gazed, and gazed again, and grew angry because of my apparent coldness. It was the coldness of white heat. All my reading, all my longing and sense of exile, rushed together into this moment, as into a bottle-neck. The release came only gradually, over a period of years, as I went across to France and learned to love the reality even more than the anticipated dream-France. I can now see England as a part of that European whole, and the coming and going between island and mainland is an easy process smoothed by a wider recognition of local values and contributions. But that glimpse of France was first love in its most acute form, an agony and an ecstasy such as never come again after the mind's virginity has been broken by experience.

The oldest building in Folkestone is the parish church, St Eanswyth's. It stands at the cliff-top and cuts the front in two. The saint after whom it is named was the granddaughter of Ethelbert, the first king of England to be baptized as a Christian. Her father returned to the worship of his Teutonic ancestors, but Eanswyth turned again, and founded the first convent in England at Folkestone. The churchyard is charming, and the old town begins here, so that some picturesque Kentish red roofs can be seen as one wanders about among the gravestones. This old town drops down the cliffside to the harbour, where the fishing fleet lies under the shelter of the railway pier at which the cross-Channel boats from Boulogne meet the trains from London. Down here too all is very southern in character, including the smell of the sea and its traffic. As I write about it I long to go there again, for it is the nearest approach that England can make to the warmer, more serene life of the Mediterranean civilization. It is delightful to watch the fleet come in with its catch. Later, the fisherfolk hang out great slabs of dogfish to dry in the sun. They are known as "Folkestone beef." When they get to London they are known as cod or rock salmon!

The seven miles between Folkestone and Dover offers some of the most interesting coastal scenery in England, The Warren is a stretch of cliff-land which remains wild because it is always being tossed about by the onslaught of the sea, and the internal underminings of fresh-water springs in the chalk. From time to time the railway which carries the boat-trains on to Dover is blocked by landslides of chalk as the cliff crumbles one stage further. Fourteen different beds of Gault clay are revealed in the Warren, varying in colour from grey to a deep blue. Many fossils are to be found in these layers. At one end of the Warren, near the Martello tower (which was the first of these grotesque objects), some Roman remains were found in 1924. They consisted of pottery, coins of Augustus minted in London in A.D. 315, some tessellated floors, plunge baths, and drains.

The interior of the Warren is a perfect picnic-place, because in miniature it presents complete wildness. Savage outbreaks of subsoil, trees thrown into extravagant gestures, small ponds formed in cracks, luxuriant undergrowth of grasses, creepers, and wildflowers. The place abounds in orchids and butterflies, which flourish here under subtropical conditions. Not only the intimacy, but also the general view, is delightful, for to look along the Warren from the town entrance, observing its trees, broken ravines, and patches of velvet turf, and to see behind it the sea and the great curve of the cliff sheltering Dover—well, that is a picture that comes back in later years upon the heart, with "thoughts that do often lie too deep for tears."

What am I to say about Dover? Obviously the first thing to say is that it is the keyhole in the lock in the front door of England. But I am not original in saying that, for two centuries ago the Kentish historian Hasted called it "the lock and key of the Kingdom." Like most garrison towns it has an atmosphere of grim drabness, of kindly severity and philistinism; the outlook of the sergeant-major. Rows of working-class dwelling-boxes (they cannot fairly be called houses) lie about on the hills of the town like red caterpillars. There seems to be no centre of the town. It is just a huddle in the hollow behind the harbour. Or it might be looked upon as the litter that has gathered round the foot of the Castle

during the passing of a thousand years. That is the first impression one gets from this slightly morose citadel. But it is not the correct one. Beneath that slightly repellent exterior character is a unique and original quality which I find it difficult to define.

It is a sort of stoical kindness, to be found in many frontier folk, and those who live within the smell of danger. Dover suffered in the 1914–18 war, and it has suffered still more in the last one. The shells from the German guns ploughed great furrows through the town, and bombardment from the air, in various forms, was incessant throughout the war. The people of Dover became cave-dwellers, and were able to emerge only about a week before the final stages of our great drive across France into Germany itself. Experiences like that have a lasting effect upon the character of a community.

In addition to this stoicism, which has recently become a feature in the bombed peoples in other parts of the country, there is a consciousness of each generation in the town being only temporary. We all know that about ourselves; but in Dover the knowledge is accentuated by the fact that the town and its monuments represent so long and so evident a history, while against this background the two principal activities of the town, Army life and Continental transport, emphasize the comings and goings rather than the static habits of man.

One cannot enter a restaurant in the town without being aware of this almost uneasy contrast. The courtesy of the people there is the courtesy of travellers. It gives one a feeling of restlessness, and a cancelling out of identity. One suspects that these people of Dover hardly think it worth while to have names. They are anonymous men, anonymous women; people with a through ticket; people on a rollcall known by a number. And behind all this stands the Castle, the Roman pharos, the Priory, and even the legend of the house of the Knights Templars, to underline by a superb survival the fact that here has been,. and is still, an impersonal city

> In which there was obscurity and Fame—
> The Glory and the Nothing of a name.

Sandwich Toll Bridge

Those lines were written by Byron about Charles Churchill, the satirist who wrote the *Rosciad*, an imitation of Pope with a touch of the sonority of Dryden. Churchill died young, and deprived the eighteenth century of a talent that might have freed it earlier from much of its stiffness. He was buried in St Martin's church, Dover.

This rather withdrawn attitude of the people of Dover may remind us, too, that for a thousand years—no, probably two thousand years—the rest of mankind have been little more than birds of passage. Dover has lived in the corridor of history. At the time of the suppression of the monasteries by Henry the Eighth the prior of Dover Priory wrote to Thomas Cromwell, pleading against the arbitrary action of the King's Government. He referred to the fact that the Priory had an important function, as a place of lodgment for famous visitors from Europe. He reminded the Lord Chancellor of the cost of such entertainment, and how it impoverished the coffers of the Priory, "for the strangers resorting be such wasteful streyers that it is not possible to keep any good stuff long in good order, and many times and especially strangers embassadors have such noyous and hurtful fellows that have packed up table cloths, napkins, sheets, coverpanes, with such other things as they could get."

Thus Dover has learned to watch the passing world with some suspicion.

I spoke of the *legend* of the house of the Knights Templars. The house has vanished, and there is even some conjecture as to its site. Some people say it stood in a valley at Temple Ewell. John Stow in the sixteenth century, recording the craven act of King John when he surrendered the Crown to the Pope, said that "King John and Pandulph, with the Nobles of the Realm, came together at the house of the Knights of the Temple by the Towne of Dover." Lambarde, at about the same time as Stow, was more precise. "There standeth yet," he said, "upon the high cliffe between the town and the peere (as it were), not far from that which was the house of Templars, some remain of a tower now called Bredenstone, which had been both a pharos for saylors, and also a watch-house for defence of the inhabitants." So we are able to piece together a record of a great historical event which took place in Dover in the thirteenth century.

Lambarde's mention of the second Roman pharos—"the first was within the precincts of the Castle"—helps to preserve the memory of another vanished monument. It stood under what is now the Drop Redoubt, and was known as the Devil's Drop. Here the Lords Warden of the Cinque Ports (of which Dover was the chief) were sworn in. These Roman lighthouses were massive structures, with walls twelve feet thick at the bottom and seven at the top. They were originally about 80 feet high, and rose in four stories. So wealth was poured out upon this key citadel at an early stage in our history. Dubræ (as the Romans called it) has been an expensive portal. Henry the Eighth, who first set up what might be called the *modern* defences of the port as a land counterpart to his establishment of a Royal Navy, sank untold wealth in stone, bricks, and mortar. Over forty million pounds, according to the Victorian history of the county, "have been thrown into the sea" at Dover, and the great harbour built in 1924 was a failure. The sea narrowing to the Straits, with the tug-of-war between the malignant demon of the North Sea and the obstinate devil of the Channel, makes the approach to Dover a constant ocean arena, where the tides, pinioned between the cliffs of France and English, lash to and fro, dragging the seabed with them. It is more than a strip of water that cuts us off from the Continent. It is a hundred-eyed Cerberus whose rage is dangerous with a million fangs, and a temper that keeps him ever awake. Small wonder that the short Channel crossing has always been a formidable matter to travellers, especially when they were dependent upon wind and tide alone. Even now, with the days (and nights) of the Channel packet gone, the hour's journey in the fast turbine boats is a beastly experience for most people. I find it dreadful, and my stomach begins to turn queasy as soon as I get into the train at Victoria. For years I waited for further news of the making of the Channel Tunnel, and I would look wistfully from the boat-train as it slipped into the tunnel through the Shakespeare Cliff, for just at that entrance stood the works where the abortive attempts to start the great undersea junction with France were begun. Now, I suppose the scheme will be shelved for ever, superseded by the airplane. I am not happy about it.

What a giant is that Shakespeare Cliff, which tradition has associated with the scene in *King Lear* where the blind Gloucester and his disguised son Edgar meet. No poet gives a more vivid sense of height than does Shakespeare when he makes Edgar describe the scene from the top of the cliff.

> Come on, sir; here's the place!—stand still.—How fearful
> And dizzy 'tis, to cast one's eyes so low!
> The crows and choughs that wing the midway air,
> Show scarce so gross as beetles : Half way down
> Hangs one that gathers samphire; dreadful trade!
> Methinks he seems no bigger than his head :
> The fishermen that walk upon the beach
> Appear like mice, and yond tall anchoring bark,
> Diminished to her cock; her cock, a buoy
> Almost too small for sight; the murmuring surge,
> That on the unnumbered idle pebbles chafes,
> Cannot be heard so high.—I'll look no more,
> Lest my brain turn and the deficient sight
> Topple down headlong.

It is instructive now to look *up* the cliff from the bottom. Matthew Arnold, in his poem "Dover Beach," written about 1867, has a reference in the last, magnificent lines which suggests that he had stood on the beach staring up at night at the moonlit chalk escarpment. It recalled to him, apparently, the scene from Thucydides' account of the Battle of Epipolæ, which was fought by moonlight, so that the combatants became confused and each side slew its own men. Arnold would have this picture as one of those imperishable recollections from childhood, for his father, the formidable Thomas Arnold of Rugby, edited an edition of the Greek historian and must have introduced his son at an early age to this immortal record of the Peloponnesian War and the Sicilian Expedition. Looking up from

> . . . the long line of spray
> Where the sea meets the moon-blanched sand

Arnold bids his companion

> Listen, you hear the grating roar
> Of pebbles which the waves suck back and fling
> At their return, up the barr'd strand,
> Cease and begin, and then again begin
> With regular cadence slow, and bring
> The eternal note of sadness in.

Reflecting nostalgically how the modern, sceptical mind can find no religious association for this sadness, as once Sophocles could when listening to the same sound on the Ægean, Arnold turns from the sea's edge and looks up the cliff, picturing himself at the top on the plain above.

> Ah, love, let us be true
> To one another! for the world, which seems
> To lie before us like a land of dreams,
> So various, so beautiful, so new,
> Hath really neither joy, nor love, nor light,
> Nor certitude, nor peace, nor help for pain;
> And we are here as on a darkling plain
> Swept with confused alarms of struggle and flight,
> Where ignorant armies clash by night.

Snatches of great poetry such as these are the best way to evoke the massive grandeur of the scene where the coast of England hinges upon this mighty bastion of chalk, to turn northward up the eastern coast of the county to Thanet. Impressionism is the only means to express the weight of feeling which seizes one by the throat as one stands, either at the top or the base of the cliff, watching the play of water and light, the pattern of the flight of the seabirds, the stillness in motion of the ships out in the Channel, the gleam and promise of beloved France a hairbreadth above the horizon.

Let us try to grasp something more tangible. Let us come to "the mayne, strong, and famose castel of Dovar," as Leland called it, and the town itself. Both town and castle are of great age—Roman and probably pre-Roman, for this place has always been the cornerstone of the island of Britain. Whoever was master of it had his foot well set for mastery of the whole, since he commanded all traffic with Europe, apart from furtive comings and goings that could bring little profit to the rival. In the fourth century the town was guarded by a fort near the harbour, which dominated the Litus Saxonicum (the Saxon Shore), so called because it faced the onslaught of the barbarian marauders from the outer darkness of the Gothic lands. Wars and rumours of wars have always been the stuff of Dover's life. Even the internal conflicts of our history have used Dover as a master-play on the board, because a combatant who was assured of quick contact with France and the Netherlands could buy assistance according to his means, or his promise.

The Castle can be seen with dramatic effect from two directions. First, the approach from the sea, or the historical approach. From this direction the Castle dominates the town and the Channel. It stands on the cliff-top eastward, frowning and authoritative, with the tall ramparts of the Constable's Tower rearing up like the bole of a tree out of the slope of the cliff. It still looks impregnable, and one is reminded instantly that throughout its long history it was never captured —but once, and then by twelve Roundheads under the leadership of a tradesman, who scaled the cliff at night, seized the sentry, and surprised the Royalist garrison.

As the Castle rises over the water before the returning traveller, it brings up with it an army of ghosts, rank upon rank of them, ten centuries deep. A few shades are survivors from the almost prehistoric makers of the earthworks on which the massive foundations stand. Clustered round the old pharos are the Romans, with a glint of bronze in their armour. They too are dim, a composite body. Nor can we distinguish individuals amongst the Saxons by the great well. Only with the community of Normans, who came and built the present Castle, after taking the Saxon structure "and the Well in it," do individual figures emerge; the villainous Odo, Bishop of Bayeux and Earl of Kent, so feared and hated by his brother King William; and after him a full company of kings, princes, prelates, nobles, and fair women. The story is so ample that I cannot give it here. It would indeed be a delightful labour to set about the task of writing a history of Dover Castle, with a few free years before one. It would turn out to be a history of Europe. That potentiality looms above the ramparts of Dover as seen from the sea.

The second dramatic aspect comes when one approaches along the road from Thanet. From here the Castle stands on a green hill, solitary and romantic, like a background to one of Scott's novels. It is also impressive, but in a more literary and poetic way than from the seaboard approach. All this stretch of the county lying behind the rounded heights of the cliffs is singular in its luxuriant growth of trees. The effect is one of melancholy, a "green thought in a green shade," but desperate in its intensity. This character marks the countryside right up inland as far as Canterbury, and behind the sea-coast round by St Margaret's Bay (another miniature Riviera), up behind Deal through the handsome park of Northbourne to Sandwich and Richborough. It is magical country, with many half-hidden little upland valleys, bits of hinterland where time stands still, and the air is heavy with a burden of memory. In these sheltered spots the Romans built their villas, and half-succeeded in establishing a simulacrum of the Virgilian garden-culture of their Mediterrean homeland. In these luscious stretches of land the heartache of exile must have been almost assuaged. But not more than almost, for beauty is its own defeat. To-day these woods, fields, and valleys of the north-eastern foothills of the south-turning Downs behind Dover carry that same sense of defeat. They are almost too beautiful, too rich, and the visitor there begins to understand the motive of Ulysses when he fled from the island of the enchantress. Over this sleep-soaked garden in the corner of Kent broods Dover Castle with an admonitory frown, and a reminder that the sea borders are very near, and beyond them a host of envious strangers. As an instance of the corruption that can spring from richness, we may recall the nursery tale of the Babes in the Wood. It is probable that this legend arose from the incident that took place at Eastry, in the time of King Egbert of Kent. He lived here and had in his charge two infant cousins. His evil servant and monitor, named Thunnor, whispered that these children were potential usurpers of the throne. The result of this suggestion is sufficiently well known.

This wild admixture of history and legend brings us back to the sea front, and the story of the Battle of Dover during the minority of Henry III. The English barons, in their fight against the Crown, asked for help from the King of France, who of course had dynastic reasons for despoiling the English kings. The help came with a fleet under the command of a renegade monk named Eustace. The Cinque Port ships, under the Regent Hubert de Burgh, put to sea to attack, but so manœuvred that the French thought a descent upon Calais was intended. Suddenly the English fleet veered round, closed upon the invaders, and threw quicklime into the air. It was carried by the wind to the French vessels and blinded their crews, who during the confusion were shot down by the English archers, while this was followed by a wholesale ramming of the French boats by the English, which had been specially fitted with iron bows. This defeat of Eustace the Monk was subsequently attributed not to the tactics of that good soldier de Burgh, but to the character of the Monk. Good had triumphed over evil, the latter being represented by the devilish figure of this Eustace, who had been educated in the black arts at Toledo, the centre of witchcraft during the Middle Ages. Eustace was believed to have made his ships invisible by necromancy, but a rival wizard in the English fleet, one Stephen Crabbe, continued to see through the temporary conjuration. He landed on the invisible French flagship, and was seen to be laying about him with a battle-axe, apparently standing in the air a few feet above the water. As soon as his axe struck off the head of Eustace, the ships appeared again, but during the breaking of the spell Crabbe was torn to pieces. It is a pretty story, based on the life of an ex-monk who became a mercenary soldier and probably did a bit of secret-service work for King John, a monarch of such unsavory reputation that even his servitors were tainted.

I have already mentioned Dover Priory. Its remains are now incorporated in the buildings of the small public school, Dover College, which may claim to go back under that title to the year 696. In 1139 the seminary for twenty-two secular canons became a Benedictine Priory subsidiary to that of Canterbury. Another ancient building is the hall of the hospital founded by Hubert de Burgh in the thirteenth century for the reception of pilgrims from abroad. Henry the Eighth, during his great build-up of Kentish defences and establishment of a Royal Fleet, turned the hospital into a Crown victualling office. It later served as a town hall until the building of a new one in 1883.

Before leaving Dover I must recall it as I saw it during the days just before the assault upon Europe in June 1944. A particular job of work in the Home Guard led me to visit these front-line coast-towns of Kent during the weeks before D-Day. The silence of them all was terrifying. I approached Dover along the road from Sandwich and Richborough. A complete area of country lying behind the coast between Pegwell Bay and Hythe had been closed to the public. At the entrance to this area we were stopped and our papers examined, but once through the barrier we could see nothing going on to warrant this scrupulous secrecy. A number of railheads ended abruptly at the waterside at Richborough, where one or two leisurely workmen appeared to be tinkering with a few outsize boilers, or what looked like boilers. That was all. The landscape was derelict. A huge cluster of last-war hutments lay in ruins, some of it caused by bombs, and more of it caused by the gradual disruption of weeds and weather. Nothing else for mile after mile, except deserted bungalows; Mon Abri, Hawaii, Joyous Garde, Ozone, Wee Kenders : these were a few of the names which I noted in a moment of ironic curiosity. Joyous Garde was a sweet little cot built of corrugated iron. It had not been painted for some years, and it stood near a barricade of rusted barbed-wire coils that ran along the foreshore over a stretch of sour marshland. Joyous Garde had suffered slightly, and one of its sheets of iron was torn loose and turned outward like a lip snarling. The wind caused this lip to tremble and to set up a humming vibration from time to time; a noise that ought to have sent the uniformed occupants of the happy little love-nest raving mad. But they appeared to be unaffected, for none of them, change and change about, took the trouble to fix the dreadful aeolian lyre and so to stop its sinister undertone of delirium.

The interior of Joyous Garde stank of soldiery that slept

in its clothes, cooked, ate, smoked, and groused, all in the same room. A large amount of stores added to the aroma; bacon, gun-oil, bread, explosives—all the stuff that drifts into the backwaters of war. It was almost impossible to realize that this particular backwater was on the very front line of the Allied effort, thirty miles from the Germans, in the centre of a much-conjectured-about spearhead which was at any moment to thrust out at the heart of Germany. Perhaps that snarl on the lip of Joyous Garde was an instinctive preparation.

The little patch of salted ground surrounding Joyous Garde was now scarred with wheelmarks, and bruised mats of sea-lavender, thistles, and broken bushes of tamarisk. An earth closet stood conspicuously some yards from the ex-bungalow. The disturbance which had torn the sheets of iron had also blown out both sides of the privy, leaving it with a door and a back. None of the relays of Home Guard had thought it necessary to replace the fallen walls. No doubt they had been instantly used for kindling wood. While I was engaged at Joyous Garde I saw one of the guard walk out to that privy and enter by the door, which he discreetly closed after him. This act of convention reminded me of the solemn rituals of make-believe to be seen in the No plays of Japan. I did not laugh at the time, for the gesture was no more unreal than the scene in which it was made.

Dover, which I entered half an hour later, was also part of that scene. It was not deserted. Indeed, it was full of soldiers, sailors, airmen, and airwomen. But they seemed all to be mute. They were a silent crowd in a silent city. The effect was impressive. Obviously they were waiting for something. But there was a staleness about this waiting, as though some long-anticipated crisis had fallen flat. The town looked flat too; indescribably dreary and sordid. Down in the centre of the town we found a place to eat a quick meal. All sorts of Service men and women, of all ranks, were eating there. Nobody spoke. The waitresses appeared to know what everyone wanted without taking an order. They looked tired. Everybody looked tired, and bored. That was the keynote—boredom, a boredom that gripped the town like a frost, making faces grey, minds muddy, eyes lustreless. It tainted the food. We ate our meal, looking out of a dirty window into a dirty square, one side of which opened down a canyon of rubble.

Just as we were about to enter our car and drive on to the next Home Guard post along the coast, the warning for shell-fire went. Nobody took any notice, and we drove off without delay. Coming some while later to the sea front, we saw a convoy in the Straits. It was these ships that were under fire from the French coast. Nothing exciting was happening, however. We stopped near a car, by which stood a much gilded naval officer looking out to sea through huge binoculars. Beside him, at attention, stood a Wren, his chauffeur. My companion and I produced a small pair of glasses and proceeded to scrutinize the convoy. Before we could focus them a sentry stepped out from behind a groyne in the sea-wall and told us that we were in danger of having those glasses confiscated. So we apologized, and he then apologized, while the naval officer and his companion continued to look out to sea, undisturbed by the miniature drama near at hand. With the naked eye we watched the ships in slow motion making their way down Channel. Between them and the French shore two destroyers were racing about like sheepdogs round a flock, leaving behind them thin whiffs of smoke that gradually unfolded, layer upon layer, like the ribbons produced by a conjurer from his hat. The smoke spread until an artificial fog lay between the convoy and France. Once we heard a heavy vibration, and some moments later it was followed by a stab of white out at sea, nowhere near any of the boats. A strange, eerie drama; the watching officer (I suspect he was supplied by Madame Tussaud), the tapestry of ships against a woolly background, the complete silence. And somehow it is all connected with the recollection of that Home Guard member walking over to the very unprivate privy and solemnly shutting the door as an act of modesty.

CHAPTER XII

THANET

I HAVE already described how the caprice of the tides in the Straits long ago closed the Roman and medieval ports of Sandwich and Richborough. History and geography primers will explain it more fully; the formation of the Goodwin Sands, quick with treachery; the quiet shelter of the Roads or Downs, between the sands and the shore, where a great fleet might ride out a storm; the blind groping of the Stour amongst the flats between Reculver on the north shore and Sandwich Haven on the east. Macaulay's schoolboy will tell you how these flats were an open sea channel in which Edward III was able, in the fourteenth century, to gather a fleet of sixteen hundred ships for the campaign that was to be victorious at the Battle of Crecy and the conquest of Calais.

The chalky island of Thanet, Earl Godwin's Saxon stronghold against his rivals and sometimes against his King Edward the Confessor, last of the Saxon semi-federal monarchs, is a closely written palimpsest. Layer upon layer, the centuries have laid their record there, for archæologist and historian to discover and exhibit. Its geographical position, especially centuries ago when it was insulated from the mainland, made it a bridgehead to be aimed at by all invaders. Julius Cæsar and William of Normandy were the only exceptions; rather whale-like exceptions, for their invasions outweighed all the others put together. The Christian doctrine was first preached by Augustine on the slopes at Minster, inland from Richborough. Many people may justifiably believe this to have been the most influential invasion of all. Hengist and Horsa landed in Thanet, at the invitation of the native British when denuded of their Roman guards. The invitees proved to be violent cuckoos in the nest, for once they were lodged firmly in this island they had a footing to leap across England.

All these riches are in the past, however, for to-day Thanet is one vast holiday camp and sanatorium. The air of Thanet is miraculous, especially for children, and a host of convalescent homes and boarding-schools have settled round about the towns, such as Margate, Ramsgate, and Broadstairs, where the tuberculous and rickety products of Victorian and Edwardian London slums were given at least a short respite from their social degradation and misery. Since the coming of the National Insurance, and the general improvement in wages and education, this morbid traffic between London and the Isle of Thanet has vastly decreased. But the improved health of the latter-day town-dwellers has given them only the more energy to seek the air and the sea, and Thanet has more visitors than ever. During the war this moving population was cut off suddenly, and for nearly six years the island was left to ruminate over its past. To visit it during that time was to come to a land where ghosts whispered at your ear, and time went into reverse. For the fastidious scholar it was a period of opportunity to explore places which in the more garish days of peace and plenty would have been unapproachable. During that time of bombs, barbed-wire, desolation, and decay, the natural character of the district emerged, just as the bone-formation of character emerges in a human face during privation and trouble. The soldiers and the guns were more in keeping with that deep-rooted quality of the island than were the peace-time vulgarities of fun fair, lido, soda fountain and fish-and-chip shops, and all the hideous paraphernalia of the petrol pump, that latest signal of philistinism.

But let us go to Thanet, instead of talking about it in this generalized way. There is plenty to see on the way up from Dover. The road runs straight to Deal, and we can turn off to right and left, exploring villages in this undulating country whose lush richness I have already described in my last chapter. Just past the Duke of York's Military School, a road to the right leads to the coast and the South Foreland lighthouse at the south-western extremity of St Margaret's Bay. That is the prosaic way of approaching this little Antibes of the North. The more rapturous path is over the cliffs from Dover, taking in the South Foreland lighthouse on the way. It needs a genius like that of George Meredith to give the sense of light, buoyancy, and sheer ecstasy of motion which takes both body and soul of the person walking over the Downs and cliffs at this point. One seems to be at the prow of a mighty ship, the ship of Time, the ship of the world itself, thrusting forward into a sea of light, a passer-by of the sun. The winds come up the Channel, or down from the North Sea, swinging the inland woods. The salt waters of the Straits sparkle and leap, even on the calmest day. The distant line of the French coast is hovering rather than static. The seabirds, gull and guillemot and other, rarer, kinds, scream in a savage triumph as they dash themselves against the wind, carving and shaping it into planes down which they glide; down and up again, following the tossing of their own wild voices, baffled but untiring as they chase these echoes of echoes beating to and fro from walls of nothingness.

The earth itself, a sort of velvety flesh over the chalk, perfumed with miniature cropped herbs, appears to be in constant motion too, for this tiny vegetation that clothes it is shaking and trembling, to the tune of a gleeful murmur hardly distinguishable amongst the larger and more spacious gestures of the sky and the wind, yet adding an undertone to give a base and a location to the welter of movement. From the clifftop by the lighthouse, four hundred feet above sea-level, the view is superb; up and down Channel, across to France, westward across the top of the Downs, fold upon fold lapped in woodland, and north up the coast, the Downs, and beyond that across the marshes past Sandwich to Thanet, whose chalk risings so often take on that cold, ghostly gleam of all northern aspects in this hemisphere. Nobody capable of a vigorous walk should miss this experience. To come to the lush and sheltered St Margaret's Bay by this route is to be prepared for luxury, just as the poet John Keats prepared himself for drinking a full claret by sprinkling his tongue with pepper. There lies the bay below, with trees to the water's edge, the broad steps leading down to the beach where the houses lie shrouded from the subtropical sunlight.

At low tide one may walk round by the shore, under the base of the cliffs; but this is laborious going, and the time has to be chosen nicely, or there is a risk of being cut off by the incoming sea. But this adventure has a sort of Robinson Crusoe quality, with its solitude, its discoveries of small items of flotsam and jetsam and unexpected sea-pieces, while the formidable ramparts of chalk rear up, their muscles strained against the constant onslaught of the tides and storms. Here again, to reach St Margaret's is to come into a southern haven. Here is the very centre of that Litus Saxonicum which it was the concern of all the masters of England to fortify against invaders. The almost prehistoric inhabitants first set about the task, and when the Romans came they found the beaches staked against them. Julius Cæsar had to grope up round the shore as far as Deal before he found a spot where he might dare commit his legions to the hazard of a landing and an attack. After he had succeeded, and during the following four centuries, a line of fortresses was established, under the command of a Count of the Saxon Shore, whose duty it was to ensure against any landings by the Gothic pirates lurking up and down the Channel.

The Saxons, however, were not altogether strange to Britain during the Roman occupation. Many were brought here willy-nilly long before they came of their own accord. A German historian named Lappenburg says that the Romans brought two hundred thousand Vandals to Britain during the reign of Emperor Probus. These were slave labour whose descendants no doubt provided a sort of Fifth Column when their untamed kinsmen came from overseas after the Romans had departed. The Saxons appear to have come as casual marauders for over a century before they settled here. According to a Roman writer, Marcellinus, about the middle of the fourth century after Christ, these sporadic attacks by the Saxons were the most formidable menace to civilization at that time. The Wagnerian heroes, feeling their way into the outer reaches of the Empire, appear from the beginning to have had a most ingenious gift for cruelty.

To a Britain which for over four centuries had been settled into ways of peace and comparative plenty, with a flow of wealth coming and going and gradually adding to the amenities of life, these cold stabs from the north-east must have been especially terrifying. Always an outrider of the Empire, Britain seemed to lack the cultural power to influence the Saxons when at last they came and decided to stay.

In Gaul, Spain, and Sicily, the Frankish invaders were impressed by what they found, and surrendered with some humility to the greater way of life into which they had blundered like bulls into a china-shop. But in England they remained Norsemen for nearly another two centuries, until the coming of Augustine with the principles of Christianity. It may have been the latent respect for individualism (which even the overlay of Rome could not disguise) in this new religion which appealed to the Saxon genius. King Ethelbert, in 597, already biased no doubt by his Christian queen, accepted Augustine's teaching wholeheartedly, and carried most of his subjects with him. From that time the Saxon in this island began to germinate a culture that has become unique. It is neither in the full Roman tradition nor is it barbaric like the Teutonic. It has welded the best of both worlds; the poetic, mystical solitariness of the Gothic with the sound and rational Roman urbanity, dropping the morbid egoism of the one and the impersonal formalism of the other. It remains to this day as a wonder and an enigma to the rest of the world, a flowering of the human spirit which has not only survived, but developed for fifteen hundred years. To-day it is being assailed by the levelling processes of science; the machine which, like a cement-mixer, is pulverizing all human and social idiosyncrasy and local differences, by means of swift transport, the cinema, and the radio. Even if our English way of life is absorbed into this generalized world-mixture, it will be the determining ingredient. And a few historians in the future may still remember that it started in Thanet.

During this small historical parenthesis we are standing on the cliff top at Hope Point looking northward at a collection of gentle heights beyond the dead flat basin of the River Stour. Those heights are the island of Thanet, and we are gradually making our way to them. We do so over the bones of a civilization, Roman-Celtic in structure, which flourished

essentially along these northern slopes of the Kentish Downs, and was utterly wiped out by the self-contained Teutonic hordes. Descending the slopes of the cliffs northward, we approach Deal through Kingsdown and Walmer. Walmer Castle, one of the string of coastal fortresses built in Tudor times as a sort of concomitant to the opening of our expansion policy, is the seat of the Lord Warden of the Cinque Ports. Mr Churchill holds that office now, and I like to think of him sitting in that frontier bulwark, now merely a nominal one since he made his famous offer of brotherhood to the French people in 1940, writing further chapters of his own adventurous life, which is so inextricably mingled with that of his country.

He is able to look out upon a handsome garden, whose magnificent trees are the result of William Pitt's period in the same office in the eighteenth century. When writing about Bromley I remarked how Pitt, who lived there, had a passion for planting trees. He indulged it at Walmer Castle. Further, he brought his niece, the famous Lady Hester Stanhope, to plan the garden. She made a success of this task, and the garden at that time was renowned. When the Duke of Wellington was made Lord Warden of the Cinque Ports he was asked to conform to what had by that time become the custom, of planting a tree in the garden. So to the acacia planted by Queen Elizabeth, the palm tree by Lord Clive, and the small forest planted by Pitt, the Iron Duke added a willow tree taken from that which grew over Napoleon's grave in St Helena.

At this point I must rescue a charming story from a history of Deal written in florid paragraphs by a local justice of the peace in 1860. He says that "shortly after the Duke of Wellington was appointed Lord Warden, a sergeant in the Peninsular War wrote to his old commander to inform him that he had received his discharge, but without pension. The day following, the sergeant received the following laconic note, 'Field Marshal the Duke of Wellington would be happy to see Sergeant —— at Apsley House, on Friday at noon.' Punctually at the time appointed, the sergeant made his appearance, and had scarcely been seated in the ante-room when the duke came in, saying, 'How d'ye do? How

Cobham Hall

d'ye do? Do you know anything about gardening?' 'No, Your Grace,' was the answer of the sergeant. 'Then learn, learn, and come here this day fortnight, same hour,' the duke leaving him to himself to ponder over in his mind the words just uttered. During the fortnight the sergeant endeavoured to learn something of gardening, but he found the art difficult to master in so limited a time. At the end of the fortnight the sergeant went as directed, to Apsley House. The duke was as punctual as himself, and on entering the room said to the sergeant, 'Take the place of gardener at Walmer Castle, twenty-eight shillings a week, a house, and all that.' 'I know very little about gardening,' said the sergeant. 'Nor do I, nor do I,' said the field marshal; 'go and take your place at once!' The sergeant lost no time in going to Walmer. On arriving there he found instructions had arrived before him, and he was immediately placed in a comfortable cottage, well furnished, and everything in it that could make his life agreeable. For several weeks he employed someone to teach him the difference between flowers and weeds, and hearing that the duke was about visiting the Castle he got a speech ready in his mind to thank His Grace for the appointment, but he never got the opportunity. On one occasion the sergeant, after a restless night meditating over what he ought to say to the duke, rose at six o'clock, purposely placed himself at the spot where His Grace was accustomed to take his early morning walk, and, touching his hat, was about to speak, but the duke simply said, 'How d'ye do, how d'ye do?' and passed on. From that time to the field marshal's death, the sergeant gardener had no means of expressing his gratitude to his noble and generous friend."

The same historian maintained that Deal and Walmer enjoyed the most healthy air in the kingdom. This is how he said it: "The open plain here in Deal and Walmer offers no hindrance to a free circulation of the air of the atmosphere; it is felt by every wind that blows. The *Zephyr*, or west wind, that blows off the land comes to us with a force and feeling that is truly refreshing and invigorating."

While Pitt was in this now merely picturesque office of Lord Warden, he was faced with the same responsibility as that which Mr Churchill fronted in 1940. He used the Castle as his headquarters, and from there planned the setting up of the string of Martello towers which still disfigure the landscape round our south-eastern coast.

Half a mile inland from St Margaret's Bay is St Margaret's-at-Cliffe church, which is a notable specimen of Norman architecture, the west doorway being one of the finest of its kind in England. The massive tower opens to the nave by a pointed arch with shafts of Norman character. I believe that the church is built mainly of stone from Caen. To-day that adds to its value. Anything which survives, and adds to our memory of Caen, one of the wonders of Europe totally destroyed in the war, is to be hugged to our souls. The rich ornamentation in several tiers over the arches, and the lozenge, embattled, and rope mouldings over the north doorway are particularly to be admired. One's eye will at once catch, too, the fine run of plain Norman clerestory windows. On some of the pillars there survive rough-scratch drawings of ships, thought to be the work of sailors in the fourteenth century. The church was built from 1130, upon Saxon foundations.

A pretty legend survives in connection with this church. From November to March a curfew is still tolled here at eight o'clock at night. The custom is said to have originated with a shepherd in the seventeenth century who was injured by falling from the cliff in the darkness. After being rescued, he left five roods of land to be held by the person who would undertake to ring the curfew during the winter nights, as a guide to all people, other than the deaf, who might be passing that way.

A mile to the west is another church, a small one with no tower, known as West Cliffe. It contains a tomb which is a reminder that Gibbon may be claimed as one of Kent's native literary figures. It commemorates his grandfather, whose family held the manor hereabouts. This man was a merchant of London, a Commissioner of Customs. He made a large fortune, and lost it in the South Sea Bubble. In spite of being fined as a director of the fraudulent company, he managed to save the remnant of his fortune, from which he proceeded to amass another. It is not possible to associate the great historian closely with Kent, for he appeared to have no dealings with the county from which his family originally sprang. He was born at Putney, and lived in Hampshire and Surrey, when he was not in Switzerland, his spiritual home, and the place where he wrote the final volumes of *The Decline and Fall of the Roman Empire*, that great symphony in prose with a somewhat hurried finale.

About ten miles inland, north-west toward Canterbury, in the little church of Bishopsbourne, there is a brass to an earlier member of the Gibbon family, one John, who was buried there in 1617. This gives me opportunity to mention another among the greatest of our English prose writers, Richard Hooker. This saintly man, whose only folly in life was to give up a good fellowship at his university in order to marry a woman who turned out to be a virago and a slut, spent the last five years of his life as vicar of Bishopsbourne, the living being given to him by Queen Elizabeth in 1595, to mark her admiration for his writing and scholarship. The matter of his *Ecclesiastical Polity* is to-day merely quaint and faded stuff, but the manner of it remains to charm us as it charmed Pope Clement VIII, to whom the book was recommended by two English cardinals at Rome during Hooker's lifetime. According to Izaak Walton, in his *Life of Hooker*, the Pope listened to the reading as far as the end of Part One, and then declared with fervour, "There is no Learning that this man hath not searched into; nothing too hard for his understanding : this man indeed deserves the name of an Author; his books will get reverence by Age, for there is in them such seeds of Eternity that if the rest be like this they shall last till the last fire shall consume all Learning." One might call that tribute the foundation of an international reputation. I doubt if this master of prose is much known to his fellow-countrymen to-day.

Another prose master, the novelist Joseph Conrad, spent 1919 to 1924, the last five years of his life, at Bishopsbourne, after twenty years lived in several other parts of the county, dogged by gout, money troubles, and a despair of ever being able to master the language which he had adopted as his literary medium. His letters to Edward Garnett make a trail of misery across the county; but the misery of a giant, a Laocoön, contending with the gods. And he won.

But we must return from this short excursion inland after paying a tribute to two word-masters. We can do so through Barham and Broome Park, a fine Caroline house where Lord Kitchener lived. He bought it in 1908 from the original family of Oxenden, which had been established there since the reign of Edward III. Their tombs are in Barham church. All along this ridge of the Downs, and stretching eastward to the coast, the antiquarian may quarter every inch of ground and find riches in profusion. Tumuli and ancient earthworks abound, relics of camps, battles, burial grounds connected with Neolithic men, Celts, Romans, Saxons, and the contending armies of historical times. King John camped here with an army of sixty thousand men in 1213, when he paid submission to the Pope with his crown. Fifty years later Simon de Montfort brought a large army here. An army for defence against the probable invasion by Napoleon sat here for years. And in the last two wars (or those two phases of what may come to be called the Second Thirty Years War of 1914–45) troops were assembled here for training in 1914, and for very serious defence in 1940, prepared to "fight on the beaches, in the streets, and in the hills," as Mr Churchill indicated in his greatest speech in those terrible days when we stood tiptoe, waiting for disaster.

So far as the systematic covering of the county is concerned, I have done a disastrous thing by turning aside from my path between Dover and Deal in order to visit Bishopsbourne, because this vagary has led me into the heart of that bit of country about which I have already written with some enthusiasm. But once caught among those miniature valleys and ranges among the Downs where they bend south-east between Chilham, near Canterbury, and Folkestone-Dover, the wanderer becomes a latter-day Ulysses on the island of Circe. Every village in this area is a gem set by a goldsmith of genius. Elham, Stelling, Waltham, Bishopsbourne with its literary as well as its architectural treasures, Patrixbourne whose church is one of the most perfect pure Norman pieces in England, Denton, and Wootton, the seat of the Bridges family, that gave us a famous littérateur at the beginning of the nineteenth century, and a great Poet Laureate at the end of it : these are only a sample of the valleyfuls of names that represent a social history to which no writer could do justice in one lifetime. That Laureate I have mentioned, Robert Bridges, was moulded in his taste by his early impressions of this, his native environment. Its conservatism is his conservatism, its ordered yet exquisite and tender beauty his beauty. To walk and explore hereabouts is to walk amongst the rolling quantitative verses of his epic poem, *The Testament of Beauty*, which is a gallery of local water-colours, landscapes and seascapes in words, to be recognized again and again in the corners and open sweeps of this land where the poet was nurtured; scenes which his imagination has revisited in old age, "glossing the mazy hieroglyph of Nature's book." The ancient history of the soil here, under the influence of the first English cathedral; the sense of tradition, and slow evolution in patience, the labour in richness amongst scenes of harvest both Theocritan and Christianized; these are all fixed in the amber of Bridges's poetry. Listen to these lines from his *Testament*:

Or what man feeleth not a new poetry of toil,
whenas on frosty evenings 'neath its clouding smoke
the engin hath huddled up its clumsy threshing-coach
against the ricks, wherefrom labourers standing aloft
toss the sheaves on its tongue; while the grain runneth out,
and in the whirr of its multitudinous hurry
it hummeth like the bee, a warm industrious boom
that comforteth the farm, and spreadeth far afield
with throbbing power; as when in a cathedral awhile
the great diapason speaketh, and the painted saints
feel their glass canopies flutter in the heav'nward prayer.

That is precisely the apt association of fundamentals to represent this countryside; for here the survivals at least of sanctity, legends in folktale, in stone, in stained glass, are as widespread as the furrows and the roots of the copse trees or those solitary arboreal giants in the parks where Roman villas were replaced by Norman castles, and these by the relaxed and peaceful mansions of the Tudor aristocracy of wealth. Nothing can be done here without stirring a host of associations; in the dairy, at the plough, by the cottage fireside, beneath the sanddropping tick of the church clock in every village; whatever human traffic is in motion, it moves with a pregnant heaviness, carrying the past within its gesture, and promising thereby a rich birth and inheritance. The faces of these Men of Kent appear to be half-alight with a consciousness of that inheritance; reserved, protective, reminiscent. It is small wonder that one of them, Richard Barham, who was born of a family rooted in the midst of this magic-ridden patch of country, found such a treasury of legends in his own neighbourhood of Tappington and Ingoldsby. Nor is it to be wondered at that Jane Austen, staying with her brother Edward at Godmersham Park or Rowling House, two of the three country seats left to him by his fairylike foster-parents, solely on the guarantee of his personal charm and virtue, should have recorded in *Emma* and *Mansfield Park* a way of life that not even the further passage of a century and the world-disrupting wars have quite dislodged. To visit Godmersham to-day is to see physically something of that sedate world with its gift for ironic observation, its tidy control of the violence of nature, which Jane Austen made her medium.

But I must turn back from this over-rich enclosure between Watling Street, Stone Street (two Roman radii from Canterbury) and the Ashford Road, or I shall find myself prematurely at Canterbury. And it would be sacrilege to approach that superb shrine out of the order planned for this book. Canterbury is the prime jewel in the fan-shape which my imagination has made of the county, and it is to be seen only when the fan is completed and outspread. I have yet to complete the edge, and link it up with the hinge along the ribs.

So we cut across country eastward toward the coast, taking up our way where we left it at Kingsdown, about to drop into Deal and the entrance to the wide levels of the Stour Estuary. We come to the town along the road under the sea-wall which, like the human fingernail, is constantly being renewed. Wind and water, sun and frost, nibble constantly at it, and man with antlike industry restores the depredations. Charles I spent six thousand pounds on it. The shingle beach below it is where Julius Cæsar and Perkin Warbeck, in that order, invaded England. Here were two extremes of human dignity and achievement. " 'Tis true, this god did shake," as Shakespeare said of Cæsar. So did Perkin Warbeck, living in his isolated, vanity-built universe, out of which he broke into active revolt, only to find that "the Kentish men working guiles promised that they would assist him if he and his company would land there. Albeit the same Perkin fearing that they meaned falsehood and craft, would not descend himself, but caused certain of his soldiers to land, which persons being a pretty way from their ships, were sore beaten and put to flight, and many of them taken prisoners, and after were condemned to dye." Anne of Cleves landed on this beach and spent her first night in England under the roof of Deal Castle. It was on this strip of beach that Fanny d'Arblay, who as Fanny Burney had been Dr Johnson's little friend and a best-selling novelist, performed a charming ceremony in 1812, when she landed in England after an absence of twelve years, due to the war with France. As she and her child were set ashore, she went down on her knees, snatched up a pebble, and kissed it with thankful lips.

So, having watched this charming, half-involuntary ceremony of kissing the pebble, we come to Deal. It is something of an anticlimax. Deal, like its name, has a certain flatness and shabbiness. One has the feeling that its townsfolk come home only to sleep and are too much concerned with their livelihood on the sea to be bothered about amenities on shore. Yet painters love it. It has so many wooden houses, boathouses, shacks, and sheds, along the sea front and in the back streets; so many boats of all sorts and sizes drawn up on the shingle, that an artist is supplied with subjects throughout the daylight hours. And there is so much tapping, caulking, trimming, painting, and varnishing going on in and around those boathouses that youngsters can be brought to Deal for holidays as they would be brought to Paradise. But they will need overalls.

What more can I say about Deal? It is not a place to rhapsodize about. I remember renting a fisherman's cottage there just after the last war, and taking a family of young children, including a newborn baby, for one of those restful, health-giving holidays which can sometimes become a nightmare of minor disasters. The cottage proved to be bug-ridden. Our nursemaid was followed by an adorer who one night produced a razor and threatened to cut her throat if she did not accept his advances. We had to invite the local police to remonstrate with him. But the police could do nothing about the bugs. We handled that problem ourselves by hiring two of the lifeboat crew (the famous lifeboat house was outside the front door of the cottage) who came in with pails of limewash, turned out all the furniture and beds, and brushed down the walls while their wives scrubbed the blankets and quilts. The remainder of the holiday was uneventful, and the infants thrived.

I recall a holiday at Deal at the opening of the century, when I was a child. The principal recollection is of wonderful breakfasts eaten in a sitting-room with a bay-window overhanging the pavement along the sea front. Every morning the landlady carried in a dish of small soles, caught the previous night, and lightly fried in butter. Ah! That makes Deal an immortal place for me, and I will not smutch that memory by further probings into the somewhat squalid back streets. It is somewhat of a Dickensian way of recalling the character of a town; but that is appropriate to Deal, and indeed to all this part of the county, which reeks with associations of the novelist. I still can sit at those immortal breakfasts, gazing out to sea, or at the tarry traffic below the projecting window, men with baskets of shrimps, men with loads of netting over their shoulders; men in blue jerseys bloomed by sun and salt air. I snuff the ozone, a composite of seaweed and fish-guts. That is Deal, of all marine places the most marine.

We continue northward along the shore across the golf links, for it is worth a snail's progress for a few miles in order to savour the sheer flatness, the sense of desolation, which this estuarial beach possesses. Human society has not been discreet with this waste-land. It seems to be littered with the throw-outs of human ingenuity, the droppings of farm life, engineering shops, garages, and the advertising world. I am ashamed to say that all this means we are approaching Thanet. However, on our right hand is the sea, the Downs, and a velvety shadow in the sea suggests the presence of the vanished lands of the Earl Godwin. The Goodwin Sands lie six miles out, and their shallows give a sheltered water between them and the land for some eight miles. Thus they make the Downs, as that shelter is named, a sort of Purgatorio of the high seas, where ships may ride safely during bad weather. The *Victory* spent three days here on her way home with Nelson's body on board, after Trafalgar. Four lightships mark the limits of the Goodwins, and no other form of warning can be placed there, because the sands are shifting and quick. That accounts for the fact that vessels are constantly being grounded there, an occurrence which during heavy storms often means destruction, ships in the non-resilient grip of the sand being cracked by the blows of the waves.

There is a sort of Atlantis legend about the Goodwins. It says that they are the relic of an island called Lomea, which belonged to the famous Earl Godwin, the first of our king-making barons. So that suggests that, in the eleventh century, the Goodwins were part of the mainland, or at least an island above sea level. It is probable that this tale is a confused account of the one-time insularity of Thanet, Earl Godwin's land, which has since disappeared as an island by being merged with the mainland. Do not ask the people of Tenterden for the true story, for they are still touchy about the Goodwins. It appears that funds intended for the maintenance of a sea-wall to protect what was once the island of Lomea were diverted by a too pious bishop toward the building of Tenterden church-steeple, with the result that the sea broke through and did its deadly work.

We walk straight on to the coastguard station and battery, turn inland past the golf-house, and come to Sandwich, the original Cinque Port of which Deal was a subordinate.

It is difficult to think of it now as a port, and the principal port in England, for between its extreme buildings and the sea stretch fertile fields and meadows. But it still bears the character of its past. It is an enchanting place, and even thousands of holiday-makers cannot spoil it, for its nature is so complete and so determined that it subdues the most frivolous and rowdy visitors to its mood. That mood is one of sleepy reminiscence over a rich and full past. The remarkable thing is that this great past came to an end so recently, with the suffocating geographical changes that carried the sea-edge some three miles from the town. So late as 1749 an Act of Parliament was passed "for enlarging and maintaining the Harbour of Ramsgate, and for cleansing, amending and preserving the Haven of Sandwich." What took place during the centuries of English life before this sad and ineffectual necessity arose may be read about at leisure, for there is much literature on the subject. One W. Boyes, in 1792, made a "collection for an history of Sandwich in Kent." Hasted of course has much to say about it. I recommend George Gray's book, *Sandwich; the story of a famous Kent Port*, or A. H. Anderson's *Practical Guide*.

It is no exaggeration to say that Sandwich has had three lives. The first and longest was as England's premier port; a proud phase, concerned with the traffic of kings, saints, and pilgrims, and with the destinies of empires. That lasted roughly from days before dates signify to the fifteenth century. By that time the sand had begun its stifling work, and big ships could no longer come up to the harbour. Ruin threatened. Instead, there came an immigration of weavers, religious refugees from Holland and Belgium, who settled with a new industry in the town, and, as was their practice wherever they went, set about at once to add to the architectural pride of the place. It is this phase of the history of Sandwich which most conspicuously remains to-day. But after three centuries the weaving went up to the industrial North, and stagnation again threatened the town. Thereupon, through the enterprise of a Scotsman, began the third phase of prosperity. The long stretch of flat sands which had been the undoing of the commerce of Sandwich were now utilized to restore it. The Scot saw that here was a perfect setting for the pursuit of his national sport, golf. He founded the Royal St George's Club, bought the freehold of the ground, and built a clubhouse. The members consist mainly of wealthy folk from the City of London, and their latter-day pilgrimage to Sandwich has brought money and life to the town. The links are amongst the finest in the country.

Sandwich began its first phase towards the end of the Roman occupation, when Richborough (Rutupæ) had already begun to lose its value as a port. It was certainly the most important coastal town for the Saxons, and therefore it suffered heavily at every further invasion. Sweyn and Canute landed there in 1013, sacking the existing settlement. It was quickly restored, however, as a bridgehead. The fortress covered some ten acres. From its walls King Ethelbert went out to listen to St Augustine. He crossed ground already sown with ancient monuments, amongst them the probable foundations of a gigantic pharos. Smaller relics are constantly being discovered; shards, coins, fragments of weapons, amulets. They symbolize the whole four centuries of the Roman occupation.

The first sign of the medieval town which we meet on our way in from the links is St Bartholomew's Hospital, an almshouse founded in 1190 by Sir Henry de Sandwich for maimed mariners and decayed townsmen. The chapel of this ancient institution is worth notice, with its two aisles in Early English style, and a west-end doorway with some notable toothed mouldings.

A few steps beyond this place we come to the first signs of the site of the fifteenth-century wall of the town, and walking along this we see the most important and much the most impressive of the three churches. St Clement's has a pure Norman tower which is one of the finest in England. It is uncommonly beautiful, being supported upon four lofty semicircular arches, all of which have well-defined mouldings, clustered shafts, and sculptured capitals. Inside the tower, above the arches, runs a tier of semicircular arches, whose piers form alternate single and clustered shafts.

The other two churches, St Peter's and St Mary's, have been so mutilated by accident and vandalism that they are negligible. The Guildhall, marred by a modern front, was built in 1579. It contains fine wood panelling, historical portraits (also a picture of the sea-fight off Deal between Admiral Blake and the Dutch van Tromp in 1666), and a rich collection of archives. We may see several old houses that belonged to Sir Roger Manwood, a town draper in Elizabethan times, who was a good representative of the growing commercial class that became so powerful in English politics and economics from that time onward, gradually engulfing the landed aristocracy. Manwood became Elizabeth's Baron of the Exchequer, and founded a grammar school (what a passion for learning swept England in those "spacious days"!) The building that now houses the school is modern, but Manwood's dwelling, built in 1564, can still be seen.

Along what was once the sea front of the town now runs the riverside Strand Street, which meets a bridge and ancient barbican before giving on to a market-place where the remains of an earlier Fish Gate survive.

Such a summary is totally inadequate. One needs several days in Sandwich, to explore and to savour the discoveries upon one's imagination, bringing them to life again, until a cavalcade of England's history is in motion through the old Cinque Port.

A mile and a half from Sandwich, going north by west, lies Richborough Castle. Here again words are not enough. At first sight it is not impressive, because it is down to ground level. But what it represents is so vast that the visitor should look about with patience. It was the first, and remained the greatest, fortification put up by the Romans. It was half of a binary work, the counterpart being at the northern end of the channel that then separated Thanet from the mainland. The channel was a mile wide, and Rutupæ was the landing-place at its southern entrance. Here the legions landed, and took the new road inland. That road was the Watling Street that stretched to Canterbury (Durovernum), Rochester (Durobrivæ), London, and out north-westwards through St Albans (Verulaneum) up to the Celtic borders at Wroxeter (Viroconium). It was thus the gate to all defence and offence. It was the door to Rome, that could be slammed against the wild and unaccountable that lay beyond the wall of the Sacred Empire. It was the centre of the most densely populated and industrialized area of Britain. A town lay round the base of the fortress, and on the eastern side the sea touched it. Granaries, a mint, large villas proved the wealth that the pensioned legionaries, intermarried with the British, were raising from the rich soil before the Saxons descended upon so fat a prize.

I need not give details of the excavations which have laid open the foundations of the castle. A local guide-book will do that. All that remains now is a system of massive roots in stone and brick and tile, revealed amongst the corn and fields of vegetables. The walls were some ten to twelve feet thick, the flint and stone so mortared that it is a solid mass. Within the great rectangle of the outer walls is a system of interior walls that suggests a barracks or village community. It also contains a crematorium, and a mysterious "platform" over a subterranean passage. This rectangle is some thirty feet thick in solid masonry. Was it the bed of a heavy watch-tower or beacon? And what was the purpose of the under-ground passage? It is an odd thing that the Roman records, often so voluble, do not explain this, any more than they explain the construction of the lead piping the Roman ducts at Bath, an alloy whose specific gravity is said to be different from that of the lead used by plumbers to-day.

During our latter-day world wars, Richborough has had a sudden ghost life. History has repeated itself belatedly. In 1916 some twenty thousand workmen, under the direction of the Royal Engineers, descended upon this derelict coast between Sandwich and Pegwell Bay. They widened and deepened the Stour, which by then was a mere trickle in the marsh; they cut a canal across a horseshoe-shaped bend; reclaimed two hundred and fifty acres of swampy ground; built a mile of modern wharves and equipped them with elec-tric cranes. The result was an up-to-date port covering nearly two thousand acres. From this secret place a fleet of inland and sea-going barges transported some million and a half tons of war material to France by the end of 1918. Further, in 1917 a train-ferry service was set up there, for the trans-port of troops, thus relieving Dover of the greater part of the burden. All this, of course, was attacked by the enemy, but Richborough's lowly position was its salvation, and the surrounding wasteland swallowed most of the bombardment.

What survived of all this mushroom growth was a sordid spectacle after the war. I believe the whole outfit was bought from the Government by heavy industry, but little use was made of it. When the second phase of the war broke out in 1939, the whole district from Richborough to Hythe (as I have already explained) was enclosed from the public, and once again mysterious engineering enterprises went on. Such matters are too recent for civilian tongues to be allowed to comment on. My own impression of that forbidden area was of vast flats of ragwort and rusty iron, one or two men here and there, sitting or squatting on patches of grass, barrels, or heaps of throw-out stuff, smoking cigarettes and just looking into space; a girl or a naval officer in uniform riding a disgraceful bicycle over a still more disgraceful cinder path; a sentry guarding a gate into an open field where a cow grazed; a six-deep railhead that ended abruptly in a long jetty where half a dozen men in dungarees were tinkering with oversize and profoundly rusty circular tanks. I realized later that those half a dozen tinkerers were making a section of the Mulberry dock, later to be assembled from many ports round our coast.

Through Richborough village and Stonar we take the round of Pegwell Bay, leaving the dead flat bend of the Stour on our left. From the midst of this crossing we can see how the island once stood off from the mainland. Behind us and before is rising ground, and Thanet stands up as a unit. Round to the east of the bay we come to Ramsgate, which like Margate, its opposite number on the north of the island, is now a holiday resort of the most popular kind; a den of landladies, aspidistras, fish and chips, concert parties on the sand, and many other things on the sand as well.

But between these two overblown fairgrounds lies Broadstairs, set in a tiny bay. It is another gem, with as much character of its own as that possessed, for example, by Polperro in Cornwall. I like it in winter, when it is deserted. To wander on a December afternoon, when dusk is falling, down the narrow central street and through the medieval gateway to the jetty, is like returning to a generalized childhood, in which everything is tinctured with the genius of Dickens and Captain Marryat. I have somewhat desperate recollections of that jetty, for when I was an infant of about ten years of age I fell so ill that my parents had to send me to a sanatorium at Broadstairs (Switzerland being beyond their means). My mother, to whom I was abnormally devoted, owing perhaps to my bad health and therefore precocious sensibility, took me down one serene winter day. Inevitably the hour came for her to say good-bye to me, and I to her. How was it to be done? She thought she might not see me again, so we went to a photographer in the town and had my portrait taken. Then we wandered about on the sands, marvelling at the warmth and light of the sunshine, while our hearts were breaking. My mother wept quietly behind her veil, and I felt my hands and feet growing colder as my spirits sank and a numbness overtook my thinking mind. She bought me a novel, and I remember to-day what it was, *The Lilac Sunbonnet*, by a Scottish parson, S. R. Crockett. But I could not see the print that day. I carried it with me to the beach and back to the sanatorium, and again to the station (for I insisted on seeing the last of her). There we parted, and the train took her away. I turned back with the person who had been sent from the hospital to take charge of me, and I walked draggedly along, the darkness of despair behind my eyes, and the book, her book, in my hand. Next day was still another serene one, with old-gold sunshine and opal glosses upon the sea. I stared out through the high windows of the great dining-room of the institution, and watched a man in the grounds hammering a stake. The sound of the blow syncopated with the image of hammer meeting wood, and I used this as a symbol for my young mind, suddenly acquainted with grief, to grasp the difference between reality and the desired object; the one lagging behind the other, so that they never meet, yet are ever interdependent. As soon as I could, I contrived to go into the town, where out of my pocket-money I bought my mother a small vase with the coat-of-arms of the town on it (there was a fashion for collecting these Goss pieces in those days). But then with terror I found that I could contrive no way to pack it and send it off to her. It did not occur to me to ask the nurses or the matron to help me, for they were the people whom somehow I had to circumvent; cold, formidable, impersonal officials. The agony increased, until it drove me again down to the sands, where in a fit of madness I dashed the vase against a rock and stamped the fragments into powder under my heel. Then suddenly the spirit of the place whispered to me, and my grief sank down into resignation. I saw the curve of the sandy cliffs, the sun shining over the town and throwing shadows upon the golden sands, where patches of weed made a strange writing that I longed to read. There seemed

to be nobody about, and I might have been on a desert island; but in fact I was with a crowd of sickly children, under the charge of two bonneted nurses who walked up and down, stopping at times to exchange a word with a boatman repairing his nets. But the revelation, a sort of apocalypse, carried me into a solitude of that strange kind of happiness that children can sometimes weave out of pure despair.

This experience, which I have so inadequately revived, set Broadstairs for ever in a special light for me, and when I go there now I cannot see it as it probably is, a mere adjunct of the larger watering-places on each side of it. It is quiet, unchanged, like the figures round Keats's Grecian Urn; a little seaside place so compact, so warm in tint and texture, set in a framework of gardens and fields that appear even to-day to have an added richness of foliage and flower and perfume. Here certainly the quality of Thanet, which is altogether luxuriant, is accentuated, and not only in the imagination of an elderly writer hynotized by recollections of childhood, but in reality; a reality of rich soil, saline air, and all the fruits of their marriage.

Thus my picture of Broadstairs is not vastly different from that which made both George Eliot and Dickens want to live there. George Eliot's desire was never fulfilled, but Dickens settled there for some time, and lived in the house now called *Bleak House* (misleadingly, for he wrote that novel much later), a castellated building set sharply against the sea-walk overlooking the harbour. He finished *David Copperfield* there, looking out just a century ago on what he described as "a little fishing-place; intensely quiet; built on a cliff, whereon—in the centre of a tiny semicircular bay—our house stands." Oddly enough, I read *David Copperfield* during those months of convalescence spent at Broadstairs, losing my own troubles in those of young David. I remember one of the nurses telling me that Dickens lived in that great house (as it seemed to me then) when we were out for one of those humiliating crocodile parades, a procession of sick infants lacking the vitality to break ranks or get into mischief. I can feel now the warm sense of glory that came over me as I looked up the brown brick wall at the windows high above me. The marvellous book with its hundreds of

P

characters, the author with his beard and his kind eyes, his immediate world and his very home, all were confused into my own personal, still morning-twilight universe. Had I been walking there hand in hand with the writer, to stop and chat with Peggotty outside his upturned boat, it would have been acceptable to me, as a natural course of events.

Turning in from the coast, we wind about at the back of the three holiday towns among lanes overhung with almost tropical verdure. We pass fields of lavender, and gardens where the sweet-pea is grown commercially, for table decoration. The rows of flowers "on tiptoe for a flight" stand seven to eight feet. Crossing the rising ground we reach Minster (which must not be confused with the Minster in the Isle of Sheppey). Here the scene is more open, with cornfields and patches of blazing poppies. It is a realm of light, for the sun comes down through this dry and salted air with a clinical purpose, kissing our skin through an ultra-violet beard. Disease, dirt, and darkness have no place here. The light soil, aerated chalk, the washed and blown air, the polished facets of the sea, the gold and crimson fields—it is sheer madness of colour and light; a very presence such as the painter van Gogh tried to capture, only to drive himself mad.

Minster is a place to linger in. Here one can pick a posy of legends as readily as daisies. The church is a survival of the nunnery founded in the seventh century by the Saxon princess Domneva, a sister of the two princes whose murder by their usurping uncle may well have given rise (as I have suggested earlier in this book) to the folk-tale of the Babes in the Wood. The wicked uncle, overcome with remorse, offered to give his niece (out of the stolen lands) as much ground as her tame doe might encircle at one running. The sagacious animal enclosed some ten thousand acres, and this so disturbed Thunnor, the king's factotum who had carried out the murders, that he expostulated, with the result that the earth opened and swallowed him. Why it did not do so earlier is not made clear in the morality of the folk-tale. About the year A.D. 670 the church and abbey were consecrated and Domneva became the first abbess. Her successor, St Mildred, worked many miracles, and was one of the many saints up and down Europe whose mortal remains preserved their lifelike form. Three hundred years afterwards, in 1027, they were given by Canute to the Abbey of St Augustine at Canterbury, together with all the possessions of the Abbey of Minster. The holy relics of the saint were removed only after a fight between the officers of the archbishop and the local folk, who of course were more concerned about the desecration of their saint than about the transfer of title-deeds and the probable increase of oppressive taxes. During those three centuries the settlement was repeatedly ravaged by Danes, and Canute's father, Sweyn, burned it to the ground.

The present church is one of the finest in the county; a large, cruciform structure with an unadulterated Norman nave and tower. The chevron and billet ornaments can still be seen in the semicircular arches of the nave. The Early English chancel has a ceiling entirely groined in stone, and the effect of this is most impressive.

Taking the road due north across the marsh, we complete the circuit of the island of Thanet by reaching Birchington, a seaside place popular with stage celebrities. It is thus like Frinton, in Essex, which it faces across the estuary of the Thames. It is clean, bright, and altogether unsuitable to have been the final resting-place of that grubby, stuffy, exotic genius, Dante Gabriel Rossetti, who spent his life behind heavy velvet curtains, bemused with drugs and dreams, a sombre personality half-regal in spite of a sordid bohemianism.

CHAPTER XIII

THE ROMAN WAY

LEAVING Thanet, we cross the wide stretch of no-man's-land which was once an open channel. Its western shore, on the old mainland, is guarded by the Roman fortress of Reculver (Regulbium), the companion of Richborough at the other end of the channel, the vanished seaway which is now the bed of the River Stour, and its other estuary the Wansum. Landing, as we may call it somewhat fancifully, at Reculver, we find ourselves at the beginning of the great northern stretch lying on the Thames side of the North Downs. Here is the oldest part of the county, at least from a historical point of view. Neolithic man, then the Celts, then the Romans, settled here because it was an open country of rich soil, protected from the wild beasts of the central and impenetrable forest of the Weald, and made easily intercommunicable by water.

Reculver now stands somewhat remote from the main road across the flats, conspicuous because it is on a patch of rising ground, the last small outpost of the spur of hills that break away from the North Downs and turn north-eastward from the woodlands west of Canterbury. It commands the approach up the Thames estuary and the outlet of the Medway. It is therefore still a cardinal point for navigational purposes, and that is why the twin towers of the church are maintained to guide mariners. While the sea is steadily receding from the Richborough end of the flats, the opposite process eats at the northern shore. Reculver in Roman times consisted not only of a fortress, but a town of rich villas where officials of the administration maintained an ample life as much like that of Rome as they could make it. As far out as Black Rock, which now stands a mile offshore, there survive tesselated pavements, broken walls, loose bricks and tiles, cisterns and arched vaults. In addition, fragments of furniture and domestic equipment, together with abundant quantities of coins from the period of Julius Cæsar to that of Honorius, are constantly being washed up. The coins are indeed so various that one may surmise that the settlement maintained an Imperial mint. These remains suggest that Regulbium was as large and as important as Rutupæ. The Latin records, *Notitia Imperii,* state that the first cohort of the Vetasii had its station here under the command of the Count of the Saxon Shore, one of the most important officers in the whole island colony.

The Roman station was oblong in shape, bounded by a ditch, and rounded at the corners. Its area was over seven and a half acres. The walls were of smaller stuff than those of Richborough, consisting of a concrete of pebbles and boulders from the beach, cemented into walls about nine feet thick. ·Within this large enclosure must have gone on for three centuries a vast amount of clerical work by busy civil servants of the great empire, men recruited in much the same way as our modern State servants, by examination, and trained in the school of official experience. A residential town spread around the government offices, and during the long periods of peaceful and highly civilized existence much cultural life must have developed there, with the amenities of literature and the fine arts, including the cultivation of that dissociated mysticism which the Romans borrowed from the surviving esoterics of Greece and the Middle East. Who knows when the first rumour of that new cult, the worship of Christ, practised by certain Jewish fanatics in Rome, came to these Roman headquarters in Britain, and exercised the nostalgia-ridden minds of some underpaid minor officials, frustrated by the weight of many ranks above them, all ambition of advancement long since spent? This teaching, heady as fresh wine, with its novel doctrine of humility as a virtue instead of a shame, its lifting up of the individual (something completely revolutionary in the history of human thought) from the prostration demanded by the State; all this must have come like a spring tide to these weary creatures, underlings of empire, bored by a traditional life of safety and monotony between office and dormitory in a land that was a simulacrum of the Latin centre, but tinged with fear and a hint of the unknown North.

All must have seemed so secure, so abiding, to those

Romans, performing their daily work, visiting each other in their villas along the slopes falling to the river mouth, right up as far as Londinium. They would come and go, with periods of leave or official journeys to Rome, taking with them local produce of Celtic origin or colonial variations of Latin arts, foods, sciences. They would bring back articles to act as restoratives of the great central culture, so that these villas and offices and temples to Diana, Apollo, and Mithra might not lose a nice sophistication or be condemned as provincial by superior visitors from Rome. But now all that remains of this solidity is a rare flotsam drawn in by fishermen, or cast up on the beach after storms. A fibula, a girl's ring with the stone gone blind, a spoon, a coin celebrating a God-Emperor—these come to shore at Regulbium, fragments of the undertow mingled with survivals of the Christian order and settlement which replaced that of the Romans, only in its turn to be swallowed by the sea.

That Christian settlement began when King Ethelbert resigned his royal palace at Canterbury to St Augustine for the foundation of a priory. He built himself a new palace on the site of the already crumpled Roman fortress at Regulbium, and it is probable that he was buried here in a newly erected church. The usurping King Sigbert, as well as founding Minster with conscience-money, also set up here a Benedictine monastery in the seventh century, and this later was made over to the see of Canterbury in Norman times. The great church of St Mary, with its twin towers, was built on the site of the Roman fort and the Saxon palace. The towers were set with spires, and their great height made them conspicuous far out at sea. Throughout the Middle Ages passing ships would doff their sails when passing, as a tribute to the Virgin. In those times the church was a noble shrine, with a spacious nave, aisles, and chancel. But gradually the sea approached, consuming first the surrounding township, then attacking the church itself. Three hundred years ago the fabric was intact, but few efforts were made to prevent the encroachment. The burial-ground disappeared, with all its names and bones. Then the walls were attacked. In 1809 the vicar held a ballot of the congregation, and by a majority of one vote it was decided to take down what was left of the material and to use it to build Hillborough church two miles away. Trinity House took over the twin steeples, deciding that they were too valuable a seamark to be allowed to vanish. Groynes and a stone wall were built against the sea, the sandy foundations of the towers were fortified, and the spires partly restored. That is all we may see to-day of Reculver, the once thriving town of the Middle Ages, the Saxons, the Romans. A coastguard station, with its cottages, an inn named after King Ethelbert; these, and the reliquary flotsam on the beach, alone survive.

Driving westward along the open country, half waste littoral and half farming ground, we pass Herne Bay. We pass it because there is nothing in particular to attract a visit of pure curiosity. One can go to this well-known watering place for a family holiday, or for a convalescence after a period of debauchery. Otherwise, one turns inland, where two miles behind the shore lies the slumbering village of Herne, with its noble Early English church, whose large west window is worth noticing, as also are the wood carvings and brasses. Bishop Ridley was vicar here, in his first curacy. In his valedictory note, before his execution in the reign of the zealous Queen Mary, he referred to the village as a "worshipful and wealthy Parish." It is still wealthy—in everything that matters; beauty, peacefulness, venerable buildings, and an open and healthy view. But it is typical only of many such villages along this side of the Downs, all the way to Canterbury. A sense of great age, and at the same time an expectancy and freshness, fills this countryside. Looking along its slopes from the clay cliffs of Herne Bay, one can see the Reculver towers, and beyond them the outline of the coast of Thanet. It is an invitation southward. Up there, in those hills, every aspect is promissory. It may be an illusion, a physiological trick which we share with sunflowers, always to turn ourselves toward the south, where the daystar treads across the sky; but it is a constant in human nature, and when the place and the time augment this inclination, the result is overwhelming. My temptation, therefore, is always to turn inland while exploring this part of the county, though I am ready to appreciate the character of the coast, with its heat-split cliffs of clay, its dwindling shore, and its wave-borne rumours of vanished men and the fruits of their hands.

So we come to Whitstable, a Mecca for gourmets. It is a pleasing little place because it is untidy and concerned completely with its special job, the breeding and marketing of the world's most famous oysters. Places, like people, always acquire some distinctive quality when they are expert in one or another art, craft, or science. A master carpenter, a skilled coal-miner, a mathematician, a pianist, a poet, a horse-trainer, an oyster-breeder—they will each, as far as they are masters in their own sphere, outwardly but unconsciously carry that distinction. And all that they gather round them, the impedimenta of their work, shares in it. Their tools are symbols of the joy and confidence with which they are handled. Like the articles in the daily life of primitive peoples —the gypsy's horse-harness, the tribesman's bow and arrow —they have a strength, and an appearance of being slightly over-used and worn-down.

That describes Whitstable. There is no laid-out waterside parade. The cottages, boat-building sheds, huts full of gear, are littered about the sea front in a rule-of-thumb fashion, amid a confusion of ropes, baskets, odd-looking tools connected with the dredging, boats, and oilskins. There are two kinds of native. One, the human, is truly so, for these men work in a close corporation that is hereditary. Half a dozen family names have been on the enrolment books of the Whitstable Oyster Fishery Company for two centuries. The organization is a sort of corporation set up by Act of Parliament in the eighteenth century. The little industry is ruled by a Water Court, consisting of a foreman, deputy foreman, twelve jurymen, and a water-bailiff, all elected annually along with a treasurer, auditor, and salesman. There are now two or three such companies, each with its allotted culture beds defined by buoys. Outside these beds the flats are "free," and these are worked by "flatsmen," who are not members of the company. They dredge for the oyster brood (which is enormously prolific) and the young bivalves in various stages of development. This stuff they sell to the company for supplying the breeding-beds. In addition to this source of local supply, however, the company buys in brood largely from the Essex flats (there is a special fleet of Essex boats engaged solely in this trade), from other parts of the English coast, from Brittany and Portugal. Wherever it comes from, it thrives here uniformly, owing to a unique admixture of salt and fresh water, and certain algæ carried down by the little streamlets which supply the fresh water. The beds are cared for as tenderly as rose gardens, and the Royal Natives that we used to buy at anything over eight shillings a dozen (and cursing the price) represented a watchful care over each individual shell and its delectable treasure whose flavour and effect can never be described in words. "Fallings from us, vanishings" perhaps may approach the reality; a phrase made by Wordsworth apropos of more celestial matters. But the flavour of an oyster has something metaphysical about it, and we can best approach it by saying what it is not. It is not fishy, it is not substantial. It is a cleansing. It wipes away the taint of the world and the flesh from our palate. It prepares the way for the most superlative of vintages. It keeps us sober, yet it makes us susceptible. It is an introduction rather than a meal. And no matter how many we may swallow, that flavour remains elusive and tantalizing. What a fool was King Henry I of England to die of an excess of lampreys when he might have died of an excess of oysters. For in the Middle Ages and indeed right up to the beginning of the nineteenth century, oysters could be bought by the bushel for a few coins. Shakespeare was able to swallow oysters at one and fourpence a hundred. No wonder he had such poetic vitality. No wonder his magic lines shone like gold, and were active as uranium.

And of all oysters the native Whitstable is the most choice. I can say that after much sampling. I have been especially to Paris in September to eat the Portuguese oysters (shaped like shoe-horns) at about one and threepence a dozen. I have been to Amsterdam upon a similar pilgrimage. But there is no oyster like the misnamed native Whitstable. I call it misnamed because it is more accurately described as the *cosmopolitan* Whitstable; for who can be sure where it was born?

How unfortunate it is that the little harbour, now owned by the railway company, should be given over to coaling. The dust and din of this trade are a blot on the otherwise extremely picturesque locality. But this trade is the somewhat sordid end to a story that began when the second railway and the first railway tunnel in the world were opened in 1830 between Whitstable and Canterbury. Sir Charles Igglesden, in his delightful *Saunter Through Kent*, quotes a local newspaper paragraph of that day which records the incident :

"The motion of the carriages is particularly easy and agreeable, and at first starting the quiet power with which the vast mass was set in motion dispelled every fear in the passengers. The entrance into the tunnel was very impressive—the total darkness, the accelerated speed, the rumbling of the cars, the loud cheering of the whole party echoing through the vault, combined to form a situation almost terrific, certainly novel and striking. Perfect confidence in the safety of the whole apparatus, however, seemed to prevail, and the company emerged from the dismal tunnel into the warm precincts of the cheerful day."

With perhaps a little less confidence (knowing what mankind has done with mechanical force during a century of misuse) we leave Whitstable and continue our progress within sight of the coast, along the road over the flats. During the war all this was front-line battleground, from which the public was excluded. Signs of the struggle are being gradually removed, or submerged. Here was the place to be in during the dark days of 1940–1, to realize how near England stood to disaster. All this open country, with its flat beaches, seemed to be too pregnable, in spite of the entanglements on the shore, the guns behind them, and the temporary airfields. But even under those nervous conditions the local folk went about their work on the land and in the water stolidly—fishermen, dredgermen, ploughmen, and market gardeners. Their work "will go onward the same, though Dynasties pass," as Thomas Hardy wrote of them in the equally dark days of 1915.

The wide waters close in as we go westward, for the Isle of Sheppey shuts our vision off from the open estuary. The figuration of waters becomes more and more difficult to comprehend. The island, with its slopes on the northern shore, the heights behind the Medway, and the distant heights of Essex across the estuary—these all rising at unexpected

places and angles, amongst a network of streams and creeks
—baffle the amateur map-reader. The only way to avoid
being caught in one blind alley after another is to stick to the
main road for a while, going through Faversham and Sittingbourne. But this main road is Watling Street, the Dover
Road which for nearly two thousand years has been the
artery connecting England with Europe. It is almost banal
nowadays to enlarge upon that theme. It has been done *ad
nauseam* from Geoffrey Chaucer to Jeffrey Farnol. Strangers
to Kent may say that the Dover Road, the old Roman road,
is the principal feature of Kent, but readers who have wandered with me through so many chapters will treat that suggestion merely as a traveller's superficial tale. The road,
shunned by the villages and sought by the towns, runs almost
dead straight from Canterbury to the outskirts of London at
Kidbrooke, the most impressive as well as the oldest highway
in the country. We shall stick to it now as far as Dartford,
with one excursion from it to explore the Isle of Sheppey.
When we reach Dartford, the outer edges of our imaginary
fan will have been visited, leaving us the centre ribs to
follow out as far as Canterbury, the fair flower, the jewel
set so skilfully in the fabric.

Soon after joining the Dover Road and turning westward
we come to Faversham. It is an ancient town, Saxon in
origin, with remains of an abbey and a priory, both Benedictine, founded in the twelfth century. It also possesses two
buildings built on pillars with an open ground floor. One is
a sixteenth-century grammar school, and the other is the
Town Hall. There are several merchants' houses and warehouses of the Tudor period. All this, and the fact that the
town stands on a U-shaped creek opening into the Swale, and
has its own oyster-bed and boat-building, make it a sufficiently
interesting place for a day's visit.

In addition to that, however, its name brings to the visitor's mind at once a famous literary recollection. No. 80
Abbey Street is only one of several fine old Tudor buildings
in this street. On 15 February 1550 a rich merchant named
Thomas Arderne, Clerk of the Court and Controller of the
Customs of the town, was murdered by his wife and her
lover, one Mosbie. They and the assassins were caught and

executed. The case might have been forgotten, except in the court records, had not some local genius written a play about it. It is a prophetic piece of work, both technically and psychologically. Its blank verse was contemporary with that of Marlowe (to whom some critics have rashly ascribed it), and its subtlety of characterization was so remarkable that other critics have said it must have been written by Shakespeare. Moreover, its theme, by treating the domestic life of middle-class and peasant folk as the vehicle of high tragedy, foretold the way that literature was to take in this country some two centuries later when the bourgeoisie had risen to greater power. The play *Arden of Faversham* is well worth reading to-day. Its anonymous author, writing in 1586, was undoubtedly a poet worthy to be put amongst the great names of Kent, the county of so many famous poets. Alice, the infatuated wife of the rich merchant, is a character that might have been created by D. H. Lawrence. The way in which her rough, class-conscious (and therefore resentful) lover accepts her passion while secretly despising her and using her for his own avaricious purpose, is a revelation of the depths of human nature which the reader cannot forget. And the author has used it with much modern dramatic effect.

There is a valuable museum, of Roman funerary remains, housed in an ancient building called the Maison Dieu, at Ospringe, west of the town, on the way to the site of the Roman camp at Syndale, which is believed to be the Durolevum about whose exact position archæologists make much debate. The Maison Dieu was originally a monastic hospital, founded by Henry III about A.D. 1230, and it covered a large area. It consisted of the hospital buildings, a church, a King's Chamber, the domestic offices of the master and brethren, with adjoining barns, mill, and stables, while on the other side of the street stood the leper-house and its outhouses. As well as being a hospital it was also a hostel, and many pilgrims accepted its shelter. After the Dissolution of the Monasteries it gradually decayed, the local folk in the customary way helping themselves to stones and other material from the buildings to feather their own nests. I believe that the site, on which the house now used as a museum was built soon after the Dissolution, belongs to-day to St John's College, Cambridge.

At the top of the hill, overlooking a pond, stands the Priory, or what is left of it. This consists of part of the mansion erected or adapted from the sacred building, after the Dissolution. At one time this Davington Court, as it is called, belonged to Sir Thomas Walsingham's daughter. Along the private road to the house runs an old wall of brick with a gateway into the kitchen garden. Over it is the following inscription : "Deus nobis hæc otia fecit, 1624," a Virgilian tag which Dryden put into English thus, "These blessings, friend, a Deity bestowed." I think that such garden walls, with disused doorways, have a more nostalgic effect even than ruins. They are a backway entrance into the past, and are still the scenes of clandestine emotions. The church was restored in the nineteenth century, but in spite of that the massive austerity of the Norman nave, with its remarkably noble west doorway (late Norman), can still be appreciated. Over the door stand three orders of mouldings and shafts with abaci and foliaged capitals.

Faversham, the Fair Town of the Saxons, is a lively monument of English history, with emphasis upon its adolescent period between the going of the Romans and the coming of the Normans. Many Saxon remains have been and continue to be found in the neighbourhood, and they all have that grace which is peculiar to the spirit of youth. I think it is no exaggeration to say that this spirit is characteristic of the Nordic peoples. It has its disadvantages, both for themselves and their more adult neighbours. From the time of King Athelstane, who held a witenagemot here in the year 930, Faversham has been favoured by royalty. It had been called "the King's little Town" for over a century before that. It was early made a member of the Cinque Port federation, because its creek met the Watling Street and thus became important as a point in transport. King Stephen, who founded the Abbey, was buried here. Henry VIII visited it three times, on the first occasion with Wolsey, who had to be entertained "with capons." The great Emperor Charles V was lodged here during his visit to England. Elizabeth and Mary both came here, Elizabeth to grace the setting up of the powder mills which two hundred years later blew up and destroyed half the town. Charles II stopped the night here on his way "home" after so many years in exile. His brother James II was arrested in Faversham by sailors, who thus bungled a convenient plot to allow him to leave the country without embarrassment to the new government. He subsequently "escaped" through Rochester, spending his last night at an inn which still stands (now a bank) in Rochester High Street.

So we leave, reluctantly, this historical little town, fair St Crispin's town, to which this cobbler-saint came and settled during the Diocletian persecutions (though Soissons in France also claims that honour). I have spent only a day here, but like the heroes of Agincourt, I can "stand tip-toe when this day is named, and rouse me at the name of Crispian."

As we proceed along the Dover Road westward, over on our right lies the estuary, with the Faversham creek and the marshes. It is a wonderful stretch of flat land and water in a bewildering confusion. Fields, boats, trees, houses, tall chimneys, and haystacks—all surrealistically juxtaposed by the caprice of chance. And over them the sun, wind, and weather race unimpeded. The exhilaration of space, an excitement shared with gulls and rooks and sailors, seizes the traveller along this road, and he feels that he must stand and throw his arms out and upward, in sheer worship of he knows not what; worship, and defiance too, at such a monstrous imposition of light and space and "that inverted bowl we call the sky."

Sittingbourne lies close under the lee of the North Downs. It is not a prepossessing place, although close by are many enchanting villages, especially those in the hills above it; Rodmersham and Tunstall in particular. It is worth climbing out of the long High Street of the town, which occupies a couple of miles of the main road, in order to visit Tunstall church, and to take a look along the avenue of enormous trees that lead from the churchyard to the manor house. Although so near the workaday world of Sittingbourne, Tunstall sleeps on the hillside under an eiderdown of centuries, snug and still. The trees of cedar, yew, and giant elms make a wall against time itself. The church is a small one, containing an Elizabethan worthy reclining, in effigy, on his elbow in the Shakespearean manner, and below him appears the record that "his dear and sorrowful wife, not without much grief, hath erected this monument." What a strange little shudder of communication with these vanished people goes through one's blood! Is it they, or their phrases, that are immortal and so potent? Is the word greater than the fact?

Before returning to the Dover Road and hurrying through Sittingbourne, we can enjoy the view not only across the estuary, or rather the estuaries, for from here we can see both the mouth of the Medway immediately below us, and further off the Thames winding round northward and east, we can turn, I say, from these, and notice the great slopes of cherry orchards along the northern side of the range. Sittingbourne has the richest cherry orchards in England. Second to this rich land is that round Goudhurst. But I have already said something about the fruitlands of west Kent. Cherries were first introduced into England at Sittingbourne, by Richard Harris, fruiterer to King Henry VII.* He obtained 105 acres here and "with great care, good choice and no small labour and cost," planted it with cherries. Sittingbourne still has the biggest orchard in the country. The cherry crop is a profitable one, and during the war has been a bonanza. I know that one orchard in the Goudhurst district, of seventeen acres, turned over some seven thousand pounds in money each season while the price was controlled by the Government.

It is worth while turning to the right out of Sittingbourne and running up along the side of Milton Creek. The country is rather spoiled by odds and ends of domestic squalor, of recent deposit; but amongst this detritus of the twentieth century will be found gems of an earlier time; cottages, farmhouses, Milton church with its great tower standing defiantly on the marsh against the four winds. We cross the Swale on to the Isle of Sheppey by the ramshackle bridge which I have already mentioned. The southern part of the island con-

* A correspondence in *The Times* has since revealed references to cherries in England some century and a half earlier.

tinues the marshland, not unlike Romney, with dykes and cattle. But the front of the island facing the open sea rises quite steeply, with an almost cliff-like approach to Minster. The church looks somewhat squat and huddled from outside, like a hen sunk down into the earth against the weather. But inside it is cavernous, cold, and has a gaunt austerity like that of William of Normandy himself. It is only a fragment of the original conventual church, built of Kentish rag and flints. There are some old tombs, including one of 1330 with French brasswork.

I stood one evening, during the peacemaking festivities of 1945, on the clay cliffs a couple of miles from Minster tower, looking westward over Sheerness and the wartime dam stretching across the estuary. It was a lonely experience, to be there in a silence loaded with significance. Not a ship, not a plane to break the pause. What comes next? I asked myself, thinking of the recent doings and restless gropings of the human race. But there was no answer. The whole universe was pausing. Then gently, from the rough old Minster walls, there floated the music of bells, rising and falling like lines from Tennyson or Virgil, unbearably melancholy, deep throat-sounds fusing together and sometimes dissolving quite away on the air, then swelling out again like a fresh pulse of sorrow. True celebration, I thought, of the end of such a war. It was too acute to bear, so I clambered down the cliff to the shore, and gathered samphire, while the bell-music rolled unheard above my head and out to sea. I stayed there for half an hour, looking across to Essex, and identifying the buoys and lightships. The pastel-shaded waters of the estuary moved gradually, merging into each other and fading. This too was mournful, and I could no longer endure the burden. Making my way up the iron-stained mudbanks (they can hardly be called cliffs) I put the basket of samphire in the car and drove away from these too potent reminders of what the world had just been through; the destruction, the moral degradation, the anguish and waste.

Through ten miles of hills and orchards on the south, marshes on the seaward side, I made my way back to Rochester.

Rochester and Canterbury are binary stars in the archæo-

logist's and the historian's heaven. To tell the story of one is to hint at the story of the other. How are we to approach Rochester? Are we to become classical and tell its Roman story, or shall we make a period piece and portray the Rochester of Dickens? Those are only two of the aspects of the history of this compact little city. In fact, the dominant feature of the place is its medieval relic of castle and cathedral. They stand side by side, gaunt and grim, on the mound above the bridge. That is certainly the physical character of Rochester. But it is increased I suspect by the sense that these austere Norman remains are Romanesque in more than one sense. They stand on sites of the stipendiary settlement which was the second halting-place of the invading Romans, after Canterbury. Any work that requires excavation in the town reveals at once the record of massive foundations, and Roman articles of war and domestic life. And after the Romans the city flourished for six hundred years under the Saxons. King Ethelbert, immediately he had embraced Christianity and relinquished his palace at Canterbury to St Augustine, set about building, in A.D. 600, the first church in Rochester.

Two and a half centuries later King Alfred saved the city from the Danes, and built a fleet of ships there, the first English navy. Then with the coming of the Normans it was decided to fortify so important a strongpoint on the great highway, where it met the water traffic of the Thames. Bishop Odo and Gundulf, bishop of Rochester, began the building of the castle in 1080, and the work went on until 1126. The great tower stands there to-day, its walls twelve feet thick. During a seven-weeks' siege of the Barons by King John, much of the main part of the castle was reduced; but the tower survived, and in 1314 it was used as a prison for the wife of King Bruce of Scotland. Another and still more bloody siege took place during the Civil War, when Fairfax came to punish the Kent folk because of their individualist outcry, in the Petition of Right, against the totalitarian government of Cromwell in 1648. Those were years of secret police, and the use of identity cards; when everyone had to register himself when travelling, or lodging for the night away from home. Our Victorian grandparents

Hop picking at Paddock Wood

would have thought such conditions of life intolerable, but we have learned to put up with them again. Fairfax slew three hundred people by the river, and took fifteen hundred prisoners. The last alarm came in 1667, when the Dutch admiral de Ruyter sailed up the Thames with seventy ships as far as the Medway, where they were held by an obstruction of guardships which General Monk had sunk to form a boom. Why this disgraceful humiliation took place is a long story. It involves a history of the provisioning of our navy, and it is a sordid tale of fraud, treachery, wicked indifference to the privations of fellow countrymen, nepotism, and peculation. A rhyme of the times suggests that the unrest and disgust were so great that

> An English pilot, too (Oh shame, Oh Sin!)
> Cheated of 's pay, 'twas he that showed them in.

The High Street of Rochester is full of interesting buildings; ancient shop-fronts, a Guildhall built in 1687, and a Corn Exchange given in 1706 by Queen Anne's admiral Sir Cloudesley Shovel, who was also a Member of Parliament. An earlier Member, elected for the city in 1563, one Richard Watts, endowed a "house for poor travellers" in the High Street, and there it stands to-day, with a quaintly worded tablet to commemorate the gift. This house at once reminds us of Dickens's reference to it in his story, *The Seven Poor Travellers*. From that we recollect his description of Sir Cloudesley Shovel's charming clock which still "projects over the pavement out of a grave red-brick building," though I question Dickens's epithet of "grave" for the charming Queen Anne front (which as far as I could see has no back!). But maybe this difference in æsthetic appeal is due to the general change in architectural taste during the past century. To call any Queen Anne architecture "grave" seems odd to-day.

The High Street still has many of the quaint gables that so delighted Dickens. There are several second-hand furniture shops, which must have appeared since his time, for as far as I recall he makes no mention of them. His eye would not have been affronted by the ugly bridges, road and rail, which now cross the river into Strood. It is probable that there was a Roman bridge over the Medway, but no definite record of it remains. The Saxons built a wooden bridge, and it survived into the fourteenth century. In the year A.D. 1300 the Crown paid twelve shillings' recompence for a hired horse that had been blown off the bridge by the wind. A stone bridge was built in 1387 which lasted until 1856, the year Dickens bought Gadshill Place, the house which he had coveted when he was a child in Rochester. A second stone bridge was built, in keeping with the charming stone balustrade which still runs along the water front below the Castle. Why this handsome bridge, with its well-placed recesses at each pier, had to be replaced by the present horror in the Meccano Tradition, I suppose was due to the need for motor-buses to have more margin to pass each other. Factors like that weigh more heavily than the obligations to preserve beauty.

While grumbling about the municipal indifference to the needs of beauty (the food of the human spirit), I can draw attention to the chimney-stacks seen on both banks up and down the river. They are mostly cement works, which use the chalk quarried from the Downs above the town. All this district, like the rest of north Kent, was working at full pressure during the years of war. This activity attracted considerable attention from the Luftwaffe. In addition, much damage was done because the Thames estuary lay under the principal airway into London. That nightmare is rapidly slipping away from our surface consciousness, for the human mechanism seems to be so constructed that memory sifts out the horrors and refuses to acknowledge that they were ever anything but a "tale told in fury." This tendency must not allow us to forget the character of the people of north Kent, who carried on their work, making munitions and vehicles of war under the canopy of the enemy's rage, for over five years. The scars are still there as I write this book.

There is a substantial literature for the person curious to know something about Dickens and Rochester, about the Castle, the Cathedral, and the ancient houses of the town. I like to browse amongst these books, and to visit the place from time to time, coming to it over the gap in the Downs from some twenty miles south where I live. It is a rich journey, for I pass through Maidstone, the capital of the county, and pass, on the ridge overlooking the Medway break-through, an archæologist's prize spot called Kit's Coty House. This eight miles between Maidstone and Rochester was "discovered to be one of the most beautiful walks in England" by Dickens. And he was right, though to-day the road has been sadly disfigured by bungalows, cocoa-shacks for carmen, and greasy little garages.

I see no virtue in passing on a lot of second-hand information about the last fourteen years of Dickens's life, which he spent at Gadshill Place; or about the dimensions of the Norman nave of the Cathedral. Statistics are dull until one has seen and been moved by the objects which they enumerate. And how is one moved by Rochester Cathedral? Like Minster Abbey, it is harsh and gaunt. The interior of the nave is a huge rectangular box, whose only concession to grace is the ambulatory that cuts a way through the massive arches and pillars high up. The chancel and choir, with a number of chapels that form the aisles, are raised up a flight of steps, in the manner of Canterbury, and beneath them is a big crypt. All this part of the church was built in the thirteenth century and is thus in the Early English manner. Sir Gilbert Scott "restored" the choir in 1874, and the less said about it the better, in spite of the fact that the woodwork is mostly the thirteenth-century original piously preserved amid this setting of Turkish-bath tiling. Much of the restoration of the exterior is also very dubious. At the south-eastern corner are some Norman fragments of the old chapter-house and cloisters. The eastern parts were much doctored in the nineteenth century, and the original tower with its short spire has been transformed into a taller but commonplace tower with battlement and pinnacles, out of harmony with the body of the Cathedral.

Returning to the High Street we must visit the Bull Hotel, a massive Georgian place flush with the narrow end of the street, with a wide gateway through to the stabling. Here is another shrine for Dickensians. Room No. 17 is still referred to as "Mr Pickwick's Room," and the "moon-faced clock" may still be seen there.

Dickens wrote that "if anyone knows to a nicety where

Rochester ends and Chatham begins, it is more than I do."
Still more complete is that welding to-day, for now the three
towns south of the Medway are mortared indissolubly
together. These three, Rochester, Chatham, and Gillingham,
are separated from Strood and Frinsbury only by the winding Medway, which is about as wide here as the Thames at
Charing Cross. Although his heart was in Rochester, Dickens
spent his childhood in Chatham, between the ages of five and
eleven (1817–23), after which the impoverished family removed to London. The child's impression was that "the
principal productions of these towns appear to be soldiers,
sailors, Jews, chalk, shrimps, officers and dockyard men. The
commodities chiefly exposed for sale in the public streets are
marine stores, hard-bake, apples, flat-fish, and oysters. The
streets present a lively and animated appearance, occasioned
chiefly by the conviviality of the military." He continues,
through the mouth of Mr Pickwick, "the consumption of
tobacco in these towns must be very great; and the smell
which pervades the streets must be exceedingly delicious to
those who are extremely fond of smoking. A superficial
traveller might object to the dirt, which is their leading
characteristic; but to those who view it as an indication of
traffic and commercial prosperity, it is truly gratifying."

The habits of the men in the Services are much different
to-day, in spite of what the pessimists tell us. I remember
that, during the war, a lofty official in the Army Education
Department told me that 11½ per cent of the Army was
unable to read or write, and that he spent most of his time
in Whitehall indenting for picture-books with which to edu-
cate the troops. That may be so. I can only record that while
I was in Chatham one day, just after the Battle of Britain,
I stopped by the road against the recreation-ground to look
back over the river to Brompton on the other side. Two
sailors, who had apparently been in conversation, stopped
talking when they saw me near. Were they discussing naval
secrets? No, they were reading aloud to each other, handing
the book over in turn. It was Palgrave's *Golden Treasury*.
That same day I was in Rochester, and in the gardens by
the Castle I chatted for ten minutes with a soldier who was
sitting at the other end of the seat. He was reading a fat

book, which I at once recognized. It was Fisher's *History of Europe*. I longed to ask him questions about it, and to discover what was this boy's attitude toward the cultured Liberalism, with its austere Greco-Victorian background, of the author. But I feared he might suspect me of being a specimen-hunter, one of those superior observers of their fellow mortals, who collect worthless statistics and feel very much above the battle. Even so, my neighbour saw me looking shyly at his book, and he in turn looked equally shyly at me. I suspect that he knew what I was dreading, and with this mutual sensibility and respect for each other, we parted, with as it were, a "nod and a wink." But there came to my mind as I walked away the recollection of that statement about the 11½ per cent. My experience in Chatham and Rochester had not disproved it; but even so I chuckled to myself. Scepticism is often as irrational as superstition.

What most impresses the visitor to Chatham, as also to that other naval barracks, Sheerness, is the quietness and discretion which pervade the town. It is almost an air of secrecy. The Silent Service, that hackneyed phrase, at once comes to one's mind. In *The Uncommercial Traveller* Dickens makes the same observation. He speaks of Chatham having "a gravity upon its red brick offices and houses, a staid pretence of having nothing to do, an avoidance of display, which I never saw out of England." So this spirit is something older than the reticence needed to guard highly technical matters about modern mechanical appliances.

Having somewhat indulged the reprehensible habit of quoting, I must take myself in hand; but I cannot do so before allowing myself one more passage in inverted commas to show how our national pride in the Royal Navy has a deep root that nourishes a leaf or two even in the most emancipated and international-minded Englishman to-day. It comes from the historian Lambarde, who is writing of Chatham :

"Even at our first entrie into the Diocese of Rochester, on the north-east part thereof, the Station, or Harborow of the Navie Royall at Gillingham and Chatham presenteth it self, a thing of all other the most woorthie the first place, whether you respect the richesse, beautie, or benefite of the same.

No Towne, nor Citie, is there (I dare say) in this whole shire comparable in the right value with this one Fleete. Not shipping any where els in the whole world to be founde, either more artificially moalded under the water, or more gorgeously decked above. And as for the benefite that our Realme may reape by these most stately and valiant vessels, it is even the same that Apollo by the mouth of Aristonice promised to Greece, when his oracle was consulted against the invasion of Xerxes, and that his woonderfull armie (or rather world of men in armes) saying,

> "Highe love doth give thee walles of wood,
> Apointed to Minerve,
> The which alone invincible
> May thee, and thine, preserve.

"And therefore, of these such excellent ornaments of peace, and trustie aides in war, I might truly affirme, that they be for wealth, almost so manie rich treasures, as they be single ships : for beautie, so many Princely Palaces, as they be several pieces : and for strength, so many moving Castles, as they be sundrie sailing vessels. Howbeit, if their swiftnesse in sayling, their furie in offending, or force in defending, be duly weighed, they shall be found as farre to passe all other in power, as they be inferiour to any in number."

How appropriate that is as a description of the descendants of that same navy which for two terrible years, 1940 and 1941, held the history of Europe in its hand, out of reach of the enemy who, had he snatched it, would have thrown it into the sewer of time.

Of all places in England, Chatham is the one where ghosts might least be expected. But on his official visit to the Dockyard in 1661 Mr Pepys anticipated such an adventure, which he has recorded in his diary :

"Then to the Hill House at Chatham, where I never was before, and I found a pretty pleasant house, and am pleased with the armes that hang up there. Here we supped very merry, and late to bed; Sir William telling me that old Edgebarrow, his predecessor, did die and walk in my chamber, did make me somewhat afraid, but not so much as for mirth's sake I did seem. So to bed in the Treasurer's chamber. Lay and slept till three in the morning, and then waking and by the light of the moon I saw my pillow (which overnight I flung from me) stand upright, but not bethinking myself what it might be I was a little afraid, but sleep overcome all, and so lay till nigh morning, at which time I had a candle brought me, and a good fire made, and in general it was a great pleasure all the time I staid here to see how I am respected and honoured by all people; and I find that I begin to know now to receive so much reverence, which at the beginning I could not tell how to do. Sir William and I by coach to the Dock, and there viewed all the storehouses and the old goods that are this day to be sold, which was a great pleasure to me, and so back again by coach home, where we had a good dinner."

Leaving Chatham upon that sensible suggestion, I intend to push on along the London road to Gravesend; but first I must diverge both to right and left. I turn off through Frindsbury to explore the tongue-shaped peninsula whose base is bounded by the wavering road that runs to Gravesend from Strood. This compact of country is cut off from the main stream of life even to-day, and I recommend it to folk who are in need of space and silence and solitude. Much of it is marshy ground, with saltings towards the shores of the Thames and Medway. Bird life abounds here, and all that attractive detritus of the sea; flotsam whose odds and ends come to shore with surprises and incongruities, some of them tragic, others ludicrous. Most of these relics are tarry, and coated with oil, so that one need be not too well dressed for a ramble by the water. It is impossible to go there and not to be overcome by curiosity; that means touching, picking up, hauling, sometimes with sad effects upon one's hands and garments.

The interior of the peninsula is undulating, with a number of ancient villages and historical pieces, notably Cooling Castle, or at least the fine double-towered gateway that is still surviving. The castle was built in the fourteenth century by an early member of the Cobham family, the Lord John Cobham whose granddaughter married the Lollard worthy, Sir John Oldcastle. This pious follower of Wyclif was taken from the castle and executed for his religious opinions. Such an event gives a somewhat sardonic twist to the meaning of the inscription which can still be seen over the doorway of the gatehouse. In wording of black and white enamel, wonderfully preserved after five hundred years' exposure to the weather, it says :

> Knowyth that beth and schul be
> That I am mad in help of the cuntre
> In knowyng of whyche thyng
> Thys is chartre and wytnessyng.

Cliffe, to the north-west of Cooling, is a Saxon village where throughout the eighth and ninth centuries national councils were held. We can make our way at leisure by the north or south shores to the extremity of the tongue, which is called the Isle of Grain, where the view is most interesting because of its extraordinary variety. The dockyard of Sheerness lies across half a mile of water opposite. On the left hand is the open estuary, which we have already contemplated (with its buoys, lightships, and seaborne traffic) from the mudbanks of Sheppey.

On the backland, as on the heights of Thanet, one is dazzled with the ardour of the light and the vast range of sky, land, and water. Fields of mustard blaze with yellow fire.

My divergence to the left from the road to Gravesend brings me to scenery in lively contrast to that of the Isle of Grain. Turning southward parallel with the Medway, the road climbs steeply out of Rochester and is already on the chalk hills before it leaves the town. Climbing steadily, on a wide sweep with woods on our left, and the hideous survival of a huge airfield, while on our right flows the river, cutting round a noble expanse which closes in upon Maidstone, still out of sight, we come at last to a clearance above the trees, and passing a quarry discover Kit's Coty House. It stands in a cornfield called Blue Bell Hill, one and a half miles north-east of Aylesford. It consists of thirty tons of stone, three megaliths on end supporting a fourth as table or altar. Local legend, of course, is vague about their origin. Like Stonehenge, they are supposed to mark the burial-place of various British and Saxon heroes. Catigern, a British chief killed near here in the battle against Hengist and Horsa (when the latter was also slain), is one theory. But their origin goes back further than recorded history, to the days probably of cave-dwellers who worshipped the sun according to creeds brought ages earlier from the Old Testament lands. Throughout the neighbourhood, between this central worshipping place and the village of Aylesford below, have been found other related relics; in one field the Countless Stones (now largely distributed by ploughing), so called because there is said to be a supernatural ban upon a correct counting of them, while in the hillside are pits that may have been rudimentary homes or refuges used by the folk who worshipped here, returning by superstition and dim hearsay to the sun-rich lands beyond the bounds of Europe, whence their ancestors migrated thousands of years earlier.

It is a baffling object, this uncommunicative cromlech. Like all such monuments, it teases the imagination, and I found myself in just the same mood of exasperated inadequacy as I felt while staring at the walls of Rochester Castle, trying, and failing, to touch them into time-animation, so that the centuries should come about them, a backward-moving panorama tangible to my imagination, with men and women in it, things and ideas, whose mode of existence should be revealed to me. In this absurd hope I hung about that field, half-going, then turning for another look, while my companion tapped an impatient foot on the turf. With not one single question answered I left the temple, and took the road again for Rochester.

CHAPTER XIV

THREE RIBS OF THE FAN

I T is a counsel not of perfection, but of despair, that makes
me presently decide to turn inland, after I have reached
Gravesend, so that I may conclude my exploration of Kent
by following paths along what I may call three ribs of the
fan. The first will run along the Downs from Wrotham, the
second through the clayey Weald from Tonbridge, and the
third from Cranbrook along the lower heights and through
the Ashford gap. They will all meet at Canterbury, the
superb crown of my pilgrimage. I suspect that when I reach
that now battered shrine I shall be as dumb as most of those
reverent folk who have preceded me through the centuries to
that place whose beauty and power are more than words can
describe.

The road to Gravesend rises steeply out of Strood to the
summit of Gad's Hill. Here is the spot where Falstaff,
Poins, and their boozing cronies proposed to come to play
at highwaymen. "But, my lads, my lads, to-morrow morning,
by four o'clock, early at Gadshill. There are pilgrims going
to Canterbury with rich offerings, and traders riding to London with fat purses. I have vizards for you all, you have
horses for yourselves. . . . I have bespoke supper to-morrow
night in Eastcheap : we may do it as secure as sleep. If you
will go, I will stuff your purses full of crowns; if you will not,
tarry at home and be hang'd." How this enterprise turned
into a practical joke, and how it came that

> Falstaff sweats to death
> And lards the lean earth as he walks along,

is recorded in Part I of Shakespeare's *King Henry IV*.

No doubt in those unruly days this stretch of road was a
fine hunting-ground for footpads and gangs of highwaymen,
for much coming and going of merchants and their wares
was maintained between the busy river ports and London.

To-day the road is comparatively quiet, and Gad's Hill ·
Place, with the Sir John Falstaff inn on the opposite side of
the road at the top of the hill, dozes through the seasons, and
the only pilgrims are literary zealots come to see the house
where Charles Dickens spent the last fourteen years of his
life (1856–70). The house is a late Georgian villa, light and
cheerful, standing in a well-wooded garden. A tunnel (made
by the novelist's brother) runs under the road to connect the
house with another part of the garden, where Dickens had
his workshop (a highly ornamental imitation Swiss chalet).
He was working here on the unfinished story of *Edwin
Drood* when he had the cerebral hæmorrhage from which he
died the following morning, at the age of fifty-eight, worn
out by working for so many years at too high a nervous
pressure. However, it was a pleasant way to end; at work,
with fame and success still ripe, and living in a house with a
noble view on four sides; a house, moreover, which he had
longed to possess since he was a small boy, poor and pre-
cociously sensitive.

Gravesend is approached in the same way as Rochester,
over a steep ridge of chalk that drops to the waterside. Many
people consider it to be spoiled by an overlay of industrialism; but I think they are blind who cannot still see a
slightly exotic, southern quality in the steep streets running
up from the waterfront. Two hundred river pilots live in
Gravesend, and their personality, which is that of a vocation,
permeates the town. Though it stands on the closing shores
of the Thames, which at this point is only a mile wide at
high tide, Gravesend is a maritime, one might even say a saline,
place. There is a certain robust, hornpipe character about its
people. One expects to see a parrot in every front room, and
a tattooist's shop round every corner. If one lands there
from the Tilbury Ferry the aspect of the old High Street,
with its many shop signs hanging out like those in a Chinese
city, gives an impression of entering a foreign country. It is a
great place for eating-houses, but rather of the forecastle
than the quarterdeck kind. If you want simplicity and quantity
in a meal, go to Gravesend.

The town is famous for two picturesque figures; the Princess Pocahontas, who was buried there, and Sir Edwin

Arnold, who was born there. Pocahontas was the daughter of Powhattan, an Indian chief in the newly founded state of Virginia. She seems to have been unduly attracted to the white people in spite of the fact that they came to cheat and destroy her own people. She saved the life of Captain John Smith, the leader of one of the groups of pioneers who came from Elizabethan England to make their fortunes, and she married one of his party, named John Rolfe, while she was held as hostage by the colonists. Her husband, bringing her back to his native Norfolk, with their little daughter, was wrecked on the Bermudas, and as a result of the hardships of the journey to England her health was permanently damaged, and after a few years the smallpox carried her off. There seems to be some doubt about the place of her burial; but the parish registry of St George's church contains the following entry: "Rebecca Wrothe, Wyff of Thomas Wrothe, gent, a Virginian born lady, here was buried in the Chauncell." In 1907, during building operations by the edge of St Mary's churchyard, a skeleton was unearthed, and it was found to be that of a female Indian.

Sir Edwin Arnold was a member of a family long established, and I believe still established, in Gravesend. He was born there in 1832, and wrote his famous poem, *The Light of Asia* (a Victorian best-seller), after many years in India as head of the Sanskrit College in Poona. He was associated for forty years with the *Daily Telegraph*, in the days when it was perhaps the foremost journal in the world for well-edited foreign news, and his work in this connection made him a great empire-builder. It was he who promoted Stanley's expedition to search for the source of the Congo. He coined the phrase "a Cape to Cairo Railway" which Cecil Rhodes subsequently shouted through his megaphone. *The Light of Asia* needs to be read when one is about eighteen, and full of the new wine of religious curiosity. It has about it a glamour of the spirit comparable to the glamour of young love. I remember making myself drunk on this poetic account of the life of Gautama Buddha when I read it over thirty years ago. Some of the perfume still remains; sufficient for me to recollect many lines of wistful beauty, and to recommend the poem to young people in a generation that is groping about once more for other-worldly values after the shock of two world wars and their aftermath.

Leaving Gravesend we can wander to advantage amongst the hills in a triangle of country with Watling Street as its base and Wrotham as its apex. There is much treasure here, of natural beauties, history, and architecture. First we come to Cobham, with the park and hall adjoining. Here is a complete survival of feudal and Renaissance England, with the great Darnley family (by collateral descent on the female side) still in possession and residence. The park is comparable to that of Knole, with wide views, and ancient timber, amongst which are oaks of tremendous girth. One giant (I have never seen one with more mass of timber) stands beside the back drive into the stables behind the great house. It must be at least five hundred years old. Behind this veteran, shaded by cedars, is the entrance to the long kitchen court-yard and stables. They are beautiful buildings, perfect examples of Tudor brickwork, ripe-pippin-coloured bricks in alternate end-and-face courses. From the village to the hall runs an avenue of lime trees in four rows, some thousand yards long. It is a scented cathedral in early July, built of living jade.

The hall stands with its turrets emerging above the trees. From the public road it appears to be lost in the woods; but this is a skilfully conjured impression, made to prepare the way for the visitor's second stage of pleasure and admiration. The lawns and flower gardens are magnificent, and even the garden troubles of wartime have not spoiled this general beauty that surrounds the house as a perfect gown adorns a woman. The view from the windows on every side of the house is one of serene loveliness. Only an artist could have foreseen, and maintained, such a visual music. The lawns, the roses, herbaceous borders and their shubberies, with the harmony of Tudor brickwork and Inigo Jones's Italianate stone dressings to his central block—all these build up into a symphony that plays itself out upon the imagination, one movement after another, until the visitor begins almost to have the illusion that an orchestra is actually performing this shapely work of art.

The first records of the house date from the year 1300,

when in the will of John de Cobham his manor house was listed as "a messuage with garden worth 6s 8d per annum." Throughout the following centuries, records of rent and expenses were kept which now make interesting reading to the student of economic history. In 1327, for example, the first Lord Cobham's property in this manor and parish was valued at £16. I wonder what is the significance of this constant depreciation of the value of money? Is it because money has no root in reality? How would a banker or a stockbroker explain this : by holding that as society becomes more civilized it grows correspondingly more arithmetically sophisticated in order to set a finer differentiation of prices upon its greater range of things in demand? Perhaps it does not matter how much money is current so long as it is easily and swiftly current, reaching every individual as surely as a copious lubricant reaches the smallest working part in an intricate engine. The trouble perhaps is for those generations who, like ourselves, are born into a period when the balance between money and real wealth (goods, materials, and craftsmanship) is unsteady. Prices should stand by habit, so that we can forget them and give our minds and emotions to more important matters. But to pay twopence for a haircut when you are a child, sixpence when you are a youth, and eighteenpence when you are silver-haired is confusing. It humiliates you because you find yourself worrying in an almost miserly way about the expense, and this can become a habit that tends toward a mean and materialistic way of life that lacks freedom and the gesture of nobility. Maybe this uncertainty of prices thus has something to do with the general decay of good manners which so oddly coincides with the growth of democracy.

But these are sordid reflections in such a setting. I prefer to enjoy myself without them, returning carefree to my surroundings.

The present buildings comprising Cobham Hall consist of long and narrow north and south wings, joined by a cross section containing the great hall. The wings were built by the last two Barons of Cobham, of the original family of Brooke, between 1584 and 1603, when disaster overtook the family. Much alteration and ornamentation was going on at this time, a sculptor named Giles de Whitt being brought over from Belgium. The mantelpiece in the great picture gallery, dated 1599, is a good example of his work. The enhancement of the house by the Brooke family was stopped suddenly in the reign of James I, when Henry Lord Cobham and his brother George were attainted on a charge of high treason. George was beheaded, but Lord Cobham punished only by the confiscation of his estates. He died in obscurity and poverty in 1619.

The estate, now Crown property, was given by the king some few years later to his cousin Lodowick Stuart, the Duke of Lennox and also Earl of Darnley. This family, blood-related to Queen Mary of Scotland and the fair-haired giant Darnley whom Bothwell murdered (see Maurice Hewlett's huge-canvased novel, *The Queen's Quair*), still holds the property and lives in it.

When the Duke of Lennox acquired the hall he pulled down the central block and commissioned Inigo Jones (then the fashionable architect who brought back from Italy the latest Renaissance modes, and also introduced the proscenium arch into the designing of theatres) to build a new connecting core between the two long wings. Something happened between the design and the execution of it (owing to the intervention of the Civil War and also of the architect's death). What Inigo Jones intended can still be seen, how-ever, in his designs published in *Vitruvius Britannicus*.

Time has mellowed everything, so that now there is no conflict of styles in the noble place. There it stands, a work both of art and of nature, like that

> Rose-red city, half as old as time,

so perfectly described in one line of poetry by an obscure Oxford don. It is good to think that still, in the rooms of this house or working in its gardens, may be met a figure with the features, and the courtesy, of a princess of France and a Queen of Scotland.

The village of Cobham is full of treasures. First amongst them is the church which contains the finest brasses in England. They date from the fourteenth century, and commemorate the Brooke family. A hundred years ago they

*"Stringing" in a hop garden in Spring
Aylesford Bridge*

were restored by a surviving member of the family, Francis Brooke of Afford Place, Suffolk. This act of family piety is pleasing to contemplate. Would a descendant of such a house to-day have the courage to undertake so pious a work, in the face of public contempt for family tradition and the aristocratic way of life? Too many of these few survivors seem determined to deny their birthright by becoming more jazzy and philistine than the crudest *nouveaux-riches*.

The oldest of these brasses, that to Dame Jone de Cobham, has an inscription in Norman French that has about it a quality of the music of the *trouvères*, or of François Villon :

> Dame Jone de Cobeham gist ici
> Dieu de sa Alme eyt merci
> Ki ke pur le alme priera
> Quarante jours de pardoun auera.

In the centre of the chancel stands a magnificent tomb, also to one of the Cobhams, made in the latter half of the sixteenth century by Flemish workmen.

Having admired the fabric of the church one must not miss the College, founded, with the consent of a Papal Bull, in 1387 by the lord of the manor. It is a monastic structure, which after the usual break in its history round about the time of the Dissolution of the Monasteries has since become a group of almshouses.

Opposite the church stands the famous inn, the Leather Bottle, now a chapel-of-ease for Dickens worshippers. Pickwick, Tupman, and Winkle are appropriately celebrated in the pictures in the Dickens Room inside. Further down the village is the house called Owletts, which I mentioned in the opening pages of this book as the home of Sir Herbert Baker, the famous architect and friend of Cecil Rhodes.

Leaving Cobham for a leisurely exploration of the rest of this small but rich triangle, we must pay a visit to another noble house, Franks Hall, which I ought more methodically to have mentioned during my journey up the Darent River, for it stands just outside Farningham, and close to Horton Kirby. I would like to describe this house too, but I am wary of tiring the reader with too many records of ancient time,

Smarden
Chilham

and vanished craftsmanship, and forgotten pieties. So instead
we will make our way into the hills, climbing up southward
over the North Downs amongst the butterflies, the profusion
of scabious flowers, the chalk cuttings and pits, and the vast
expanses of open views north, south, and eastward, until we
reach the hinterland of Kent once more at Wrotham.

So we have left the Thames Valley. Our journey along
Watling Street, with the excursions into Sheppey and the
Isle of Grain, has been a skirmish rather than an exploration.
All this part of the county, much of it overlain by industrialism and the appalling pleasure haunts that cater for the
tumid populations spawned by industry, consists more of
buried than of patent historical treasure. But the treasure is
there in abundance, and in a geographical setting that is
almost unspoilable, so that the traveller who would appreciate its riches will need a great leisure and a large library to
direct him.

Yet the whole of Kent is lavish, and now that I am preparing to wander along the Weald and the internal slopes of
the saucer-edge hills that enclose it, I feel my inadequacy
just as acutely. Not even a Hasted or a Charles Igglesden
can do justice to so much. This interior stretch of the county
has touched the poets shrewdly, and driven them to despair.
Notably Robert Bridges, a Man of Kent, and Frank Kendon,
Edmund Blunden, Kentish men, with V. Sackville-West, a
Kentish woman, have sought to capture the spirit of the
Weald. Bridges has sung its winds, skies, and approaches to
the sea. Blunden has made his music from its close network
of streams, where pike and roach haunt, and where mill-
wheels turn below ponds draped with shawls of green weed.
Kendon, a southern Wordsworth, has found a panic mysticism in a small district round the warm, undulating country
between Tunbridge Wells and Goudhurst. V. Sackville-West,
in her gracious and stately verse, and particularly in the long
bucolic poem "The Land," has sung that fourth dimension of the local landscape, its time-growth, its encrustation
of habit and the secular ritual of the labourer with his tools,
and the country gentleman with his sacred obligations to
gardens and estates. Miss Sackville-West knows and loves
the Kentish folk, the fields and gardens they work in, and

the hand-worn tools they use. She celebrates the culture of the hop-vine, which in her own part of the county dominates the life of the people as the cult of the wine-grape is the more frankly Dionysiac shaper of life in the Châteaux country of France.

From the gap at Wrotham we enter this inner garden of a garden-county, and realize at once that the word "garden" tends to be misleading. I recollect that many people speak disparagingly of the Home Counties. When I published a volume of essays about life in Kent during the days and nights when our villages were being dishevelled and our landscape cratered (a damage that has destroyed much that is irreplaceable), a North Country critic, a Dalesman poet named Norman Nicholson, wrote with some element of contempt for my delight in what he called the suburban scenery of Kent. I went about with rage in my heart for days. I wanted to bring him down south and confront him with a southwesterly gale roaring up the great funnel of the Weald. I wanted to show him a few of our farms, where agriculture is a science and every inch of worthy soil is made to yield. I would have shown him the complete rusticity of village life here. But I doubt if this Mercian would have been convinced. As well try to persuade a Bulgarian of the glories of Transylvania.

From Wrotham we have first to visit Ightham Moat, and poke about over Oldbury Hill on the site of the Roman camp. We overlook a hinterland lying between Otford and behind Knole. The chalk hills here rise steeply from both north and south, with cuttings, quarries (some disused and now mantled with green and breasted with orchids and deadly-nightshade bushes). At the top is a stretch of Trust ground where one may lie in the bracken and fancy oneself alone on a boyhood island awaiting tremendous perils. Birches sigh in the wind, and kestrels hover above the scrub. This is the place to come with a volume of Richard Jefferies or W. H. Hudson, a pair of binoculars, and a picnic basket. And the day should be the twenty-first of June. If you come up from Shipbourne or Tonbridge, and your car is an old one, take care that your radiator does not boil as you climb through the woods at the last stage of the ascent.

Across the little valley on the northern side, some way up the further slopes, runs the Pilgrims' Way, through Otford and Kemsing. The latter village is well set, sheltered from the north and east by the Downs, and facing the serene wooded slopes of Knole. Many artists have lived there, and one of them, Herbert Cole, made a reputation in the early part of the century as a book illustrator and designer of stained glass windows. Built above the village is a modern house which is a good example of what present-day craftsmen can do when not restricted by costs. Sited almost on the edge of the precipitous drop of the hill-top, this expensive piece of domestic architecture had to be based on a great platform supported on brick bastions of great strength and size. The bricks for this, and for the house itself, were made on the site, slightly smaller than the regulation size. The house stands as a proof that English craftsmen do not lag behind the mastermen of Italy when they are given a chance to work without hindrance by costing clerk or trade union official. What an unhappy age we live in, while all these parasitic flunkies hang on to the man with the tools, robbing his arm of its freedom of movement, and his soul of pride in the work done.

Having spent our timeless and magic midsummer day on the heights known as Wilderness (and rightly named!) we go east to Ightham through the woods and over Oldbury Hill. The ancient fortifications, probably pre-Roman, cover a hundred and twenty acres of the hill. Geologists as well as archæologists find a hunting-ground here, for the stony outcrop of this hill represents a survival of one of the great moraines formed by the glaciers that slid down the heights where now the Weald stretches, and gradually wore them away. Pit dwellings, and other evidences of Paleolithic man's sojourn here, survive, although the latter-day quarrying of stone for road-metal has disturbed this chapter in the story of the human race.

To make our topography hereabouts more complicated, another little valley cuts the ridge just east of Ightham, to conduct the small River Shode southward through Plaxtol and Hadlow to join the upper reaches of the Medway. Here again is a profusion of small places, each having its surprises for the visitor; something unique in church, houses, or other memorial. If I begin to explore them all in detail I shall become a perpetual pilgrim, destined never to reach Canterbury. Through the valley of the Shode, and turning sharply left and northward again, we may come over another isolated patch of wooded heights, through Mereworth to West Malling, where we shall look from another angle down the opening valley of the Medway, over the cement-making district of Snodland to Halling, Cuxton, and Rochester.

Ightham has held a weekly fair since it was granted a licence in 1315, though nowadays this Cockscomb Fair as it is called has become the usual annual, a token occasion for a holiday break. The village played a pioneer part in the fomenting of Jack Cade's Rebellion. Later, it propitiated this disloyal (if it can be so called) conduct by providing the squire's wife who was said to have deciphered a letter, illegibly written, warning Lord Mounteagle of the intended Gunpowder Plot. This lady, Dame Dorothy Selby, was wife of the squire whose family lived at Ightham Mote for three centuries, subsequent to that patriotic bit of secret-service work. The house stands some way beyond the village in an isolated corner of the ridge facing south-east to Shipbourne. The Shode provides the water for the moat which still surrounds the house, whose ragstone walls rise abruptly out of it. It is a miniature mansion, built in the fourteenth century and added to in Elizabethan times. It is still a romantic place, a moated grange where we might expect Mariana to lean from one of the mullioned windows, murmuring, "He cometh not, I would that I were dead." And in the countryside around it still lie the relics of earlier hopes and disappointments, joys and sorrows. At Plaxtol an exquisite bronze statuette of the Roman Minerva was dug up in 1857, one of those pieces of evidence that help us suddenly to break through the routine unimaginativeness in which we inhabit the present, so that for a second the past comes really to life, warm flesh and blood, words, tears, and laughter. We almost stretch out a hand, shy with welcome, but in that instant the vision is gone.

The Mallings, East and West, with Leybourne and Mereworth, within a few miles of each other, are a representative sample of the riches of this stretch of foothills under the southern shelter of the Downs. Undoubtedly this strip of country is the most romantic and beautiful in Kent. It has an almost Roman quality, as of the Alban Hills. Its mansions, parks, ruined castles, steep slopes densely wooded and broken by ravines and quarries, offer scenery characteristic of Turner's water-colours. No photograph can reproduce such country. I could travel backwards and forwards along this slope, just above tree-height from the Weald, and drive myself to distraction in the effort to describe one village after another. The result would be wearisome to the reader, and I will not attempt it. I can merely pick out one jewel here and there.

West Malling, in addition to several good examples of medieval domestic architecture, has the ruined tower of a Benedictine abbey built by Gundulph, that Norman priest-artist who did so much massive and austere work, including the Great Keep of the Tower of London and the castle at Rochester. East Malling to-day centres round the Fruit Growing Research Station, whose scientific and practical experts go about the county working with the farmers in the ceaseless effort to perfect disease-resisting strains of apples, cherries, hops, plums, pears, and the soft fruits. The station has recently added Bradbourne House to its premises, in preparation for a great expansion of its activities. This, together with the fact that Wye Agricultural College has now amalgamated with Swanley Horticultural College for the purpose of co-ordinating their work in a much more progressive way, shows how England is preparing to develop and keep up-to-date the farming industry, which still employs the largest number of people in the country. Already the improved wages and conditions of the agricultural workers have made the lot of the women less dreary. Hitherto the women of Kent have had a harder time than the wives of labourers in other counties, because they have to turn out for most of the spring, summer, and autumn seasons to work in the fields and hop-gardens. Living in tied cottages, they cannot refuse the work. Some people say that the farm worker to-day is no better off than he was in Victorian times, when his wages were twelve shillings a week, with various perquisites in kind.

With his minimum wage fixed by Government decree, he is said to have lost the close relationship and goodwill of the employer, especially as with increased wages he has acquired an appetite for independence of spirit and "bolshie" ideas. That is the argument one hears on market day when the dealers and farmers are gathered in the hotel bars in Maidstone. Yet I have never seen the farms looking in better trim than they are to-day in Kent, and indeed all over the country. The hedges and ditches groomed, the barns and cottages repaired, the children better shod and clothed and fed—these are signs of the general revival of the oldest industry. And if the promises hold good, the rural prosperity will continue, offering a means of livelihood once more acceptable to men back from the wars, and to youngsters who will no more be driven by the squalor of country life to find a dubious escape into the factory towns.

All this is involved in the future balance of our national economics and scientific technique as a whole. The next few decades of the twentieth century are bound to be experimental and transitional, with much uprooting of decayed institutions, processes, and the physical environment that went with them. Much that we have cherished will have to go. The last surviving practices of the system of the squirearchy, the rule from the country house, for good or for bad, must disappear, and we do not yet know what is to take its place. It has been a way of country life that has put its mark upon the habits and allegiances of the people, and the very aspect of the fields, woods, and hedgerows (particularly the hedgerows!) Will the new dispensation alter everything and make our England unrecognizable, not to be differentiated from an agricultural scene in Russia or the Middle West of America? It is a question which makes my flesh creep. God forbid, I say; though I want no reactionary putting back of the clock to the wicked old days of the past, with its enclosures, its poaching laws, its tied cottages, and its degraded serfdom.

Leybourne is a suitable memorial to that system of the squirearchy, for it has been for many centuries the seat of one of the richest Kent families. One of its early members, a Crusader named Sir Roger de Leyburn, instituted a novel form of memorial in the village church. He built into the wall (the east end of the north wall) a recess, to contain a shrine where should be lodged the hearts of members of the family. He died in 1271, and his heart was duly enshrined there. I believe no others followed, perhaps because his descendants recoiled from the somewhat grisly process involved in the ceremony. One member of this family, who lived in the time of Edward I, was known as the "Infanta of Kent." Her name was Juliana of Leybourne. She augmented her inheritance by three judicious marriages, and died in the possession of twelve rich manors, which she left to the Church and the Crown. Such a disposition of property always depresses me. I like to think of some fortunate person enjoying the sudden access of riches. It is a contemptible thought, unworthy of our modern political science. But the Crown or the Church, so vast, so calm, so impersonal! To send the means of endless delight and cultural expansiveness back to them is like pouring a bottle of vintage Burgundy as a libation over the sands of the Sahara.

Before we look further along the magical southern slope, we come to the great break in the hills where the Medway begins to grow proud and mature. And in the middle of this gap, set in a triangle of hills, lies Maidstone, the great capital of the county. It is a city, with a metropolitan atmosphere, though at first one is inclined to overlook its character and its urban riches. Its historical treasures are many and beautiful, but the city fathers appear to be indifferent to their worth. While the town is well run from a practical point of view (it is clean, well lighted, and its enormous traffic problem efficiently controlled), it is shamefully neglected in æsthetic and cultural matters. In the very heart of its most picturesque centre, where the river flows past the great fourteenth-century church, the college and the remains of the archiepiscopal palace, the Corporation has allowed the omnibus company to dump its central station. The magnificent medieval stables of the palace, one of the finest buildings in Kent, is overshadowed to-day by this noisy, greasy, stinking terminus, from which the great two-decker buses have to be edged out by nervous inspectors, inch by inch, while the engines roar, and the petrol fumes creep like poison gas along the waterside. And next-door to this abomination the munici-

pal parking-place for private cars stands back to back with a
huge commercial motor garage whose factory buildings
stretch along the other bank of the stream, a tributary about
to drop into the Medway, making a junction which could
have been the ornamental centre of the city. As for the other
cultural amenities of this capital of so great a county, I have
not yet found a worthy bookshop, while the museum and art
gallery (whose pictures are beneath contempt) offer a con-
ventionally accumulated mass of archæological and miscel-
laneous material that with a little expense of money and good
taste might be made an entrancing record of all that Maidstone and the county it capitalizes have experienced during
the last two thousand years or more. Further, this dusty
cache is housed in a building which is one of the most handsome in the town, Chillington Manor, in Faith Street, once
the town house of the Cobhams. What an opportunity
wasted! Good theatrical companies, and the more intelligent
films, appear to shun Maidstone. The cultural life of the city
is even more moribund than that of Tunbridge Wells.

I do not know why this should be so. Is the government
of Maidstone entirely in the hands of hop and corn brokers,
and the tradesmen and manufacturers whose sole interest is
in touchable wealth, money and goods? Certainly in these
assets the city is overflowing, and that is all to the good. But
we want something more in the capital of our beloved Kent.
We want a city that is proud of its inheritance, the richest
history in north-western Europe. We want Maidstone to
wear that history openly, displaying its dignity, pride and
beauty. Instead, we have a bus terminus stinking in the centre
of the town, and we have no place where Kentish artists can
show their work, or Kentish musicians perform their com-
positions. Why does not Maidstone maintain a Kentish symphony orchestra and a municipal theatre?—both of which
would attract a constant inflow of visitors not only from the
principality but from all over England. In this beautiful
setting among the hills, with a valuable river winding its way
through the heart of the town, Maidstone could be a civilized
centre of the south, representing the present life of Kent and
England as Canterbury enshrines their past. The lack of consciousness, of vision and proud enthusiasm in the City

Fathers is lamentable. One needs the astringent prose style of a William Hazlitt to lash them.

In a little street just off the High Street William Hazlitt was born in 1778. His father, an Irishman, came to the town as minister of the Unitarian Church which can still be seen opposite a small hotel called the Mitre, where one may go for a good market-day meal. Two years later the pastor quarrelled with his flock, and returned to Ireland; so the future painter, critic, and amorist had nothing further to do with the town of his birth.

Having railed so vigorously against the centrepiece of my book, I must now make amends by praising its shops, which are excellent. Here one may still find some antique furniture and old silver at not too fantastic a price. There are some surviving county tailors in the town, who will make a suit for something more than fifty shillings, which will not convert its wearer into a cross between a smart cheapjack and a Broadway film-fan. And I must also pay a tribute to the County Library, so well housed, and so courteously run.

The principal attraction of the town, after one has somewhat gloomily inspected its historical treasures, is the weekly market of country produce. This is a joyous affair; with dense crowds, animals, flowers, fruits, and vegetables, and a section for non-perishable goods such as pottery, linens, and cutlery. The auctions, the side-shows, the comings and goings and the finding of meals at the hotels; all this is something which one feels is deep-rooted, really English, really Kentish. For that alone Maidstone is to be cherished amid its rich manufacturers, its paper mills and breweries, its motor works and toffee factories. I will leave its now static architectural treasures, and its non-existent arts, until there is more justification for discussing them.

Returning to the Downs, or at least the lower reaches of them, north-east from the town, we stop at Boxley to look at the remains of the Cistercian abbey which was once famous for its Rood of Grace, a cross with a Christ image believed to have been gifted with movement and speech. Archbishop Warham wrote to Wolsey of Boxley as "so holy a place, where so many miracles be showed." This of course attracted many and profitable pilgrims. However, after the Dissolu-

tion, when the Crown official took over the rich effects of
the monastery, a disconcerting discovery was made. This
man, one Geoffrey Chamber, was employed in defacing and
pulling down the buildings in 1538, and he wrote to Thomas
Cromwell (that financial spider) that he found in the Rood of
Grace "certain engines and old wire, with old rotten sticks
in the back, which caused the eyes to move and stir in the
head thereof, like unto a lively thing, and also the nether lip
likewise to move as though it should speak, which was not a
little strange to him and to others present." This of course
was admirable propaganda material for the iconoclasts, and
the elaborate model, so reminiscent of the ingenuities of
Leonardo da Vinci, was put up in Maidstone market-place
and shown to the people by the officers of the Crown, with
much consequent damage to the cause of the Pope. and his
claim to interfere in English politics and the taxation of
England's folk.

At Park House, which we pass on our way to Boxley
village, lived Tennyson's sister. The poet often stayed here,
and he describes it in the opening lines of that wearisome
pseudo-epic, *The Princess*, in which lie buried some of the
most exquisite lyrics in the language. He speaks of the house
party coming out to mingle with the tenants on the occasion
of the garden party given to celebrate the opening of the
institute, and one marvels at the difficulty of setting such a
comically prosy word as "institute" in a line of blank verse.
But there they are, those Victorian men in their stove-pipe
hats, and those women in their crinolines and Paisley shawls,
walking amongst the docile tenantry, while

overhead

The broad ambrosial aisles of lofty lime
Made noise with bees and breeze from end to end.

Strange was the sight and smacking of the time;
And long we gazed, but satiated at length
Came to the ruins. High-arch'd and ivy-claspt,
Of finest Gothic lighter than a fire,
Thro' one wide chasm of time and frost they gave
The park, the crowd, the house; but all within
The sward was trim as any garden lawn:

And here we lit on Aunt Elizabeth,
And Lilia with the rest, and lady friends
From neighbour seats . . .

We leave that gathering before our ears are startled by the very unperiod outbreak of passionate feminism from the young women posing in front of

A Gothic ruin and a Grecian house.

All that is now exactly a hundred years ago, for *The Princess* was published in 1847; and every member of that crowd, parsons, squires, and peasants, gay undergraduates and girls with silk slippers and parasols, has vanished from the face of Kent. So let us move on, before our bones melt, and the sense of inexorable time comes down on us like a shroud.

From Boxley we follow the Pilgrims' Way, past the great airfield of Detling, which suffered so much during the war. This road, tree-height above the present main London to Folkestone road, runs almost parallel with it, resuming the same geographical stance which it had along the ridge further west by Otford and Kemsing. But now we are tending southeast instead of due east, following down the run of the Downs which is soon to be broken at the Ashford Gap. We need to make many turns to explore villages on the southern side of the main road. There is a constant ribbing of small lanes for this purpose, and each one of them has its particular secrets of beauty, while all have in common the great view across the Weald. Leeds village stands back somewhat from the highway, though the famous moated castle can best be seen by running along the main road for half a mile after turning into it from the village. The church, survivor of an old priory dedicated to SS Mary and Nicholas by its founder Robert de Crepido Crevecœur in 1119, is almost square, with a great gaunt tower, and a handsome ceiling over the chancel. The castle, once among the most impregnable strongholds in England, has had many owners and has been used for many purposes. It still looks formidable, even in these days of the atomic bomb. At different periods it was Crown property. Richard II was imprisoned here, and so was the Irish chieftain Desmond.

During the war it was used as a military hospital, though I believe that the owner lived on there also. In 1665 John Evelyn was in charge of French and Dutch prisoners of war who were kept there. It was to Leeds Castle that Froissart, the French historian and poet, came to present the King of England with an illuminated volume of his work bound in crimson velvet. The scene must have been wonderfully picturesque, and should have been imitated, I think, for the presentation by the grand old poet Robert Bridges, that Man of Kent, of his *Testament of Beauty* to King George V, to whom it was dedicated.

Just south of Lenham (a spongy village on the main road, where two rivers rise and the inhabitants are riddled with rheumatism) lies the tail-end of a ridge of hills that runs back westward to Linton, below Maidstone. This ridge is set with several jewels, appropriately named: Linton, Boughton Monchelsea, Chart Sutton, Sutton Valence, Ulcombe, and Boughton Malherbe. The last one takes the palm both for its name and its situation. It stands high up, on what gives the effect of a precipitous drop into the Weald proper. It thus appears to be a cul-de-sac, cut off from much contact with the world. A stranger comes here only out of curiosity, and is repaid by an even greater curiosity from the few natives. It is the seat of the Wotton family, the most famous of whom was Sir Henry Wotton, a poet and diplomat in the reign of James I, who reprimanded him for saying that an ambassador is a man "sent to lie abroad for the good of his country." Wotton was Provost of Eton, a scholar of much skill in verse, a lively wit, and a devout spirit. It was he who pointed out

> How happy is he born and taught
> That serveth not another's will.

This forgotten little village survives to-day as it was when described by our dear old prose master Izaak Walton, in the opening of his biography of his friend Wotton, who was "born in the Year of our Redemption 1568, in Bocton-Hall, in the Parish of Bocton Malherb, in the fruitful Country of Kent: Bocton Hall being an ancient and goodly structure, beautifying, and being beautified by the Parish Church of

Bocton Malherb adjoyning unto it; and both seated within a fair Park of the Wottons, on the brow of such a Hill, as gives the advantage of a large Prospect, and of equal pleasure to all Beholders." The pleasure may still be found there, in that little churchyard sloping down the hill, with the "large Prospect" beyond, and the scent of the rose bushes mingling with that of the many aromatic chalk-born wild flowers with which the hill is covered.

The same view continues, as we take our way along this isolated ridge to the other names on this lovely necklace. Each of these villages is rich in Elizabethan domestic architecture, and Sutton Valence has a fine bit of modern work in the new chapel of the public-school. Ulcombe, on somewhat lower ground and watered by one of the outlying tributaries of the River Beult (which drains so much of the hop country into the Medway) is worth a visit if only to look at its astonishing yew trees, vast in size, that grow horizontally for many yards.

From here we can turn back to the main road at Lenham, and retrace our steps westward in order to look at Hollingbourne, one of the prettiest villages in England. Its main street rises abruptly into the Downs, narrow and lined with one perfect specimen after another of Early English and Tudor houses and cottages. To crown this almost theatrical effect, there stands in the middle of the village a Tudor manor house, called by the locals Colepeper Hall. The brickwork is elaborate, with ornamental facings and a bravura of chimney-stacks. The Colepeper family at one time was rooted like poppies all over the county, and held high office. The owner of this house in the time of Henry VIII was a cousin of Anne Boleyn. He got himself into trouble by becoming something more than cousin to that exuberant and dangerous young woman; and Katherine Howard, one of the king's more unfortunate wives, regretted in her last words before her execution that she had not married this worthy suitor, instead of flying higher into the sun of royalty, and burning her wings.

I cannot think of a more suitable village than Hollingbourne in which to spend one's latter years. To settle there, in one of its period houses (I should choose a William and

Mary piece higher up the village), with a devoted gardener, a good cellar of claret, and rooms in the Albany so that comfortable reading could be done in London when in the mood, seems to me the height of civilized living. Merely to mention such an old-age programme shows at once how our standards have declined. So I climb the hill somewhat sadly, out of this dream village to the woods above it, turning to look back from time to time at the increasing range of the view. From the top, some 600 feet above sea-level, we can stare right across to the Isle of Oxney. It is an awe-inspiring scene, and induces a mood which I suspect I have already discussed too frequently in the course of writing this book. So without repeating myself I will push on to the hilltop villages of Bredgar, Bicknor and Tunstall, which must stand as representatives of many upland settlements that have hidden in these hills since the Saxons came. After that break northward, almost to the Thames Valley again, we return to the southern sweep and ride down the High Street of Charing, another village rich in period pieces, and notably in two fine Georgian town houses, one of which I should decide to live in had I not already made my choice in Hollingbourne.

Charing stands on an elaborate junction of roads, which meet rather giddily on the steep slope of the Downs. The village has Roman foundations (probably the Durolenum whose site is still in some dispute), and for centuries it saw much coming and going of men of destiny, because a large archiepiscopal palace was maintained here. Henry VIII stayed in it while on his way to the meeting with the Emperor Charles V at the Field of the Cloth of Gold, that crowning ceremony of the Age of Chivalry. A few crumbled remains of the palace may still be seen near the church. Above the town (for Charing has somewhat of that character owing to the dignity of its houses) lie great chestnut woods, while below it, across the main road, is a beautiful stretch of country still sleeping in almost feudal slumber, in spite of the horrid damage done to such hamlets as Little Chart, whose church had a direct hit from a V.1 in 1944, and was totally destroyed. The church at Pluckley too was damaged, and several old houses near it.

These terrors, however, appear to have disturbed the local

life hardly at all, and since the return of peace, atlhough it is still an uneasy and impoverished peace, these two villages, like the others in this triangle of country whose apex runs into Ashford, have slipped back into their old ways, and one is moved to overlook the underlying changes such as the broken fences round the great park of the Derings, whose family tradition is stamped so markedly on the countryside.

At Little Chart lives the poet H. E. Bates, in a converted tithe barn round which he has made, in the course of some twelve years, a garden that reflects his general good taste and knowledge. Here is a writer about the English country-side who has magic in his prose and verse. His work stands, at least for me, along with that of Gilbert White and W. H. Hudson.

Pluckley makes bricks and tiles. Its situation is magnificent, like that of Linton further west. From the top of a pre-cipitous High Street the view of the Weald, seen behind the silhouette of church tower, cottage eaves, and the trees of the village, is grand, though it can be bettered a little higher up if we go to Egerton. All about here the houses are stamped with the Dering mark, which consists of a window with narrow panes and rounded tops. This character is found all over the huge estate, and it dates from the Civil Wars, when a Royalist squire of the village escaped through a similarly shaped window in the manor house, which had been captured by the Parliamentarians. He vowed that if ever he returned home he would find a way to commemorate this happy adventure. He did.

The house, Surrenden, stands at the end of a drive which runs for a mile from Pluckley church through a grove of elms, limes, and sycamores. The family have been at Surren-den-Dering since the time of Harold—over thirty genera-tions of them. John de Surrenden rebuilt·the house in the reign of Edward III, and a Sir Edward Dering added to it in the eighteenth century. During the period between 1811 and 1896 the title was held, for this eighty-five years, by one member of the family, another Sir Edward who succeeded at the age of three. Such statistics impress me. Maybe I am antiquarian-minded. An old house, an old family, an old person, always move me to a complicated storm of emotions.

Canterbury Cathedral (from the air)

Even an old toad squatting under and indistinguishable from a stone does so. I don't know why! Maybe it is because they *contain* so much, like a Beethoven symphony, or a Titian canvas, or a night sky when the Milky Way stands up with the individual stars of heaven in perspective around it. I cannot hear of a heart-rotten old tree being felled without my own heart feeling a twinge of dismay. What is this conservatism? I am not content to hear it called mere sentimentality. I know it has a more sound basis, deep in the regions of the mind where a sense of order, of sane growth and continuity, of an appreciation of ripeness and things well rounded off, has settled into a philosophy of the nerves and emotions.

Because a family has been living for centuries on one great estate, marrying discreetly and educating its rising generations upon the edge of pride, while being enabled to make the grand gesture ensured by wealth and leisure; because of these right ferments I expect, when I meet a present-day representative of such a family, to find wisdom and grace and a profound courtesy. I am not always disappointed.

Leaving the question of family trees, we will push on to Ashford, a town which is older than it looks at first sight. For since it became a railway town, where the Southern Railway has its building and repairing shops, a certain amount of dreary brickwork of the factory-dormitory kind has inevitably overlaid the more acceptable original town. Already, from our position in the middle of the twentieth century, we begin to see the æsthetic effects of the nineteenth century upon the face of our beloved country. And in hardly one instance do we find them anything but disgusting, something to turn from with shame and bewilderment. To-day, here and there and still very sparsely, in spite of all the conscious effort of the planners, a few buildings are going up which may survive as additions to the character and grace of the country. But how meagre a contribution, when we compare it with what the earlier centuries, each in turn, have bequeathed to us. It means, of course, that in the future two centuries of English historical evolution will leave little trace, at least in static form through stone, brick or concrete, of a too mobile phase of civilization. We have much to be proud of, but little of it is in the æsthetic field. And what our final

Canterbury Cathedral (from the town)

monument will be nobody can say. Probably it will have to take the formless form of some abstract conception, a fitting symbol of our restless, dynamic mode of life, in which the static things, such as the family, the home, the tradition, have been broken down and consumed in the fire of this new aerial, high-speed existence whose technique we are now so painfully learning.

Ashford has a character which becomes more endearing as one learns to live with the town; to shop in it, day by day, and thus to appreciate its well-run municipal life and its cleanliness. It has its interesting corners too. The parish church is a noble one, built of Kentish ragstone with a great central tower possessing four corner turrets.

Now the second of the three central ribs of the fan comprises the very centre of the county. It runs through the low-lying Weald that was once the forest of Anderida, a jungle too thick and too dangerous for settlement, until some of it had been thinned by the gradual burning of the trees during the centuries when the iron foundries were flourishing. Riding east from Tonbridge, along this wide, gigantic valley, one is impressed by the touch of heaviness of the scene, and its close particularity. Here the emphasis is not on landscape, but on individual things; a copse, a bridge over a stream, a water-mill, a lush meadow where the cattle stand belly-deep in buttercups, and finally and most emphatically a hop garden.

For here is the true hop-growing country. I should place its very centre round about East Peckham, where one may see a cluster of hop kilns comprising some dozens, a city of them, giving a foreign aspect to the landscape. The hop gardens are not restricted to this stretch of the Weald proper, this clayey, water-netted land where rheumatism lurks like a malevolent old pike in wait for lingerers. The lonely ridge bordering the Weald on the south is also rich in hop gardens, though those upland farmers usually combine hops with fruit and dairy farming, and also with corn since the advent of the Government subsidy for ploughed land. But every farm there has its oasts, and they are the feature by which Kent is singled out from the rest of England.

I have already said something about the sacred nature of this culture of the hop, and how the whole economy of the natives turns upon it. That is why it has become almost a religious ritual. Even to-day, with superstitions being washed away by the antiseptic of materialism (leaving sterility behind!), there remains a certain mysticism in the minds of the farmers and their workpeople about their hop gardens. The way in which the vines are tended, one process after another through the seasons of the year, is comparable only with that given to the grape-vines in France. The culture is a sort of pale, northern version of the great Mediterranean labour-tribute to Dionysus, just as the beer it goes to produce is a chilly substitute for the sacred clarets and burgundies and chiantis of the South.

But there is nothing pale and chilly in the character of the hop gardens and of the life that circles round them. The warmth, the richness of the scene when the hops are ready for picking, standing eight feet high along the green aisles, bring Bacchus "and all his pards" rioting from the Orient into the Kentish countryside. But they also bring more than this symbolic procession. Each year, at the end of August, an invasion from the slums of London, and the gypsy settlements of the county towns, comes down on the Weald and the upland gardens, completely disturbing the whole way of life of the natives, and stamping the green solitudes into the ground. This lasts from four to six weeks, and then suddenly the tide of humanity recedes, is gone overnight like the swallows, and the farmers are left with their own folk to clear up the mess, burn the bine stems, and scour and disinfect the huts where the hoppers have slept and cooked.

The poet of this part of Kent, Edmund Blunden, was born at Yalding, one of the most handsome villages in the Weald. The great bulk of his early poetry consists of word-paintings of this land which he has always loved so intimately. His genius is truly its spokesman, and I know of no more direct way to penetrate into the secret nature of the Weald than by reading quietly through Blunden's collected poems, especially the first large volume. Here, for example, is a set of verses describing the coming of the hop-pickers:

The hoptime came with sun and shower
That made the hops hang hale and good;
The village swarmed with motley folk,
For through the morning calm awoke
Noise of the toiling multitude
Who stripped the tall bines' bower.

Slatternly folk from sombre streets
And crowded courts like narrow wells
Are picking in that fragrant air;
Gipsies with jewelled fingers there
Gaze dark, speak low; their manner tells
Of thievings and deceits.

And country dames with mittened wrists,
Grandams and girls and mothers stand
And stretch the bine-head on the bin,
And deftly jerk the loosed hops in.
Black stains the never-resting hand
So white for springtide trysts.

And by and by the little boys,
Tired with the work and women's talk,
Make slyly off, and run at large
Down to the river, board the barge
Roped in to shore, and stand to baulk
The bargee's angry noise :

While through the avenues of hops
The measurers and the poke-boys go.
The measurers scoop the heaped hops out,
While gaitered binmen move about
With sharpened hopdog, at whose blow
The stubborn cluster drops.

Such was the scene that autumn morn,
But when the dryer in his oast
Had loaded up his lattice-floors,
He called a binman at the doors,
"We want no more; the kilns are closed.
Bid measurers blow the horn."

The binman found the measurer pleased,
For hops were clean and work was through;
He told him what the dryer said,
The measurer nodded his grey head,
Lifted the battered horn and blew.
And so the day's work ceased.

That is not only beautifully made verse. It is also a minutely accurate picture of the technical process of picking, measuring, carrying, and drying. This last, the drying, is the fine and hazardous stage in the culture of the hop. The drier is always the farmer's most trusted and experienced man. During this period of his glorification (for the drier becomes a high-priest at this time of the year, and is treated as one) he puts aside his regular habits, and spends day and night in the oasts. The time needed to dry the hops in the kiln, over the carefully tended fire and draught doors, is continuous and does not coincide with the working day. Therefore the drier makes a bed of sacks in a corner of the upper drying floor of the barn adjoining the kilns, and from time to time during the night he gets up and attends, with an artist's touch, to his fires and regulators. The hops have to be of an exactly calculated dryness, and must not be singed, or their flavour is spoiled and they fetch a poor price.

The fire stands on a brick table on the ground floor, and it burns anthracite coal. A small pan of sulphur fumes on the edge of the fire, to keep the hops from the spores of mildew, should they not be used by the brewer for some time. The hops are spread on the drying floor, which is of open slats about halfway (some twenty feet) up the kiln; but to prevent them from falling through, a hair mat is first spread over the slats, and the hops are piled on this to a thickness of about sixteen inches. This mass of hops will weigh about a ton at a time.

During the drying the scene is wonderful. The drier, his eyes bloodshot with heat and fumes, his skin smeared with the vine-stain, moves about half-drugged by the perfume of the shrinking pods. The light from the fire throws grotesque shadows up the circular walls, menacing shapes that leap and bow and mow like gigantic bats flickering round the more substantial objects, though they too have lost all semblance of form and solidity. It is a Walpurgis Night scene, and one suspects the making of strange potions, and communications from Endor. The scent of the drying hops is unforgettable; but it cannot be described. It floats out over the countryside from the open hoods at the top of the kilns; a keen, half-medicinal tang, with something bracing about it, yet old-fashioned and reminiscent of moods, moments, and far-off things that we strive vainly and intensely to remember as we stand at some lane-end or under the shelter of a wood where the scent lingers under the moonlit sky. The very moths floundering about seem to be drunk, and the shouts and maundering songs from the pickers drinking outside the village pub come upon the ear expectedly; for what place has sobriety in this Bacchic setting?

When the hops are dry they are raked out with great wooden or open shovels like rackets, down to the drying floor, whence they are again scooped toward the hole under which is attached a new "pocket" from the neatly piled reserve on the ground floor. These pockets are used only once. They are sacks about five feet long, and the farmer's name and mark are stamped on them. The hops are pushed down at first by the scoops into the open sack, and then as it fills the press comes into play. The filler turns the winch of this elementary apparatus and the hops are steadily rammed down into the pocket until it is as tight as a drum, and rings to the touch. Then the neck is sewn up, and the pocket, round and firm, is rolled aside to await transport to the brewery, where it will be opened by slitting the stitching down one side. As each pocket is filled the score is chalked up on one of the beams of the barn. In my old barn such numbers are still to be reckoned, and the initials of the men who scrawled them there may still be read. I hesitate to remove them, for they are a history-book of Kent, which from time to time I like to re-read. Nor do I want to scrape up from the boards of my barn the sage-green layer of hop-juice, pressed hard as linoleum. For it is still alive and potent. With every change of the weather, especially when rain is coming, it sends out a ghost-perfume from vanished summers and forgotten vintages, until the house reeks and we grow drowsy over our domestic tasks. The hop is a great soporific. The local folk stuff pillows with it, to sleep on as a cure for neuralgia. And they say that a hop drier, in spite of being exposed to so much heat and draughts (those draughts keep up a steady roar that can be heard a mile away), never catches cold.

All these processes, which I have described with the help of Edmund Blunden's lovely verses, are part only of the final ceremonies of the culture of the hop-vine. During the rest of the year, beginning immediately the last of the seasonal hoppers have departed, the work goes on. In October, great piles of the discarded bine stems and leaves are collected from among the permanent poles and wires with which the gardens are staged, and on days when the wind is away from the farmhouse the sacrificial fires are set going.

The smoke is dead white, and it drifts through the gardens, across open fields, and is tattered among the flaming fingers of the cherry orchards. Colour rolls upon colour, vast shapeless masses of white over coral (the changing leaves of the cherry), umber of the oaks, the warm brown of the newly ploughed and sown fields, the yellow and scarlet hedges. The beauty of it all comes almost too poignantly upon the watcher. Time, life itself, seems to be going up in this annual oblation of colour and movement, slowly, majestically, and with an infinite sadness. And to add to this ministry of the religion of the eye, there is an accompaniment for the other senses. The rooks beat up against the rains and gusts of October, cawing hoarsely. The slashing drives of starlings, now in crowded flocks, sweep down with shrill whistlings and screwings of sound. And the robins and trooping finches, working frantically against the coming privation of winter, chatter and protest through the shortening days, until at night the owls take up their complaint and give it a diabolical turn, fierce and predatory.

During the first weeks of winter the gardens are ploughed between the poles, and fertilizer scattered to feed the roots that are waiting for next spring before they send up their fresh shoots to climb the strings that will be tuned for them. Feathers, or waste shoddy from the Yorkshire woollen mills, come down by the trainload, stinking like greasy slums. The gardens look dilapidated after this muck is spread, and they smell like middens. If a wind blows immediately, the bits of coloured wool—violet, blue, red, yellow—spin and dance about the poles, and float off into the lanes and among the branches of the trees in wood and orchard, until the whole countryside, usually so kempt, is littered afresh. But somehow the mess all disappears, some of it to add a glint of exotic dyes to the lining of many a nest.

The next process comes in early spring, when the women go out again on the land (after their winter respite) to string the poles afresh. First the men go up and down the rows, either walking on stilts or using rustic-made step-ladders, to reach the top wires with the upright strings. These are pegged down by the women, and drawn into cone-shaped groups by a central band of string. After the garden is prepared it has the appearance of a gigantic cat's cradle, or a diagram of geometry, so accurate is the setting of the strings, which make avenues of acute triangles, diminishing down the perspective until each avenue closes into itself.

Some weeks after that job the women have to turn out again into the gardens, leaving their domestic chores and the care of their families until the evening, for now the springing tendrils of the new season's shoots have to be persuaded up the strings, anti-clockwise. This job, known as "twiddling," goes on for weeks, as the vines grow overnight, like Jack's beanstalk. Thus the Kentish folk find their main service in the care of the vine, and everything else has to take a subsidiary place.

Meanwhile, against next year's invasion from the towns, the farmer must clear out the huts and cooking places, and cut and pile great stacks of cordwood and kindling for the visitors to use as fuel. As the autumn approaches, more personal preparations have to be made. Doctors and nurses prepare temporary first-aid posts, and Salvation Army workers come down to the huts owned by their organization. The casualties are frequent every year, for a wandering population of some fifty thousand people, mostly from the slum districts of London, is liable to trouble. During the war many were wounded by machine-gun bullets. I remember an incident that happened during the Battle of Britain in 1940 in a hop garden near Marden. A German pilot, seeing so many people gathered together in one place, probably mistook them for soldiers. He swept down and machine-gunned the rows, and one woman, who was sitting nursing her baby under a hedge, was wounded in the back. The pilot turned, and was about to repeat the dose, when he was driven down by two of our fighters. He landed in the next field, to be confronted by a platoon of enraged women rushing at him with hatpins, hatchets, and knives. He would certainly have been torn to pieces had not the Home Guard beaten the Amazons to the prize. And the Home Guard were not too gentle with him either; especially when he demanded, in authoritative English, for an officer to be produced to whom he might surrender!

The roughest of the hop-pickers are the pseudo-gypsies, who come in their tumbledown caravans and covered carts, their men greasy and their women dishevelled. They are not true gypsies, of fastidious Indian cleanliness, high cheekbones, the Romany tongue, and a strict code of morals. Nor are they the misfits of the working-class world. Nobody knows quite what their origin is. There is something "different" about them, and it takes an ugly turn when they are inflamed by drink. Their men have a nasty habit of extemporizing weapons when a quarrel begins in a country pub. They will snatch a glass, break it against the table, and hold the jagged butt in the palm of the hand. The unfortunate victim is then likely to have this horrible weapon ground by a circular twist of the assailant's hand into his face. At Goudhurst, a few years ago, a young cyclist was mutilated in this way. He had stopped for an evening drink while on tour, and happened to come out of the bar door into the darkness at the moment when some participants in a hop-time vendetta were expected to emerge. The innocent man received a wound that laid open his face and nearly blinded him.

The pickers from the slums have great faith in the health-giving results of this annual pilgrimage. For many of them it is a sort of journey to Lourdes or Walsingham. Thus they bring their invalids with them. Among the cases tended this year in the Goudhurst area were an old woman crippled with arthritis, another old woman who died in the night in one of the huts, a youth in an advanced stage of tuberculosis, who died on the way to hospital, and several children with broken limbs who had fallen down banks or out of trees.

Many of these family groups come year after year to the same farm, and bring a temporary home with them; tables, beds, chairs, and even wall-paper to paste up in the huts. They become expert in cooking over the open fire. Now that the blackout restrictions are removed, those fires can once more be seen at night twinkling like the bivouac fires of an army, as described in Thomas Hardy's *The Dynasts*. I have watched them this year, on the slopes two miles away across my valley, and listened to the sound of voices calling, snatches of song, the music of concertinas, and the undercurrent of babbling speech. It comes so strangely, and somewhat sadly, from the darkness that for the rest of the year is silent, except for the slippered tread of the wind, or the occasional night-cry of some little creature being done to death.

One could write many chapters about these hop-pickers, the last stragglers in that riotous procession which began to wind its musical way out of the hills of India long before the days of Homer, when the gods were half-human and Bacchus came to earth in quest of pleasure and led mortals and beasts astray.

> Within his car, aloft, young Bacchus stood,
> Trifling his ivy-dart, in dancing mood,
> With sidelong laughing;
> And little rills of crimson wine imbrued
> His plump, white arms, and shoulders, enough white
> For Venus pearly bite :
> And near him rode Silenus on his ass,
> Pelted with flowers as he on did pass
> Tipsily quaffing.

The procession is not quite so corybantic as that nowadays. It tends to broken prams, farm carts, and special hopper-trains waiting for hours in railway sidings; to young girls and boys dressed not in lionskins and berry-wreaths, but shoddy garments of a flash cut, high-heeled and pointed shoes, the more odorous forms of face powder and hair grease. To see these townfolk, in all their livery of cheap-

jack industrialism, their habits a grotesque imitation of
Hollywood smartness—to see all this suddenly set amid the
ancient fields and woods and by the side of the Kentish rivers
is to see a pathetic satire upon our latter-day civilization.

For a detailed account of this annual invasion I recommend a book called *A Boy in Kent*, by C. Henry Warren, a
writer who has done for the English countryside of to-day
what Richard Jefferies did for that of nearly a century ago.
It is a delightful book, sincere, accurate, and full of poetic
sensibility. The author's knowledge of the ways, morals,
eccentricities, and virtues of hop-pickers is first-hand, and
it is faithfully recorded in this book, from the moment when
his father's shop is stocked up, until that when the last of
the gypsies, the "whining pikies," have withdrawn. He
describes how "down in the chilly cellar under the shop,
Dutch cheeses, like bright-red cannon-balls, were piled in tremendous pyramids. The miller, wearing a white sack over
his head, like a Carmelite monk, came stumbling up the yard
with so much flour that George's meal-shed was soon
crammed to the door. Sacks of sugar were stacked in another
shed, and as I passed by I could hear the sated wasps buzz-
ing there in hundreds. And all day Alfred seemed to be
winding and unwinding the squealing, primitive hand-crane
that carried boxes and crates and bags from the yard up into
the warehouse."

He also describes how the village carpenter goes round
fitting up barricades of wire netting before the shop counters,
to prevent the stock from being pilfered or even rushed.
That practice still holds; and so does that of the pubs, many
of whom will serve the pickers with beer only outside the
premises, over half-doors well padlocked, while notices are
nailed to the doors of the saloon and public bars, "No hop-
pickers served here." It sounds rather grim and hostile, but
there are reasons for this precautionary attitude toward the
September visitors.

The mid-Weald country, stretching for some twenty-five
miles between Tonbridge and Ashford, has a uniformity of
scene that at first is monotonous. But with acquaintance it
becomes subtle, every detail taking on a pronunciation that
has a special significance for the ear and the eye. I love the

little mazy streams, most of which go to feed the Medway. They trickle past willows and under tumbledown bridges of brick, or ragstone, or chestnut, where the only traffic is that of farm creatures, and the butterflies who make no wear and tear. Nor do the pike and trout who slide beneath, with the sun shining through their bodies, or seeming to do so. All this is a world of solitude and silence, and the poet Blunden has made it his own, just as John Clare appropriated the wild flowers and elms of Northamptonshire. I could best present this part of Kent by quoting a dozen poems. But I must be content with two stanzas from a poem called *Leisure*, since leisure is the presiding mood of this low-lying clay-land, with its lush meadows, its wise indolent cattle, its lavish treasury of flowers, beetles, glow-worms, flies and moths, and its great, heavy-throated birds whose song is heavy with too much green. In this part of the country it is the miscroscopic things that matter, and Mr Blunden misses none of them.

> Gentle and dewy-bright the landscape fills
> Through the serene and crystal atmosphere;
> Night's blackamoors sink into reedy ghylls
> To skulk unsunned till eve's pale lantern peer;
> And silver elvish gossamers go dance
> On twinkling voyages at the caprice
> Of autumn half-asleep and idly playing
> With fancies as they chance,
> The feather's fall, the doomed red leaf delaying,
> And all the tiny circumstance of peace.
>
> Tranquilly beats the country's heart to-day,
> Golden-age-beckonings, lost pastoral things,
> Fantastically near and far-away,
> Stretch in the sunny calm their blazoned wings.
> Then tarry, tiptoe moments, nor too soon
> Let death beat down your saffron butterflies
> Nor crush your gleaming autumn crocuses,
> But in a gradual swoon
> Let long dreams flaunt till eve accomplishes
> And round the down the tide-mist multiplies.

Part of that "tiny circumstance of peace," we may pick our

way here and there, at the vagary of whim, drawn first to one village, then to another, amongst these "lost pastoral things," beating across from the northern to the southern slopes that enclose this sleeping land. Through Marden, Staplehurst, Headcorn, and Smarden, we come by this labyrinth of lanes and streams at last to Ashford, and arrive there dusted with pollen on our shoes, and some of it in our hair where we have collided with over-freighted bees.

The third of the central ribs of my imaginary fan runs along higher ground, the central ridge of the county that breaks into the western boundary at Tunbridge Wells and cuts off the Weald proper from the Romney Marsh and the coast. For me it is the inmost heart of Kent. I live in the middle of it, and have already written one book about it, and have attempted in many bouts of verse to capture its personality. What makes it so remote, so withdrawn, is the fact that it is a casket within a casket. North and east of it, beyond the cushioning emptiness of the Weald, lie the North Downs, much higher and therefore protective. And on its southern slopes rest the warm airs and the ardent sunlight of the Channel.

It is thus subtropical in climate, while it is blessed geologically by the outcrop of that magical soil which grows the best apples and cherries in the world. I have already described how I made a garden in one of its upland valleys during the war, and in five years was gathering ripe black grapes and Turkey figs from a southern wall of the house. The Romans had vineyards here, and I see no reason why we should not do so to-day. Below me lies a meadow which would make a capital vineyard. But the farmer will not sell it. The possession of the land is an instinct with farmers, and especially Kentish farmers. To ask them to sell their land is like asking them to sell their daughters into prostitution. They take it as an insult, becoming at once suspicious, especially if the person approaching them on the matter is a townsman. So in spite of my several efforts to acquire the field (which before the war lay idle, except for an old horse grazing as pensioner) have been in vain, and my plan to plant a vineyard of Royal Muscadines remains in abeyance.

However, my ambition is merely one of many pieces of evidence of the rich abundance of this part of Kent. How to write further about it puzzles me. There is so much to be said. For one thing, the villages along these heights are the most picturesque in the county. Goudhurst, Cranbrook, Benenden, Biddenden and Tenterden, High Halden and Bethersden; what a necklace of pearls! Each one of these little places could be made the subject of a book copiously illustrated. Merely to touch upon them in passing is to give them a similarity which they do not possess, except that they are all beautiful. Cranbrook with its old schoolhouse, its mill, and its cathedral-like church, its bent-elbow High Street; Biddenden with its rows of Early English cottages and shops, its old weaving hall with a whole street of gables, and its annual distribution of "Biddenden cakes," which has gone on since the twelfth century, the benefice of the famous Biddenden Maids, two sisters who were born in A.D. 1100 joined at the hips and shoulders, and who lived thus for some thirty years: there is no end to all this historical and natural interest. I have forgotten Brenchley, for example, that enchanting village standing on a steep hill about six miles east of Tunbridge Wells. But I do not need to write of it here, for the several volumes of Siegfried Sassoon's autobiography have already preserved it in the amber of his elegant prose.

Proudest of all these sister villages, perhaps, is Tenterden, with its magnificent broad High Street, that until recently had a tollgate in the middle of the street. The small town lies surrounded by parks, and from its approaches one looks over gentle undulations of woodland, miles and miles, surviving from the fabulous Anderida. It is like a joyous-melancholy landscape by Giorgione. As one approaches the town, more and more Elizabethan houses appear, relics of the rich days of the weavers and the ironmasters, and the shipowners too, for in the Middle Ages Tenterden was a subsidiary Cinque Port, with its dock at Smallhythe, two miles to the south, where the sea once came up an inlet behind the Isle of Oxney.

The town is quite a miniature metropolis, with its air of business, its surviving shops still possessing that elusive quality called style. It even had its own theatre, which stood off the High Street in an alley called Bells Lane. On each side of the High Street runs a variety of architectural delights; rows of cottages under a single roof, Georgian houses, a fine Jacobean house, shops with original bow fronts, several coaching hostels (where one could be served with a good meal even during the war). Between the two rows lies the great wide road, broad stretches of common-grassland, and indeterminate paths. The handsome buildings, and the ample width of the highway, give the place a majesty that is most impressive. The church of St Mildred has a tower similar to that of Lydd down in the Marsh. It is probably by the same architect, who has varied his work here by putting at each angle of the tower an octagonal turret surmounted by a large crocketed pinnacle. I have already told the story about the connection of this tower with the Goodwin Sands, how it was built at the expense of the necessary repairs to the sea wall, with the result that the sea broke through and submerged the lands where the sands now lie. It is a pretty legend. I always like to hear of the triumph of æsthetic enthusiasm over utility, and I must always have a soft spot in my heart for that ruffian Nero because he fiddled while Rome burned.

From this tower there was hung the beacon which was fired at the approach of the Spanish Armada. It was an iron cage suspended from an eight-foot beam of timber. The tower is built of the famous marble from Bethersden, quarried still at Tuesnode. It is a stone that weathers rather badly, but in doing so gives out an ever-fresh glow of blues and browns, with a glitter of minute shell-like particles.

The church itself is a good example of Perpendicular work, marred by the usual conglomeration of pews. How much I agree with old William Cobbett in his condemnation of this philistinish, comfort-loving practice of filling our English churches, and often even our cathedrals, with pews, and thus destroying their whole character. The next stage, I suppose, in the efforts of the church to compete with the comforts and cushiness of the cinemas will be to put in rows of tip-up lounge seats. Congregations will then be on a much more equalitarian basis with the object of their worship. How wonderful these churches can look if restored to their original interior habits may be seen from the Essex church of Thaxted, whose vicar, Conrad Noel, cleared out all the stuffy nineteenth-century junk—the pews and the ugly stained glass. The result was that the church became in itself a prayer in stone, clear and free and awe-striking.

One of the few impressive Protestant chapels in the country is to be seen at Tenterden. Here the Unitarians have worshipped for over two centuries, in a faith as solid and uncompromising as the woodwork and furniture of their chapel.

Amongst the families who have lived in Tenterden for centuries there have been the ubiquitous Culpeppers, and also the Austens, who are still widely spread in the county. Another family of the same quality is named Hales. It was a Catholic family and thus has had considerable trouble since the Reformation. They settled in Tenterden in the reign of Edward III, and one John Hales was the first mayor of the borough when it received its Royal Charter. Hales Place, standing off the eastern side of the High Street, was rebuilt by a Sir Edward Hales in the eighteenth century. It is pleasing to think that to-day, in the middle of the twentieth century, the Ministry of Education Inspector for the county of Kent is a Mr Edward Hales, a former history-master at Uppingham.

The greatest son of Tenterden, however, was William Caxton, born in 1422. He was a fine representative specimen of the great class of merchants and manufacturers who laid the foundation of England's wealth, following Edward III's wise act of statesmanship in bringing over the Flemish weavers and settling them at Cranbrook and other towns in the Weald. Caxton became a member of the rich Mercers' Company, one of the greatest of our proud Guilds, and he lived for over thirty years in Bruges as representative of the Merchant Adventurers in the Low Countries, a corporation whose title still explains its purpose. While there he came into contact with a prince later destined to be another of our wise kings, Edward IV. In Bruges he learned the new art of printing, for his interests were in scholarship, like so many of his fellow merchant-princes. In 1476 he came home and established a press, the first in England, in the almonry at Westminster, under the patronage of the king who had already met and appreciated him. One cannot say anything new to-day about the importance of this means of spreading the growth of learning and the influence of the magic of the written word. Some bright cynic might point out its culmination to-day in the influence of the Press barons, and the universal substitution of reading for thinking and the cultivation of memory. But we all know, in our bones, what new power Caxton brought into the lives of Englishmen. How appropriate it was that this Kentish man should print, among the most important of his works, the *Canterbury Tales* of Chaucer, as well as the poems of Gower and Lydgate.

It would be fitting if a perpetual monument, a library of books showing the whole history of English printing, might be established at Tenterden. It would be a suitable crown to a queenly village, and a symbol of our own reverence for the things of worth in our island. Perhaps the National Book League, or some future Ministry of the Arts, will see to this.

T

CHAPTER XV

THE BELATED PILGRIM

Now that the time has come to approach Canterbury, I call myself a belated pilgrim because I come in an age of a different faith from that which has moved millions along the Kent roads in the past. Some readers may dispute this frightening statement, but I do not see how they can evade the historical rightness of it. For whatever we may or may not believe to-day we are worlds away from the outlook on life, the habits of mind and morals, which once led the sick in body and soul to go seeking miracles at the shrines of the dead. I know that there are survivals of the once universal practice, at such places as Lourdes and Walsingham; but how pitiful they are, how self-conscious. And how they have been degraded by shameless and ugly commercial exploitation.

G. M. Trevelyan has pointed out, in his *Social History of England*, how the vitality, the fervour, had already gone out of the pilgrimages to Canterbury before the Dissolution of the Monasteries came as a broom to sweep away so much that was already in decay. Human nature being what it is (that is, prone to inertia like all other natural organisms), the Christian religion has had its many phases of inspired organization, each of them flowering and then setting hard, to become an outmoded crust which has had to be broken so that the ever-fluid religious force beneath it should not be bottled up. Religious institutions are no exception. All our moments of glory, of illumination, are succeeded by some form of organized legend or dogma, in art, politics, science. And we outgrow those forms. The cycle of that metabolism continues, giving us an incessant stream of seers, administrators, rebels; and in that order.

The Christ-idea persists, or we must perish. This century sees us fighting for it desperately against the forces of economics which are tending to degrade us into an antlike way of life that will permit of no individual mystery. But though we fight so resolutely, and are so clearly determined about the issue, our faith can no longer express itself in the forms that attracted the Canterbury pilgrims. We go to Canterbury nowadays by a more roundabout way, along the path of æsthetic worship. And in this book there is no occasion to link up that worship in its sources with that of the miracle-mongering of the Middle Ages.

What we must bring home to our imaginations, however, is the vastness of that practice during the centuries from 1170, when Becket was murdered, to 1539 when the Crown forbade the practice and destroyed the shrine. It is no exaggeration to say that Canterbury for those three hundred and fifty years was the centre of a great industry, whose wealth flowed in to fatten and corrode the Church and all the eleemosynaries who fed upon it. Already by the time of Chaucer gross abuses had crept in, the summoners and pardoners playing their cynical, materialist game, just as to-day the brokers and middlemen batten on the credulities and enthusiasms of the worshippers of the machine and its miraculous products. Pilgrims, including kings, emperors, and princes of the all-powerful Church (that vast, international organization), approached from all parts of the known world to pay their spiritual tribute at the shrine of Thomas à Becket, who because he died at a suitable moment in the ceaseless war between two central ideas in the human way of life (nationalism against internationalism) was canonized. Wolsey, though his opposite in morals and appetites, fought the same fight with larger and more elaborate weapons, but he was defeated, and nationalism triumphed.

With those pilgrims, however, came many others who had a more mundane purpose, and in the end these grosser traffickers brought all into disrepute. Chaucer watched their goings on, and reported what he saw in the *Canterbury Tales*. An institution as sophisticated as that devoutly religious poet described it at the end of the fourteenth century was more and more saturated in political and sordidly commercial elements before the end came a century and a half later.

We look on to-day and see the whole process in its historical entirety; but it is not so easy to realize the fire and the dimensions of the blaze. The shrine itself has gone from the

T*   275

great corona chapel which was built to house it behind the high altar of the Cathedral. At the height of the cult, that shrine was one of the most richly emblazoned tombs in the Christian world. The rulers of that world showered symbols of their fervour upon it. Louis VII, the first King of France to visit England, nine years after the death of Becket, left in the Cathedral a gold cup, and the Regale Ruby of France. That opulent heading of the subscription was a criterion for all who came after, and wealth, in terms of that childlike, semi-barbaric way of life, continued to be poured out before the shrine of the martyr, and to overflow into the most sultry alleys of the city.

All that remains to-day is the Cathedral itself, relic of a greater impulse than that represented by the tomb of Becket. It is all that we can appreciate, perhaps, because it is in itself an achievement on so superb a scale, with nothing tawdry or squalid, or physically disgusting. The cult of saints and their miracle-working bones can never be said to be free of those dubious qualities. To-day, we see only self-interest in the person with a passion for being healed, whether it be by crawling to some insanitary grotto, or by swallowing patent medicines. The motive is the same, and it is not one which commands respect. So the crutches, the bandages, and all the rest of the filth which must have accumulated in the precincts of the Shrine of St Thomas, have gone the way of the superstition that collected them there. The Cathedral, impersonal sign of a vast, anonymous outlay of individual genius and creative faith, remains.

We come then, by way of Ashford, from the spine of the Weald to Canterbury, not in the various company depicted by Chaucer, but in a new solitude, and towards a new austerity. For what always strikes me about Canterbury, as about most cathedral cities, is that the devotional activities constantly in progress there are nowadays set apart from the daily life and interests of the majority of the community; just as the fabric of the cathedral, that "frozen music," is a music within whose mode we no longer can express ourselves.

All this contemplation raises questions which are outside the scope of a book on the county of Kent. Yet I suspect that even a book on this theme is affected by them, and that my attempt to put them aside in this over-polite way is an action typical of our modern moral cowardice. Without faith, and without a faculty for worship, it is futile to come to Canterbury. The city with its cathedral still demands an oblation in which the whole imagination of man is exercised to its utmost. Poetry, music, all the arts, together with a sense of history, and the dominance of religious vision in all its manifestations of power—these are the forces demanded from the mind and soul of the pilgrim to Canterbury, belated though he may be.

To-day it is difficult to combine those forces into a natural, unself-conscious unity. We are creatures looking at Canterbury, and at its values, from a post at the beginning of a new civilization. The values represented by Canterbury are static, absolute. Those of our new world are likely to be fluid, relative. From a self-expression in architecture, with all that it implies in love of home and a settled worship in communities, we are turning to a self-expression in engineering. Maybe we are entering on a period of nomadic life, a recurrence of one of the first phases in the history of mankind. We shall live on the road and in the air, with hordes of shock workers being constantly transported from one vast field of labour to another. It will mean entirely different emotional values and orientations. They will not be those of Canterbury.

But these are misgivings, and we need not come to the end of our journey, and to the crown of our delight, in such a mood. There is enough to fulfil the purpose of our quartering of the county. Canterbury stands to-day, as it has always stood, as one of the most beautiful monuments, with city and shrine, in the whole of Europe. Hitherto, man has not made a more perfect civic work of art, or expressed himself in a more exultant mysticism. From whatever road we approach the city, the Cathedral overshadows everything else. It lives. It is a personality. It appears to be issuing some authoritative utterance. But the utterance is one of thrice-meditated stone. I say thrice, because this is the third building on the site; and it incorporates the ghosts, and indeed some of the physical body, of the others.

I believe that I do not need to give its history in detail, for I have already outlined it in the course of this book. One cannot write about Kent without the story of Canterbury and its Cathedral becoming incorporated in the tale. The early Roman Christian settlement on this site; its erasing by the barbarians from northern Europe; the second coming of the Cross in the hand of Augustine, and the building of the first Cathedral; the second deluge from Denmark in A.D. 839, 850, and 1011; the first martyrdom, that of St Elphege; the great administrations of Lanfranc and Anselm after the Conquest; the destruction of the Cathedral by fire in 1067; the century of the Martyrdom and the subsequent glory which lasted for over three hundred years, and in its last stages degenerated into the sordid and vulgar pantomime which Erasmus and Colet watched with such scorn and loathing just before the Dissolution put an end to it; the economic plight of the city when the golden tide of pilgrims suddenly ceased : these are chapters in the history of Canterbury which have already been told, or implied, in our circuitous approach by way of the rest of the county.

For those who are curious to read more, there is ample literature. Two particularly good books, from the literary and historical points of view, are M. A. Babington's book on the Cathedral and D. Gardiner's on the city. Both are a history of Europe in miniature, because that is what the Cathedral and the medieval city represent. Here is the scene not only of the first establishment of Christianity in Britain, but also of that long-contested struggle between monarch and priest, state and international authority, which has raged throughout Europe and has shaped the historical form in which it has grown during two thousand years. Dante told one version of that story at a time when the opposition of the two great ideologies was first firmly set. Italy and middle Europe has not even to-day finally resolved it. For England the issue was made clear in 1538, and for France in 1789. But even in these countries it survives in another guise.

Coming into Canterbury to-day, it is hard to realize that so much has been focused within this quiet cathedral city. I was there only recently, on a Sunday afternoon in autumn. One would expect to find at that hour, on that day, a great

concourse of people moving about the streets of the capital
of English Christianity. But Canterbury was a city of the
dead. After luncheon in a silent hotel we went through the
town toward the precincts. Every shop, every restaurant, was
shut. One or two sightseers were drifting towards the Cathedral, and later we saw them under its roof, dumb, bewildered
folk, most of them obviously without the slightest comprehension of what it all signified. The only lively place in the
city was a garage. Before it stood a smart, low-built sports
car, round which two Air Force men and one or two civilian
youths were gathered, spellbound.

Behind the Cathedral there was nobody. We wandered
out past the ruins where a bomb had fallen by the library,
creating havoc in the most intimate and ancient part of the
precincts. We had seen no soul in the great cloisters, nor
along the dark passage leading round by the infirmary
cloisters. All this part has been horribly mutilated by the
bomb, and it is hard to trace the significance of the debris
of venerable stone and brick lying about there, the spot
where the domestic life of the monks went on for so many
centuries. We came out, through a low, dark arch under the
Cheker Tower (already showing signs of repair), to the
Deanery garden, where once stood the Prior's mansion. The
garden had run wild over the tumbled masonry, and now
all was gowned with a garment of warm autumnal leaves.
The level sunshine was golden, and trees, roofs, walls shone
in an unearthly light, dazzlingly clear yet unreal in their
glory of colour. Behind us the Cathedral soared backward
and upward, the sunshine picking out protrusions and doub-
ling them with purple clusters of shadow. Pigeons moved on
ledges high up, sometimes taking wing for a few yards out
and then relapsing into the gleaming confusion of light and
shadow-shapes among the stone. They moaned to each other,
and starlings carried on an impossible carpentry up in the
great tower, sawing and tapping to no purpose. Time stood
still again. The war was over, and the new ruin was already
sinking into the old. Which was Henry VIII's doing; which
was Hitler's? The willow-herb and buddleia hid the answer.

The ruined Deanery was already in process of repair, and
the multicoloured tiling of the new roof, like that over the

old granary and adjoining buildings, shone like Joseph's coat. A stonemason's tent stood in front of the walls, and in and about it a number of shaped blocks numbered in red. It was wonderful to see the rebuilt portions of walling and cornering. Here was a craftsman's signature in stone, the work of hand and brain. This was the same activity which William of Sens and William the Englishman, the two most noteworthy of the many architects connected with the Cathedral, must have overseen on this same spot six hundred years ago.

At the southern end of the garden, under the gloomy side of the surviving Norman wall of the old Infirmary Hall, with the cliff of the Cathedral behind it, played a small fountain, its crystals falling into then jumping out of the choked basin and alighting on mats of clotted grass. This water, surely, was another symbol of continuity, for it must come through the conduit laid by Prior Wibert between 1151 and 1167, some of the most creative years in the growth of the monastery. This water he brought down from the hills northeast of the town, through a series of filters that purified it, and made it safe during the recurring periods of plague. His leaden pipes were made in sections round wooden moulds and fused together. Since before the death of Becket those pipes have brought water to the Deanery and the domestic parts of the monastery. Still the little fountain shines in the ruins, the only living and moving relic. It is like the still small voice that Elijah heard after the storm. But how many, in this new world, speak its language?

One can walk through the arches of the Infirmary Wall out to the eastern end of the Cathedral, called the Gymewes, where on the site of the old piscina an A.R.P. water-tank stood during the war. One needs to take two paces, then to stop and examine the fresh aspect of the building which this advance opens. Take a thousand such snapshots with the camera of the intelligence, piece them together, and keep them in the mind for "recollection in tranquillity." That may be one way to come at this mighty achievement of man. But then the Cathedral is a living thing, and the light, the air, the moods of day and night, change it from moment to moment. It cannot be seen and accepted statically. It moves, like a column of smoke serenely rising fold upon fold in a muscular rhythm. But it has been rising thus for a thousand years, soaring in stillness, a paradox in stone.

Coming round halfway up the southern side, stop, and look back at the protruding circular chapels, Trinity and Becket's Crown, with the small Norman tower in the angle of the south-east transept. That tower was consecrated in 1130, and it stands there austerely among so much ornament of later date, a reminder of the terrible earnestness and enthusiasm, pure emanations of the spirit, which later became diluted with more fanciful and humane vagaries.

As I reached this spot that autumn afternoon, the great bell-tower suddenly spoke, its peal of ten running and changing, the first few phrases breaking about the town like water over sand. Then the mass gathered into a tide of sound, with the overtone separating out and hovering, a ceiling held up by the thrusting changes piling one upon the other. I suppose a book could be written on the story of these great bells and their makers. It would be another tale of continuity, with that of water, stone, and timber. Everything about the Cathedral leads to that—continuity, and the serene confidence that follows it, through war, devastation, solitude, and the fluctuations of faith. Intellectual and emotional fashions change. Sometimes they fancy one attribute, sometimes another; it may be miracles, with crowds round the shrine; or as to-day, it may be mathematics, with the crowds round the amazing piece of machinery outside the garage. Behind these phenomena, these momentary demonstrations, there survive the fountain, the stone, the rhythm of music from the bells, immediate aspects of the creative source of all this that is ever changing, ever the same.

Now we come to the door at the extreme south-western end of the Cathedral, facing the entrance from the town through Christ Church gate, an ornamental piece of Late Perpendicular work whose figure of Christ, which stood in a central niche, was destroyed by forty discharges of cannon from the artillery of Colonel Sandys on 27 May 1642, who at the same time, according to the vice-Dean, "entered the Cathedral and overthrew the communion table, violated the monuments of the dead, spoiled the organ, brake down the ancient rails and seats with the brazen eagle that did support the Bible, mangled all our service books, bestrewing the whole pavement with leaves thereof." Was that action the gesture of the zealot, the purifier, in man, or was it just the mischievous brute which is ever on the alert in our blood?

Before going in, let us allow that question, with its trouble to the mind, to die down, while we walk over to stand and turn by the gate, so that we may see the Cathedral as a whole, with the Bell Harry Tower rightly lighted at this angle of the sunshine. It is a mighty thing, 235 feet in height, elaborate in ornament. It succeeded the Norman "Angel Steeple," being started in 1333, and completed some forty years after the Dissolution. At the top is a single bell which tolls for the death of the king or the primate only. A delightful as well as instructive contrast is offered between this magnificent and flamboyant giant and the small Norman tower which I have already mentioned. Here, side by side, the one under the shadow of the other, are two of the outstanding characteristics of the religious way of life. It is like comparing Handel's Hallelujah Chorus with a primitive little carol about the peasant Virgin and her Babe.

Now comes the moment which I might well place as the crown of my travels in this joyous county of Kent : for the first sight of the interior of the Cathedral as one enters at that south-western corner is an experience that "out-soars the shadow of our night." My immediate desire, when I first saw the massive but featherweight pillars receding in perspective up the aisle, with their fellows along the nave crowding together through the angle from which I saw them, was to lift my arms likewise, and to seek a high place to add to my endeavour. I wanted to shout with the voice of an army of men entering somewhere in triumph. But of course I stood there, doltlike and dumb, staring no doubt as blankly as those young men had been staring at the streamlined little sports car by the garage. Exultation, like a pearl, is the fruit of some sort of irritation, and it lurks inside a drab casing. I can see myself standing there, hat in hand, with an agonized attention flickering away from the superb spectacle before and above me, flickering away to read the tickets on the collection-boxes and the booklets inside the door, then coming hopelessly back to that grandeur again, and once more failing.

This bafflement of mind and imagination is familiar to everybody. It is that midday blackout which comes on a summer noon amid a riot of light, colour, and heat. It is that which makes us lose the power of attention in a concert hall at the moment when the chorus breaks in during the last movement of Beethoven's Ninth Symphony. It is that which makes us put down the book at certain passages in Dante's *Divine Comedy*, or Wordsworth's *Prelude*, because we "can read no more that day." I believe, with Lessing, that one art cannot trespass successfully upon the field of another. Architecture, the great communal art, certainly cannot be represented in words, even though they are chiselled by such marmoreal masters as Dryden or Landor. Therefore I will not attempt the impossible. I can only try to describe my private sensations as I reacted, with all my emotions and all that I had acquired during one man's lifetime of contemplation and study, to the beauty and symbolism of the interior of Canterbury Cathedral.

The reader can see by now that my effort is in vain. It is futile to walk round, with an armful of guide-books, examining technical details, and recounting, by crib, the historical titbits about each of the famous tombs. The tomb that impresses me most is that of Archbishop Chicheley, for he was one of the first as well as the finest examples of the Englishmen whose life-stories were a happy contradiction of the theories of medieval class distinction. So many of the primates whose tombs adorn the Cathedral were blood-cousins of kings. Chicheley was the son of a Midland yeoman, that new social order peculiar to England, which had emerged out of the economic break-up of the feudal system (a process greatly accelerated by the Black Death in 1348, which cut right across Edward III's statesmanlike economic experiment in promoting the making of cloth in England instead of the raw wool being exported). I imagine Chicheley to have had some of the characteristics of the late W. P. Ker, a great scholar whose father was a farm-worker, and of the late Tom Snell, who began his career scaring rooks in a field (like Hardy's Jude) and ended as leader of the House of

Lords. Ker had scholarship and humility. Snell had wisdom and humility. Chicheley, like them, seems to have been untouched by that arrogance and self-assertion which so often characterize the self-made man on the look-out for anybody who may dare to patronize him. Wolsey is a glaring example.

No doubt overmuch has been made of Chicheley's humble origin. Early historians and biographers loved vivid dramatic contrasts. In fact, he had as excellent an education as was possible in those or any later days. He was one of the first scholars of William of Wykeham's new foundation, Winchester School, and therefore one of the first Fellows of New College, Oxford. This training determined his tastes. He became a subtle Civil Servant, as sophisticated in his public life as he was sensitive and scholarly in his private interests. That is a tendency amongst men to-day who have gone that way of learning through Wykeham's foundations. Chicheley played what must have been a skilful hand in solving the problem of the two rival papacies in 1409. His power at home was assured after this, and he soon became Archbishop of Canterbury, while continuing to hold a plurality of offices that brought in a great revenue. Unlike Wolsey, he preferred to spend it on scholarship rather than on pomanders. He founded a school at his native place, Higham Ferrers, for the study of "grammar and song" (how much wiser than teaching a boy chemistry!), and at Oxford he copied his mother-college in the foundation of All Souls'. To-day, to be a Fellow of All Souls' is to be a Levite of the Levites. St John's College, Oxford, is based on another foundation by Chicheley. He was also instrumental in the foundation of Eton and King's College, Cambridge.

All this talk about scholarship, devotion to things of the mind and spirit, and to the making of abiding monuments, that will maintain an assertion of the genius of man, is a roundabout way of trying to come at what Canterbury Cathedral stands for. And not only the Cathedral, but all the other surviving glories in the city—the pilgrims' hospital in Westgate; the pitifully few relics of the Benedictine monastery of St Augustine, which he founded along with the restored Cathedral in A.D. 598; the two Roman-Saxon

churches of St Pancras and St Martin, probably the first
Christian shrines in Britain—these, and a hundred other
monuments both religious and secular, survive to-day as
something more than museum pieces. It depends upon the
pilgrim whether or not these relics are able to blossom again,
and to yield the perfume of history in all its fullness and
sensuousness.

Take as much reading as you can carry to Canterbury, and
this great city will give you a tangible example, in stone and
timber, of the whole civilization of Europe as it has grown
up, through blood and poverty, human wickedness, and the
thin but enduring vein of faith and other-worldliness, out of
the "glory that was Greece and the grandeur that was
Rome," into the strange, sad sunlight of Christianity.

In this city is a record of that last and greatest spiritual
idea in all its manifestations, including the ill-use to which it
has been put by zealots, cynics, and power-hungry men.
Already, in Saxon times, ease and routine custom had softened
the Church, and with the coming of the Normans, Lanfranc
came also to find the original church of St Augustine a
burned-out husk, and a lethargy seeping through the monastic
life of the Abbey. It did not take many years, even after so
tremendous an inspiration as that given by the idea of the
Agony and Sacrifice of Christ, for the impulse to become
standardized and reduced to a dogma capable of being
manipulated by political chicanery. The stones of Canterbury
tell us all about this, and if we read them intelligently and
with the dictionary of imagination, they will "make the man
wise," as Francis Bacon said of a study of history from
books.

Follow the many guide-books in this way, and you will
want to come again and again to Canterbury, quartering it
methodically, and at other times wandering about like a
lover, savouring the general beauty of the place in a sort of
rapturous evocation. I would like to come along too, but it
would mean continuing this book for another four hundred
pages, in order to tell the civic tale alone, apart from that of
the comings and goings of the pilgrims and the kings and
ecclesiastics. I should want to say something too about such
citizens as Christopher Marlowe, that scholar of the King's

School, a shoemaker's son who was one of the first to benefit by Cranmer's determination to open a way for the education of Englishmen by their native merit and not by the purse of their fathers. Marlowe, like other literary figures, such as Shelton, the translator of *Don Quixote*, got himself mixed up in the Secret Service, and was finally assassinated by his own masters because he knew too much. But even so early and so sticky an end did not prevent him from carrying into the somewhat bawdy and pedantic sixteenth-century poetic drama a new and infinitely purer fire of sheer poetry. The "topless towers" of which he spoke so nobly in his *Dr Faustus* were surely reared out of his boyhood familiarity with the towers of the Cathedral, beneath which he studied. The influence of the great shrine, and of the subsidiary beauty which has gathered round it, is infinite. Poets still come there, seeking more than they know. And the less eloquent citizen, no matter how rebellious against the past and the pull of tradition, follows him there and is forced to look back through the centuries, as I have attempted to look in this book, to find in one place an epitome of life in all its forms, past, present, and future.

INDEX